11.95

RUDI

14 YEARS
WITH MY
TEACHER

RUDI

14 YEARS WITH MY TEACHER

BY JOHN MANN

RUDRA PRESS
Cambridge, Massachusetts

Rudra Press
P.O. Box 1973
Cambridge, Massachusetts 02238

Manufactured in the United States of America.

First Edition
ISBN 0-915801-04-3

Book and cover design by Bill Stanton

Contents

PART ONE

Meeting Rudi

Rudi (Swami Rudrananda).

1

Meeting Rudi

ON A CRISP FALL DAY IN 1959, I found myself on the northern border of West Greenwich Village, where the neat rectangular grid of mid-Manhattan begins to break down into irregular streets that intersect at odd angles. An area known for artistic expression, free living, runaways, and drug users, it was inhabited by almost anyone other than a college professor like myself. I was in search of an Eastern art dealer I had learned about through my interest in Chinese landscape painting.

I looked at the simple business card I had been given: Rudi Oriental Arts, 184 Seventh Avenue South. Seventh Avenue South is a main thoroughfare for traffic headed toward the tip of Manhattan or out to New Jersey via the Holland Tunnel. I walked past the block-long edifice of St. Vincent's Hospital, following the descending street numbers. But even though I was counting carefully, I almost walked past the store, it was so small.

A bronze reclining Buddha, six or seven feet long, completely filled the store's window. The store itself was shaped like a distorted pie section, cut at an acute angle about ten to twelve feet in depth. It was crammed with art, and seemed barely to contain Rudi, who completely filled the space with an air of expectancy, as if he were just waiting for *you* to walk through the door. With his short hair, gentle but extraordinarily bright eyes, and informal dress of old corduroy pants and a worn pullover sweater, he didn't fit my image of an antique dealer. He looked more like a happy Sumo wrestler whose most striking quality was an unusually intense awareness of his surroundings.

"Do you have any monochrome Chinese landscapes?" I asked.

"No," he said.

And with that, I was ready to leave. It had been a pointless trip.

"Just look around," Rudi suggested, interrupting my disappointment. "Maybe you'll see something you like."

It was an ordinary enough thing for a storekeeper to say, but if he had not said it, I might have walked out and never come back.

I looked in the semi-gloom with halfhearted interest. Buddhas smiled benignly from five different levels of shelves, chests, and boxes. Many-limbed statues extended their various arms toward paintings, tapestries, and mysterious objects in unknown materials. The profusion of art was overwhelming. A faint smell of incense enhanced the exotic flavor of the tiny space.

I finally came upon two circular plaques painted in gold. They were owls done in a Chinese style, each about a foot in diameter.

"How much are these?" I asked.

"Sixty-five dollars for the pair," said Rudi.

"They're interesting," I said, mostly to be agreeable, "but I wasn't thinking of anything like that. What are they?"

"They're wood carvings from the outer doors of a Chinese temple."

"Oh," I said, with mild enthusiasm.

"I'll hold them for a few days, if you like," he said, moving them under his small desk.

"All right," I said politely, "thank you."

As I walked out, I had the sudden feeling that both he and the store might vanish behind me without a trace, but I shrugged it off as ridiculous.

A few days later, I went back to buy the owls. I was puzzled by my own actions because I hadn't liked them that much. Rudi, however, didn't seem surprised. He wrapped them up in a brown paper bag, as I wrote him a check. There was nothing else to do, so I left. Outside the store, I suddenly felt that I should not leave without asking him to visit me. I struggled with the impulse but gave in to it.

Rudi looked at me quizzically as I re-entered the store.

"I just came back to ask if you would like to come to supper next week."

"Sure," he said, "I'd be happy to come."

We arranged a date. I left, feeling more at ease though bemused by my impulsiveness.

The intervening days were full. I was getting ready to move from a Manhattan apartment to a house in the country. I had been born in upper Manhattan and had lived there all my life. I was 31 years old, married with two small children, and held a teaching position as Assistant Professor in the Graduate Department of Sociology at New York University. To an outside observer I must have looked like a moderate American success story with academic overtones. I had never really wanted for anything on the material level, but inwardly I was starving and inaccessible.

Our apartment was a mess the night Rudi came, with boxes and crates everywhere, but the disorder didn't bother him.

He cleared some of the books and papers off the biggest chair and sat down, completely at ease. Rudi ate with great enthusiasm the food I had ordered from a neighborhood Chinese restaurant — wonton soup, egg rolls, sweet and sour shrimp — and he talked to me as if we were old friends.

"A woman at a Subud* meeting gave me your card."

"I am in Subud myself," said Rudi. "Pak Subuh is my teacher. When I last saw him, he told me to sell my business and move to New Zealand."

"Are you going to?" I asked casually.

"Yes," he said. "I am leaving with a few people who are close to me."

"Such as who?" I asked.

He described them; mostly young unsettled kids, hanging around the fringes of Greenwich Village. As he spoke, I had the very clear thought that the last thing on earth I would ever do was move to New Zealand with such a bunch of characters.

"How do you like the temple owls?" Rudi asked, interrupting my thoughts.

"They're fine," I said. I didn't really know how I felt about them, but it no longer mattered. "Have you been in your store long?" I asked.

"A few years," said Rudi, sipping some tea. "You probably think it's a small place, but it still seems big to me. In the beginning, I didn't have a store at all. Just a room to live in. I bought a few things with the little money I had. The rest I found by getting up at five in the morning and going through the neighborhood garbage cans for anything that could be fixed and sold — toasters, lamps, pieces of antique metal. I used the money to buy more art. I always loved Eastern art, but I only had forty dollars when I started the

---

* Subud is a spiritual work developed in Indonesia by its founder, Pak Subuh and is based on complete surrender to a spiritual force that has a deep cleansing action on the individual who opens to it.

store. I was out of work at the time, although I had been offered a good job at a factory. But I would have been doing one simple task over and over all day long and that terrified me. In desperation I walked for miles down Seventh Avenue. As I passed this block, I heard a voice whisper to me, 'This is your store.' I looked around and saw an empty hole in the wall. I wanted to walk away but the voice kept repeating, 'This is your store. This is your store.' I trusted the voice because I thought that working in the factory would drive me insane. I hunted down the landlord and we came to an agreement. It was a major undertaking to open the store. When you start from nothing, anything seems tremendous.

"I bought a few prints and a vase with the little money I had. I supported myself by washing dishes at the Village Vanguard down the street.

"When I had saved about four hundred dollars, someone offered me two Japanese figures that cost exactly four hundred dollars. I didn't see how I could spend it all on those two figures. But they were very beautiful, so I decided to buy them. I have never regretted it."

I found it difficult to visualize Rudi with so little. He seemed surrounded by an atmosphere of riches.

Since he had stopped talking, I returned to the subject of Subud.

"It's strange that I never saw you in any of the classes," I said. "I have been going for several months."

"You didn't see me because I haven't been there very much lately." He paused in recollection. "I helped to start Subud in New York. It was better then; we were a small dedicated group. Now it is getting too big. As soon as something starts to get packaged for mass consumption, it is already dying."

"It's all very new for me," I said. "I don't really care about politics. I just want to use the sessions to get into a better state."

Rudi smiled. "You're right. But for me, it's harder. I am too visible. I gave a talk a few weeks ago, and before I was done, half the people were sobbing. They all thought it was wonderful, but it only made the Subud leaders envious. And jealousy can sour anything. But there are still good things happening in Subud.

"Just a few weeks ago, I met with some of the founding members in my apartment and we decided to have a session. One of them had brought along his girlfriend, and she wasn't particularly interested in what we were doing. But as the force started to work, she got caught up in the whole experience. Suddenly, the room was filled with a blinding light. At first, I thought the electricity had overloaded. I looked at the light bulbs, but they weren't any brighter. Then I glanced around the room and saw that the light was pouring out of this girl. Her soul had opened up like a great flower. I don't know if it meant much to her, but it certainly was wonderful for me."

"What did you do before you were in Subud?" I asked, not knowing how to respond to what he had just said.

"I studied for four months with the Shankaracharya of Puri, and I was in the Gurdjieff work for five years."

I was shocked by the coincidence — I had been in the Gurdjieff work myself for about five years. We had never met during that time because I had worked at their country retreat while he had been with a group in the city.

At ten-thirty, he got up to go. I walked him to the subway. Night had come. Our footsteps resounded on the deserted sidewalk as we walked along Broadway near 123rd Street, where the subway emerges from underground. In a few minutes we reached the bottom of the long escalator that runs from the street to the elevated subway station at 125th Street and Seventh Avenue. Rudi said a friendly goodbye and stepped onto the escalator. As I watched him slowly being carried up and away from me, I suddenly felt that no matter how hard I worked for the rest of my life, I would never catch up to him. But this didn't bother me. Even at that moment, I knew he was my greatest protection.

.   .   .

I began to stop in at Rudi's store regularly to look at the art and talk with him. The store was less than a mile from my office at NYU, and I visited often. If it was a warm day, we would sit outdoors on folding chairs enveloped by the sounds of the ceaseless Seventh Avenue traffic. His idea of warmth was about ten degrees lower than mine, so I looked forward to moving into the store where he had a small gas heater. There was only room for about two people, so if a customer came, I took a walk. I can hardly remember what we said. Often he was silent. I watched and waited; for what, I didn't know at the time.

When he had visited my apartment, Rudi had mentioned his students. They soon appeared — a pretty ragged crew of young kids looking for hope with varying degrees of interest and desperation. He had begun working with them about six months before I had met him.

I couldn't help seeing what he was doing, though, in a way, there was nothing to see. He simply sat opposite one of his students and gazed intently at him for perhaps five to ten minutes. No words were spoken.

I was intrigued. I felt like an anthropologist who had stumbled on a previously unreported phenomenon, but I did not seriously consider the possibility of working with Rudi myself. I felt above the level of his students; I looked at them with the interest and detached superiority of the observer. Rudi said nothing, allowing me to watch and occasionally talking to me about their backgrounds. The most interesting and promising student was a young jazz drummer named Roy, who lived around the corner from the store.

Roy was a redhead with temperament to match. He was struggling to make it as a musician and to support a young family through a series of weekly and one-night stands.

"I watched him walk by every day for a whole year," Rudi said, "knowing he would be my first real student. Not once in all that time did he look in the window, until one day something caught his eye and he came in. We started talking. Before he left, we had begun to work together."

"How could you wait all that time?" I asked, surprised by such patience.

"I knew it was necessary. He had to make the first move. But the most remarkable thing was that Roy could have been so oblivious of my existence, since he is very psychic."

"In what way is he psychic?" I asked, only mildly curious. My whole attitude toward such abilities was quite negative at the time.

"He can find answers to my questions. I can get my own answers if I need them, but it takes a lot of effort. Because Roy is lighter inside than I am, he can go where the answer is and bring it back."

"I don't know what you are talking about," I said, feeling vaguely uncomfortable.

"The whole problem with getting an answer to any question," said Rudi, ignoring my reaction, "is to ask the right person. That's where a lot of people make a big mistake. Just because a psychic is in contact with some spirit, they assume the answer he gives is correct. In everyday life, they wouldn't be so gullible. You have to be able to go to the right place. Otherwise, you might end up with some minor official who only pretends to know and gives you a confident but stupid answer."

"But how can you know where to go?" I asked, curious, but without any conviction about the reality of the discussion.

"You ask to be sent to the place in the universe where the answer exists. Then you surrender and open to whatever happens. It's very helpful for me to have Roy check things out. Anyone who relies solely on his own judgment is a fool. It may work for a while, but at the crucial moment it will fail. Everyone's work needs to be checked out. That's what a teacher's for."

As I spent time in the store, I got to know Roy better. He was very easy-going, as interested in being a jazz drummer as in developing his psychic and spiritual abilities. Rudi advised him on both. I remember once walking in just as Rudi was telling Roy how to work to absorb the inner qualities of his idol, the jazz drummer Buddy Rich.

"When you are with him," said Rudi, "you have to be completely open. Approach him as if he were your guru, with love and devotion. He will feel it even if he doesn't understand what's happening. He'll have to open to you in return."

"But what if I don't really like him?" Roy asked.

"Look," said Rudi, gesturing excitedly, "you want something from him. It is up to you to consciously create the conditions that will help you get it. What I am telling you is fundamental. You are dealing with a man who represents a remarkable quantity in a particular area. He's not going to give anything away; you almost have to steal it when he isn't looking. And he will be looking, unless he feels that you love him."

"But how do I find out how he plays certain things that seem physically impossible?"

"It is partly technique and partly his inner state," said Rudi. "He can do it because he knows he can. You have to let him work through you in order to understand."

"How can I do that?" asked Roy.

"I've already given you the first step: open to him unconditionally. When you can really do that, no matter how he reacts, then I'll give you the next step."

I listened to their conversation with interest and skepticism. Although Roy was struggling at the time, he was still able to support his small family. The other students were less fortunate. Most of them were on the borderline economically, and some of them were deeply troubled emotionally. But it didn't matter to Rudi; he took them as they came. He told me, "I don't choose my students so much as I attract them by the level of my being. They appear and choose me. I open to the possibility that they represent and do everything I can to fulfill it. Sure, I'd just as soon attract people who didn't have problems, who were clean and even glamorous. But I accept whoever comes and do everything I can to raise their level."

One day after Rudi had been working with one of his students, we were left alone. A few minutes passed in silence. I felt a growing sense of anticipation.

Rudi broke the silence. "John, would you like me to work with you?"

Left on my own, a year might have gone by before I said anything. Maybe I would never have taken the initiative. But he made it easy for me, and without giving the matter any more thought, I said, "Yes."

We sat in his tiny store and I looked at him. I had no idea what to expect, though I had watched the process numerous times. At one moment, I saw his familiar, round, friendly face in front of me, then his expression changed and I felt power flowing into me. It lasted for several minutes, then he looked away.

It was the essence of simplicity — pure vitality given from one human being to another. Yet I suspected, with increasing intensity during the following weeks, that this experience, invisible, silent, and almost off-hand, was the most important thing that had ever happened to me. I also had the immediate conviction that what I had experienced was available nowhere else in the world. Later, I realized that Rudi himself assumed that there were other people working as he did. As he traveled over the earth, buying art and pursuing his spiritual development, he always expected to find them. But he never did.

During the next month I continued working with him whenever there was an opportunity and he was willing. Each time, I was drawn a little further in a direction I could only dimly sense, but nevertheless knew to be real. Other students saw lights and visions, figures appearing and disappearing, as Rudi worked. I saw nothing, but it was not necessary. I could feel the force. We did not talk about it. There was nothing to say. With each passing week, I increasingly came to feel that my one opportunity for inner growth lay in working with Rudi. It is hard for me to explain why I felt this way, just as it is difficult for anyone to explain why they have fallen in love. But this was not as simple as falling in love. I had walked through a door and in front of me was a path. I had been looking for such a path for a long time. Fifteen years before, I had started reading mystical literature. I had written a paper in college on various forms of Yoga, at a time when most people had never heard of Yoga. I had been actively involved in various forms of spiritual work for over ten years. My main conclusion as a result of all this effort was that I was virtually unreachable, spiritually frozen solid. I also realized that as long as that was my fundamental condition, there was no hope. But in Rudi's work, I had found something that could reach me. I was honest enough to realize the truth of my situation and desperate enough to appreciate the opportunity presented to me. Nothing else seemed important.

When I came to this conclusion, I was faced with an immediate problem. Rudi was moving to New Zealand in the late spring. It was not what he particularly wanted to do, but his spiritual teacher had told him to go and he had agreed. To my own amazement, I found myself also deciding to go, regardless of the practical implications. I was married and had two children. I had just bought a home in the country. The complications were daunting, but I was not going to let anything hold me back.

I told Rudi what I was feeling late one afternoon during the waning of winter. "When you first came to my apartment and talked about going to New Zealand," I started hesitantly, "my immediate reaction was that it would absolutely be the last thing I would ever want to do." I paused as Rudi smiled.

"I know," he said. "I understand."

"But now everything's changed. I feel you are the one chance I am going to have. If you move to New Zealand, I want to go too."

Rudi smiled again and said, "I'll have to work on it. Come back tomorrow. I'll let you know then."

I was puzzled that he couldn't give me an immediate answer, but at least he was taking my request seriously.

The next day I was waiting for him when he came to open the store. In the interval, I had become pretty nervous. "Well?" I said, as soon as he had unlocked the door and walked inside.

"I worked on your question," he said. "The answer is yes, if I go, you should come."

Since he was going, it seemed to be an unnecessary qualification. But on the basis of his answer, I began to collect travel folders and books on New Zealand. I spent hours looking at pictures of the beautiful scenery; the glaciers and waterfalls, the high alpine fields with grazing sheep; the natural Polynesian beauty of the native Maoris, the totally foreign setting pleasantly combined with the familiarity of English language and culture. It all excited my imagination. But at the same time, it didn't really matter. I realized we would be in a world of our own that I couldn't visualize beforehand. Rudi never even opened a travel folder. It didn't interest him. He was going because he had been told to go.

As winter turned to spring, I arranged a leave of absence from the college that could be extended to two years if necessary, and I looked into the process of immigration. My family had reluctantly agreed to accompany me.

Rudi, for his part, liquidated his business. He owned more art than I had realized. A number of his larger pieces, too big to fit in the store, were on loan. In the end, he sold much of his stock at a loss so he would be free to leave.

By early summer he was ready. He set out on a trip to disband the network of people in India and elsewhere in the East that he had organized to locate, buy, and ship art goods for him. On the way back, he intended to stop in New Zealand, look over the country, and possibly purchase a sheep farm.

I settled down to my normal routine and waited for his return in a state of suspended animation. Two weeks after he left, I was surprised to receive an overseas airmail letter in my mailbox. It was the first and only letter I ever got from Rudi. He had written from India. I hurried to open it, puzzled but excited to read what he might have to say. Probably he was just sharing impressions of his trip.

"Dear John, I hope you won't be angry, but I have changed my plans. I am not going to New Zealand. I'll be home shortly and explain everything. Love, Rudi."

My only reaction was great relief. I had never wanted to go anywhere.

A week later, Rudi returned and quickly re-established his business. He found a larger store on the same block and bought back most of his old goods. After a while he told me what had happened in India to change his life.

"As I traveled through the East," Rudi began one day as we sat outside his new store on two wooden folding chairs, "I contacted the people connected with my business. It was hard to tell them I was disbanding everything I'd built up. Most of them were pretty upset. But I did what I had to do.

"During my trip I met a number of people connected with Subud. Some of the things they told me were disturbing. They said that Pak Subuh was buying vast tracts of land for himself in Indonesia with money from Subud centers around the world. They told me stories about the politics in various centers in India. All of this shook me but I took it as a test of my sincerity and carried on. After all, Pak Subuh was my teacher; it was not for me to question his actions.

"When most of my work was done, I went to stay with my friend Beebee. Beebee is a multimillionaire whose hobby is saint hunting. When he hears about a new saint, he goes to pay his respects, leaves some money, and then begins to spread the word. When I got to his house, the first thing he said to me was, 'I just found a new saint, Bhagavan Nityananda. He's only about two and a half hours from Bombay. Do you want to meet him?' Never knowing what I might find, I agreed, though my mind was on my own affairs.

"The next morning, without really thinking about it, I found myself in Beebee's car on a road that grew steadily worse until it ended in Ganeshpuri, a town carved out of the jungle by the man we were going to meet. We left the car and walked to a plain building and then through a doorway that led to the large room where the saint held audience. The first impression was overwhelming. There were people crowded in every corner in a state of religious hysteria. In the front of the room sat a large, dark man in a semi-trance. I was completely repelled. What was I, a sophisticated westerner, doing in this weird scene? How could this utterly strange man have anything important to give me? He didn't even seem to be aware of his physical surroundings. For one long moment, I was filled with the impulse to turn around and walk away. But I have learned not to trust my instinctive reactions. Instead, Beebee and I watched as people streamed by the saint, receiving a blessing or asking him a question.

"A few minutes passed. Then, to my dismay, we were led to the front of the room. Before I could say anything, I found myself being presented to the holy man, who seemed completely indifferent to me. I was asked if I had a question. Only one thing occurred to me, so I told him I was planning to move to New Zealand shortly and asked if this was the right thing for me to do. I wasn't sure why I asked since I already knew the answer.

"The saint's response was unbelievable. 'You are completely out of your mind,' he said. 'Any decision that you make must be wrong. Go home!'

"I was deeply shocked. With one stroke, he had cut through the fabric of my whole life. I left the room in a daze.

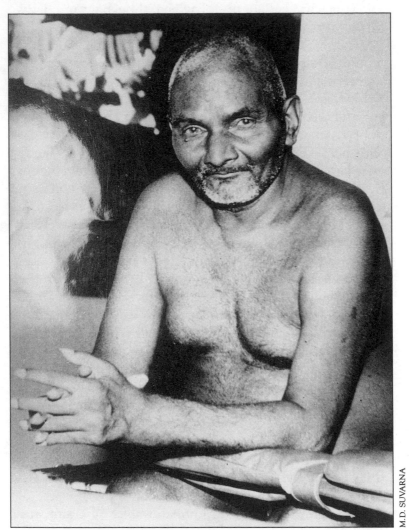

M.D. SUVARNA

Bhagavan Nityananda at Ganeshpuri, India.

"On the way back to Bombay, Beebee asked me what I had thought of the experience. Before I could answer he told me that Nityananda was considered to be an incarnation of the elephant god, Ganesh. I asked him who Ganesh was, trying to cover my shocked condition.

"'He is the god who is propitiated at the beginning of any new undertaking,' said Beebee.

"As the day passed, I had the growing conviction that Nityananda had spoken the truth. Since I am not one to hesitate, I wrote to you and a few other people the next day. Then I did what I could to pull the pieces of my business back together, to the relief of everyone concerned. A week later I was on the plane, and here I am talking to you," Rudi concluded, raising his arms to take in the surrounding scene of West Greenwich Village, which had been transformed into India while he talked.

Rudi's meeting with Nityananda was a major event in his spiritual development, but this was far from evident at the time. When he went back to India the next year on one of his regular business trips, Rudi hoped to visit Nityananda again, but he was relatively casual about it.

On his return from that trip he was very subdued.

"I don't really know what I expected," he said, "but I was totally unprepared to find that Nityananda had taken mahasamadhi."

"What do you mean?" I asked.

"When a great saint dies, he enters into mahasamadhi. It is a conscious act. His body dies but his soul-force remains. It is hard to understand unless you visit his shrine. The pure essence of the man is there, ringing in the atmosphere and saturating the walls. All I had to do was open and breathe it in.

"As I sat by his tomb absorbing what had happened, I realized that I'd been in a state of shock ever since I met him. The power that poured out of him had completely paralyzed my psychic system. It was more than I could bear. It has taken all this time for me to begin to digest it.

"He is not dead in any spiritual sense. That is the important thing to understand. The essence of a holy man is the level of the energy working in him. The higher the energy, the nearer he is to God. This energy remains after his body disappears.

"If I died, you might be upset because of our personal relationship. But if the energy that you find in me were still available, then it wouldn't really matter. You could continue on. If you ever go to India, you'll understand what I mean. There are many sacred places where you can feel a special sense of presence. There are locations where higher forces naturally focus or where work done by holy men in the past has magnetized these forces.

"Nityananda made no effort to appoint a successor before he died," Rudi said, returning to his original theme. "That wasn't his way. He was totally disinterested in any kind of organization. Consequently, after his death things were rather chaotic.

"The first time I was in Ganeshpuri, I met a man who was acting as one of Nityananda's lieutenants, Swami Muktananda. We seemed to understand each other, even though he spoke no English, but then I often get along better with the lieutenants than the generals. Last time, after Nityananda's death, the situation was very uncertain. Eventually it will either fall apart or one of the older students will emerge to fill the vacuum. I have a feeling that it might be Muktananda."

2

The Store:
Rudi's Microcosm

SLOWLY THE FAMILIAR pattern of Rudi's life returned. He sat all day in his new store. People came seeking art, friendship, and spiritual guidance. Generally he gave each more than they expected.

The new store was six times larger than the old one, but soon was just as crowded. Rudi sat behind a small desk where he could survey the passing scene through the front window and keep an eye on the entrance.

One day in 1960, a strange-looking young man with wild eyes, unwashed jeans, and a partially buttoned shirt flung open the front door and slammed it closed behind him. Rudi seemed to know him and motioned him to a chair.

The man glared at Rudi, refusing to sit. Rudi shrugged. The man sat. His first words were, "I am on my way to Bellevue."

"That's good," said Rudi. "How have you been?"

"I'm going crazy. You look like a Buddha sitting there."

"That's what a lot of people tell me," Rudi responded, smiling, though I didn't see what there was to smile about. I tried to blend into the shadows, hoping the man wouldn't get violent.

"What are you smiling about?" he demanded suddenly.

"It's nice to see you," said Rudi quietly.

"I must really be going crazy," the man said. "I see light coming out of your head."

Rudi didn't respond and they just made small talk until a customer walked in. Rudi excused himself; the man glared at the customer as if he wished him dead. After a minute, he threw over his chair and stalked out without a word. I was relieved to see him go. Rudi's comment was, "I'm his last stop before he checks in at Bellevue. He's sane enough to know when he is going crazy. If he would come here on the way out, instead of on the way in, maybe I could help him. But either way, I like to see him once in a while."

"Why?" I asked. I was still shaking inside.

"When you're with a person like that, you have to be totally aware. He senses every breath you take. If my attention wavers a moment, he knows it. Crazy people are a hundred times more sensitive than normal ones. I wouldn't like him for a steady diet, but he forces me to function at a higher level and for that I am grateful.

"What really fascinates me is that I could see the force that is driving him crazy, slowly wrapping itself around his head. When it gets all the way around, he will be totally psychotic. I hope he's in the hospital by then."

The next time I came to the store, Rudi greeted me with an announcement: "You just missed an Indian saint."

That was hard for me to believe. What would an Indian saint be doing in Greenwich Village?

"All day long as I was sitting here," said Rudi, "I felt an unusual energy. I didn't know what it was, but it was very strong and pure. It didn't seem to belong to the environment.

"And then an hour ago, in walks a Swami along with two of his followers. He didn't speak any English, but we got along just fine. He seemed more surprised by my existence than I was by his. But then, I knew he was coming. You can still feel his presence in the atmosphere."

It did seem as if a silvery light filled the air. Rudi looked wonderful. We sat together quietly, bathing in the afterglow. Then Rudi started to work with me and the rest was forgotten.

As the day ended, Rudi invited me to supper at his apartment. I gratefully accepted, knowing that he was an excellent cook and curious to see where he lived.

His apartment was quite small, essentially a bedroom and a living room, both filled with art. He had recently received a small shipment that was partially unpacked. The contents were spread out on a table, mostly jewelry and small statues. I watched as he picked Indian necklaces made of semi-precious stones from the pile and held them up to a lamp made from a Japanese bronze vessel. He seemed completely ordinary and yet, at the same time, totally strange, like a character from the *Arabian Nights* surrounded by his treasures. As I watched him, a cold chill spread through me. I had never known anyone like him. He almost shouldn't exist. And yet in so many ways he was more real than I.

He looked up and spoke, breaking the spell, "How about potato pancakes with sour cream for supper? They're one of my specialties."

I smiled in agreement.

.   .   .

My role during this time was almost totally passive. I sat and waited, slowly absorbing the energy that flowed and overflowed from Rudi's being. He tolerated my presence endlessly and fate cooperated with me.

One evening, a student at New York University asked me to evaluate a project being developed at St. Vincent's Hospital. Shortly thereafter, I was invited to talk with the director of Social Services at the hospital. She had just submitted my evaluation as a proposal to the Office of Vocational Rehabilitation. She wanted me to act as the Research Director. I agreed, because the project seemed interesting, but mainly because, by remarkable coincidence, the hospital was directly across from Rudi's shop.

In due course the project was funded, and for the next three years I had a professional reason for being in the immediate neighborhood of the store where I consequently spent several hours a day.

In spite of all this exposure, if I had been asked at the time about the nature of Rudi's work, I could hardly have given a coherent reply. I knew Rudi was a natural psychic. I watched him casually tell people what they were thinking, announce who was calling him when the telephone started ringing, and analyze a person's character at a glance. I very quickly came to take it for granted. My whole attitude puzzled me when I thought about it. As a social scientist, I should have been impressed and excited to see such evidence of paranormal ability on a daily basis. But it seemed entirely natural that Rudi should know these things. It would somehow have been much stranger if he had not.

I could not, however, classify the experience of formally sitting with him. I knew it was real and that it constituted a trail that I was slowly following through the maze of my own wilderness. That was enough.

In any case, he refused to give it a name.

"What difference does it make what it's called?" he said. "If I give it a name, you will think you understand it. As soon as people can name things and get them organized, the vitality is already diminishing."

What was clear was that when Rudi worked he generated and transmitted a higher energy. This was an immediate sensation for his students as they looked at him during class, and also had lasting after-effects of well-being, even radiance. At the same time, Rudi said, he took into himself psychic poison given off by the student.

"Why would anyone consciously want to take poison from anyone else?" I asked him one day. It seemed crazy to me.

"How else can it be?" he said. "If something of a higher nature comes into you, something must come out to make room for it. What comes out of you is poison. What goes into you is nourishment.

"I am very strong inside. In some ways, I am a mutant. I have more energy than I know what to do with, and it drives me crazy. I need to find ways to use it. So I give it to my students and take their problems and tensions into myself. My psychic mechanism is able to break most of it down into a form I can digest and use for my own growth. What I can't digest, I drop. The student has to open his heart and draw in the energy that flows from me. I do the rest."

"But I still don't know what is really happening," I said.

"Did you need to know what was happening in order to come with me to New Zealand?"

"No."

"Then stop worrying about it. Take what is given. Absorb it deeply within you. The rest will take care of itself."

. . .

Spending so much time in the store, I couldn't ignore the art. Although my original interest had been solely Chinese landscape paintings, as I saw how much Rudi valued Tibetan art, my interest grew.

One day in a quiet moment, I picked out a Tibetan tanka. I knew absolutely nothing about the figure represented in the painting, but something about his expression touched me. Rudi also seemed surprised at my choice.

"What do you like about the painting, John?"

"That's hard to say. Maybe it's the mysterious smile of the central figure."

"It's a very mystical painting," Rudi said as he rolled it up for me. Years later I discovered that the figure was Padmasambhava, the magician-saint who founded Tibetan Buddhism. That was my first purchase of Tibetan art. Even at that time it was rare and expensive. But whenever a shipment arrived, I bought whatever Tibetan pieces were available after Rudi had removed those he was keeping for himself. I had a sum of money saved toward the construction of a modern house. This gradually got diverted into Eastern art.

Rudi loved to discover art, buy it, and unpack it. He was not so interested in selling it. He would just as soon have given it away to people who shared his love for it. But being in the store gave him the opportunity to sit quietly, do his own inner work, and, at the same time, relate to the large number of people who were constantly passing through the doorway of his miniature world.

One day a man walked in and removed some wrapped objects that he wanted to sell. I caught a glimpse of them. They were golden Tibetan and Siamese statues. I withdrew until the bargaining was over. To my surprise, Rudi let them go by.

When the man left, I asked, "Were they too expensive?"

"No," he said. "They were too cheap."

"I don't understand. I never saw you turn down a bargain. I would have been happy to buy them."

"You don't get the picture, John. He started cheap and when I hesitated, he immediately cut the price in half. They must have been stolen. It is very dangerous to buy something from an unknown person who walks in off the street. If you end up with stolen goods, you can lose your money and also ruin your reputation. It just isn't worth taking the chance, no matter how tempting it might look."

While I was thinking that over, a station wagon pulled up unexpectedly and the driver called out:

"Hey Rudi! We've only got three plants left. Take them off my hands. You can have all three for five bucks."

Rudi knew the man. He bought the plants, put two in the window, and sold one to me — it is still alive, 25 years later.

. . .

The most exciting and difficult time in Rudi's business was during the arrival of a shipment. When it had cleared customs, and was about to be delivered to a nearby warehouse, Rudi closed the store or got someone to take care of it. He recruited all available help including friends, students, and customers, to go around the corner and unpack the crates. It was a collector's Christmas. Before the arrival of the shipment, Rudi would often have black and white pictures of the merchandise, but until it came you couldn't be sure what it would really be like.

The scene at the warehouse was wild — an amazing mixture of types and motivations. The professional warehouse men were entertained and dismayed by the rest of us. They took charge of unloading the crates from the truck, and helped to break the metal bands and pry open the carefully nailed crates. Then we got into the act with hammers, crowbars, and screwdrivers. Each opened crate revealed a new treasure. I was constantly torn between stopping to look at each object and getting on with the job.

Rudi was everywhere — telling people what to do, yelling at them for doing the wrong thing, calling someone over to look at a particular piece that had just been removed from its packing. Somehow, in the midst of all this confusion, the shipment emerged and was lined up along the wall of the warehouse. We took the shipment to the store a few pieces at a time on a small four-wheel dolly. With one of us pulling and the other pushing, we rolled along a bumpy side street and then, in an amazing, if only mildly risky maneuver, onto Seventh Avenue and halfway down the block, against traffic, to Rudi's store.

After five hours of this, the shipment would be in place and we would all be exhausted. But that wasn't the end. Once it was in the store, the inspection of the art would begin in earnest. Collectors would suddenly materialize out of the woodwork, somehow sensing the arrival of the art like mice smelling cheese. All of them were haunted by the fear that someone else might snatch up a desired object before they discovered it. I was no different, except that I usually felt so dazed by that time that I hardly knew what I was doing. Contact with large amounts of Eastern art is an intense, even shocking, experience, not only because of all the impressions involved, but because of the energy contained in the art itself. During the shipping process this energy accumulates. When the art is unpacked, the energy is released. Handling hundreds of such objects produces an overpowering effect. After another hour or so of sorting and selling, Rudi would close the store and I'd go home to collapse.

•   •   •

I went to Rudi's store almost every day. If it was warm enough, he might be sitting on a wooden chair on the sidewalk, working with a student. He used to work with his students one at a time between customers. The sight was always surprising; on that busy street, the two of them seemed to be sitting in an enchanted circle, and unconsciously, people reacted. More than once, a stranger rushing purposefully past would be unaccountably pulled short, staring at the pair who were at once ordinary and very strange. Rudi would fix the confounded passerby with his piercing eyes and ask, "Is there something you want?," The spell broken by the sound of his voice, the person would move on.

Such awkward encounters didn't arise when Rudi taught in the store, and the students didn't mind waiting until Rudi was free from serving customers. I certainly didn't. I waited for hours if necessary. But sometimes the customers were puzzled. Even though Rudi stopped teaching whenever a customer came in, often they would sense that something they didn't understand was going on. It must have felt like opening a familiar door and finding a waterfall. Some people took a quick look and ran. Others stayed, but often were distinctly ill at ease.

For these reasons, it wasn't a complete surprise when, in the fall of 1960, Rudi announced, "Next Thursday I will hold a group class in my apartment."

Even though I was curious to see what Rudi had in mind, I wasn't really pleased with this development. Unconsciously, I had built up a pattern of expectation about Rudi's work and how it was supposed to be done. To me, it involved a transmission of higher force between Rudi and a single individual. I didn't see how it could possibly be the same if he worked with ten or fifteen people at once. But of course I went.

His apartment was diagonally across the street from the store, in a small brownstone building on the second floor.

I ascended the stairs with mixed emotions, curious about what was going to happen, but dubious that it could be as effective as working with one person at a time.

The door was slightly ajar so I rang the bell and walked in. That evening, every available chair had been moved into the living room. Rudi sat on a sofa facing the rest of us and said only, "Work as you usually do and look at me whether I am working with you or not." With that brief prologue he began the class. The familiar silence that rang with energy descended upon us.

We sat for about thirty minutes. I tried to absorb his vitality, but my heart wasn't in it. How could working in a group compare with working individually? I felt cheated, but I kept my mouth shut.

When the class ended, we quietly dispersed. As I walked along the street to my parked car, I became more certain that it was all a big mistake. Hardly anything had happened to me.

The next afternoon when I saw Rudi, I decided to express myself: "I know I'm not in a position to judge what you're trying to do, but I felt that last night was a let down."

"How do you mean?" Rudi sounded tired and resigned.

"I didn't feel anything much happening. It just wasn't as strong as working with you alone. I can see it might be easier for you to work with everyone at once rather than spend a lot of time with each of us separately. But it isn't the same for us."

"Actually, it was a wonderful class for most people," said Rudi. "But the thing that really gets me, John, is that here I sit, hardly able to move, feeling like someone kicked me in the head because of the effort I put into giving that class, and what happens? You pick this moment to tell me that as far as you were concerned, it was nothing."

"I'm sorry," I said. "I should have kept my mouth shut."

"That's the way it always is. You never say anything until the minute I'm down, when you decide to unburden yourself. Do me a favor, go away and leave me to my misery. But don't worry. You will get used to the group."

I felt ashamed as I left the store, although I was still unconvinced. But, of course, Rudi was right. After I got used to the idea of not being the whole focus of Rudi's attention, I gradually realized that the energy was there to draw on whether Rudi was looking at me or not. After a few weeks of group classes, I could hardly remember it being any other way. He never stopped working with individuals in the coming years when time and setting permitted, but the group format was the more efficient and usual approach.

As long as I can remember, there were always people coming and going, with Rudi as an island in the stream of their lives. They would stop to spend an hour or an evening, and move on to return in a week or a month. Some were expected, others simply walked through the door of the store to make a purchase and were caught in the energy that Rudi wore around him like a psychic garment.

One day a thin, intense-looking man appeared and began to ask about various Indian gods. I retired to the hallway next to the bathroom to get out of the way until he had gone.

When I returned, Rudi said, "That was really something. This man walks in from the street and asks me, 'Which are the main Hindu gods?' I tell him and he says, 'I'll take one of each.' He's coming back for them tonight."

Several hours later, the man returned on a motorcycle to pick up the statues. Thus Wayne entered the scene. He was fascinated by Rudi, who in turn enjoyed Wayne's directness and intensity. He lived only a few blocks from the store and often came by on his way home. He loved to roar out of the Seventh Avenue traffic on his motorcycle and screech to a stop in front of the store.

During the next few months, Wayne bought more art and talked about becoming one of Rudi's students. Occasionally he took Rudi for a ride on the back of his motorcycle. It helped to break up the long day Rudi spent sitting in the store. I always watched with mixed emotions as the two of them disappeared into the endless impersonal traffic that flowed down Seventh Avenue. I waited on the sidewalk and didn't relax until they reappeared from the opposite direction.

A few days later, during a quiet period at the store, I said to Rudi, "It's a pleasure just to sit here with you without a million different things going on simultaneously."

"Appreciate it while you can," he said.

"Haven't you always been surrounded by people?" I asked.

"I used to be before I opened the store. But when I started my business I had to change my pattern. I knew lots of creative and artistic people. I loved to go to their parties, but it wasn't what I needed. I wanted to grow, so I sat in the store from ten in the morning until ten at night, as if it were an egg and I were a hen waiting for it to hatch, except I was the egg and it was the hen. I used to watch couples walking along the street, going to the corner movies or just out for the evening. Sometimes I felt so totally alone, I would sit here with tears streaming down my face. But it didn't matter. I understood the necessity and that made it possible for me to do it."

A customer came in. Rudi got up to wait on him. I drifted toward the back of the store and idly began to unroll some paintings I had not seen before. I came upon a Tibetan tanka that fascinated me, though I could not exactly say why. Rudi quietly walked up behind me and interrupted my thought.

"You don't like that one do you, John?"

"It's really unusual."

"It certainly is. I had put it aside to take home."

"Can I buy it?" I asked uncertainly.

"I was going to keep it," Rudi repeated, in case I hadn't understood him the first time.

I waited. I would do whatever he wanted, but I was very interested in the piece. After a short pause, he shrugged his shoulders: "All right, you can have it. But appreciate what you have. It is a picture of this work."

I didn't ask him what he meant and he didn't explain further. All he said was, "You can listen to this picture. It radiates music."

I looked at it intensely for a minute and I understood what he meant; it did seem to sing. I suddenly felt very happy.

Rudi walked over to his desk and motioned me over to a chair, indicating he would work with me. We sat toward the back of the store, out of the immediate sight of any customers who might wander in unexpectedly.

The familiar but always unknown process of energy transfer began. I submerged myself in it with a sense of necessity and dedication. The flow strengthened, but I felt partially anesthetized. It continued for perhaps ten minutes. Then Rudi said, "How do you feel, John?" It was unusual for him to ask.

"O.K. Why?"

"Because you are about to have a breakthrough," he said.

"I don't feel very different."

"It'll probably hit you in a minute. I'm going to step outside for some air." He left.

I sat there afraid to do the wrong thing, uncertain if there was anything to be afraid of. The silence deepened. The force working within me began to strengthen and swell. I felt unaccountably sad. Then, like sound heard first in the distance, a great wave began to break through me. I started to sob, more out of gratitude that something was actually happening than any sorrow. I felt carried out of myself. I could not say where I was, but I could hear singing around me. It sounded like a chorus by Bach or Handel, but not one I had ever heard. After a few minutes, the experience subsided and I walked outside, feeling purged and renewed. Rudi was standing under the awning of the nightclub where he had once washed dishes. He looked at me and smiled, but said nothing.

"How did you know it was going to happen?" I asked, finally.

"Does it really matter?"

"No, I guess not."

"But what does matter is that if you had followed your own inclinations, you would have walked out here with me after we worked, and the whole experience might never have taken place. You don't have enough sensitivity to your inner condition to know what's good for you."

I stood there feeling stupid and grateful.

Rudi smiled and looked around the Greenwich Village scene, but he didn't seem to be seeing the little stores, hearing the screeching brakes, or smelling the polluted air of New York City. I waited patiently until he started to speak.

"When you work," he said, "it is like surfing on the waves of cosmic energy as they move through the universe. These waves uphold creation. They are the freshest energy that exists. When you contact them it is like drinking rain water before it hits the ground.

"I ride these waves as they break through the atmosphere, absorbing, absorbing, absorbing. It is the most wonderful thing in the world. Sometimes during a long afternoon, the energy changes abruptly. I don't know why or how, but it is immediately obvious. Occasionally I phone up an as-

trologer friend of mine and ask him, 'What happened at
4:10 this afternoon?'

"He calls me back in a few minutes to say, 'How did you
know that Venus and Jupiter were in alignment at just
that time?'

"I doubt that he would believe me if I told him I can't
help knowing. The waves change continually. Every day is
different. Sometimes every hour is different. There are
some astrological events that occur only once in several
hundred years. The energy at such times is unique. If you
don't happen to be working, then you miss the chance to
absorb the energy. You will have to wait hundreds of years
for the same opportunity to recur. And that particular
quality of energy may be necessary to fill a vital gap in your
own development. That is one reason why it is necessary,
once you undertake this work, to do it faithfully every day
for the rest of your life."

The next time I saw Rudi, he looked very strange, as if
he had been through a remarkable ordeal. He didn't seem
to want to talk about it so I left him alone.

Finally with a sigh he spoke. "Last Sunday I was feeling
very peculiar. I looked down at my hands and I got the
shock of my life. They weren't my hands. They were much
larger and longer. I don't mind admitting I was frightened.
I had no idea what was happening to me. But I haven't
worked all my life just to throw away such an experience
because of fear.

"I immediately surrendered everything. I could feel the
energy of another being entering me, obliterating my personality, but leaving me a central core of awareness that
could observe what was happening. I looked down at my
hands again and suddenly I understood. They were
Nityananda's hands. He was coming into me. My whole
mind rejected the possibility, so I surrendered my mind.

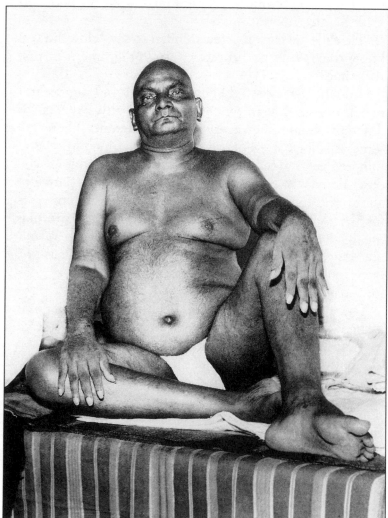

"I looked down at my hands again and suddenly I understood. They were
Nityananda's hands."

"For the last three days as I've gone about my normal routine, Nityananda has been moving in and out of me continually. My whole internal chemistry is in an uproar. But by now I am getting used to it. It is absolutely remarkable what a person can accept after a few days. By next week I probably won't be able to remember a time when he wasn't part of me. But right now I feel that every bone and muscle, every nerve cell in my body has been altered. I can never return to what I was before."

Rudi said no more about that, but on another day he talked about working with Indian saints. I mentioned that I had never had any particular desire to visit the East.

"It would be a waste of time if you did," he replied. "You haven't got the background or the capacity to get anything from the saints you might meet. And don't think that they would tell you what to do. They wouldn't. I make it very easy in comparison. Not only do I give energy away, but I teach people how to take it. None of you really understand how simple I'm making it for you."

"It doesn't seem simple to me," I said.

"There is a difference between difficult and impossible. To work in the East is more or less impossible. To work with me is difficult, just because growth is hard. It isn't really natural to grow. Everything in the universe is against it. The whole pattern of one's existence is based on an equilibrium. Anything that threatens the balance creates a complex counter-reaction, inside and out. Every significant move a person makes is tested by how he handles the reaction it produces. It must be that way. First you have to find something. Then you have to be able to hold onto it.

"And the worst of it is that the relatively few people who seek a path are often destroyed by the schools and teachers they approach. If you survive an esoteric school, that is a major test in itself."

"You survived the Gurdjieff work all right," I said.

"They told me that I would die when I reached thirty-one. Can you imagine telling anyone a thing like that? Most people would have been scared shitless by such a prediction and died just to be agreeable. It was a hard thing for me to fight because there was truth to what they said. There was a break in my life line during my thirty-first year. If I had denied it, I would still have been vulnerable. But I had a vision of how I would die and it didn't fit their image. So I decided that what they were calling death, would be death and rebirth. And so it was. You met me a few months after the rebirth."

I felt a cold chill and couldn't speak for a few moments. Then I said, "How could they tell you such a thing?"

"I was a threat," said Rudi. "I stood out too much. In class I was the only person who would ever ask questions. No one could shut me up. Experiences they described as difficult to attain seemed to happen to me effortlessly. When they tried to withhold something from me, I just reached inside them and took it. It was my need that helped me to tap the nourishment within them even when it was hidden by a ten-foot stone wall or sunk a hundred fathoms deep. I found it because I had to find it. They didn't want to give it to me.

"But that is the way most schools are. They want to fit the student to the method. If the student doesn't fit, they cut him to size. If you live through such treatment, you get stronger. If not, you hobble away. Most people don't survive. You were lucky that you were so deeply buried at the time that they didn't know how to get to you."

"That's a hell of a thing to say."

"But it's true, John. And you know it's true, or you wouldn't be so patient now. It may not flatter your ego, but the only hope anyone has is to accept his condition and begin to want to change it.

"When you were five years old, you decided to give up the world. Now you are retracing your steps. That's one reason it takes so long. You have to get back to what you left behind, and then begin again.

"A person pays a terrible price for his fantasies about himself. It takes a great deal of energy to sustain them. And even worse, it deprives him of the one motivation for change that he needs to get through the inevitable difficulties he must encounter."

"It doesn't seem fair," I said, "that people who are searching should be subjected to such treatment."

"Who said anything about fair? It is the way things are. They have always been this way. The earth is perfect. It's performing a certain function in the universe that has nothing to do with what we want or how we imagine things should be. Fairy tales are nearer the truth. There is always a search for some inaccessible treasure, with endless obstacles and temptations lying in wait. The hero may succeed, but it is never easy. And in life you never know who the hero is until the story is over."

. . .

So Rudi spoke to me on different occasions, until it seemed as if I had always been there in the store listening, watching, waiting. But it was not so. There had been many years of searching before I met him. When I was fifteen, I underwent my first inner experience. I began to hear an inner dialogue between myself and a presence whom I sensed as utterly alien. This other being told me that I was condemned to live alone in a haunted house for a long period of time. As the dialogue proceeded, I had the

39

chilling realization that the alien being was my real self, and that the familiar person to whom it was talking was an artificial creation.

During the next fifteen years I led an outwardly normal life, but nothing that occurred, except a love affair, ever really touched the inner isolation to which I was condemned without knowing why. It took several years after I met Rudi for anything to change.

In spite of the drama of some of the events I have described, I was still fundamentally buried throughout this period. When I sat in the store, it was as a shadowy and silent presence. It did not greatly matter, since Rudi talked enough to fill any vacuum that existed. He understood my condition and tolerated it, knowing that nothing but effort and patience would gradually lead to a change.

One day we were standing outside on the street. The weather was cool and the sky cloudless. Then the phone rang and Rudi went back in the store. I had been feeling strange, but that was not unusual when spending time around Rudi. Whenever something was occurring within him, it inevitably affected those around him, leaving them dizzy and disoriented.

As I waited for his return, I found myself unaccountably remembering that alien dialogue half a lifetime before. I thought how prophetic the words had been. And then, like the gentle flicker of wind caused by a passing bird, I realized that the spell had been lifted. The door to the haunted house was unlocked. I was free to emerge.

It was not a moment of high drama, but I knew it was real. When Rudi returned from his phone call, I was feeling very light and happy. I didn't say anything. There was no need.

3

Teaching

SEVERAL MONTHS BEFORE my thirty-third birthday, in 1961, I spoke to Rudi about my prospects in the work he was developing. "Do I have any chance of becoming a teacher?" I asked hesitantly.

"Is that what you really want, John?" Rudi looked up from an Agatha Christie mystery.

"I think so," I said.

"That isn't good enough. You have to be absolutely sure. Teaching is opening a door to the unknown. If you don't like what comes through, you might want to quit. It doesn't matter too much what a student does, except to himself. But a teacher is the connection between his students and a higher force. If he quits or falters, all his students are affected. If you want to teach, you have to have the capacity to persist, regardless of what happens. Otherwise, it's better to forget about it."

"I would like to say I'm absolutely sure," I said, "but it wouldn't be true and you wouldn't believe it. However, if I *were* sure, would it be possible? That's my question."

"Yes," he said.

"Any buts?"

"Many."

"What should I do about it?"

"You have to find a place inside yourself that is sincere and then ask from there to become a teacher. But if you ask, you have to be willing to pay the price. You can't figure out the price beforehand, and you can't know what you are going to get. Unless you're ready to pay, don't bother to ask. It's the only way to approach such a situation."

"What specifically should I ask for?"

"Say to yourself, 'I wish to become a teacher. I am willing to do whatever is necessary.' Beyond that, you can only surrender everything, even the wish, and wait for some inner response. If you want to try it, ask on your thirty-third birthday. Traditionally, that's a significant date for inner development. Let me know what happens." With that, Rudi went back to his mystery.

When my birthday came, several months later, I was at home in the country. During the afternoon, a great thunderstorm struck. I went upstairs to be alone. There was a picture window that looked out over a vast apple orchard. I sat down in front of it and quietly started to work. I was scared, and I still wasn't sure if I was sincere, but waiting wasn't going to help me decide. I watched the trees shudder in the wind as the lightning blazed and thunder reverberated through the skies. The power of the storm quieted me. I was not going to turn back.

"If it is possible for me ever to become a teacher," I said inside myself, "I want it to happen. I am willing to pay whatever is required."

I surrendered everything. The storm seemed to fill the void. Beyond that, nothing happened, but perhaps nothing was supposed to happen. I asked again, with more intensity.

"I want to become a teacher if it is right for me to do so. I am willing to pay whatever price is necessary." I surrendered again. This time, there seemed to be a mildly affirmative inner response.

I repeated the sequence a third time. The answer seemed clearer. It was positive. I could become a teacher.

But I honestly didn't know if the whole thing wasn't some form of self-suggestion.

The next day I was in New York and I spoke to Rudi about my experience.

"I did as you said."

"And?"

"It seemed to take."

"Good!"

"Don't you have anything else to say?"

"No."

The next thing I knew, Rudi had told Roy, who greeted me with, "Hey, that's great about teaching!"

"I'm not sure I believe it yet," I said.

"You'll get used to the idea," said Roy.

I was relieved that my experience hadn't been passed off as a fantasy, but I didn't entirely believe it either.

The following day, as we sat drinking coffee, I said to Rudi, "I have a thousand dollars. What's the best thing I could buy?"

"The standing Chinese Buddha," he replied without a moment's hesitation, pointing to a life-size wooden figure that stood in the shadows. "It is the most spiritual piece I have in the store, and just by good fortune it costs exactly a thousand dollars."

"I don't know whether you're joking or not," I said, "but I'll take it."

"It's a wonderful piece," said Rudi. "You can work with it."

"I don't quite understand."

"It's very simple," said Rudi. "You sit in front of the statue, look into its eyes, and connect with the energy that it emanates. You can work with any spiritual art in this way, or you can use a photograph of a saint as a point of contact. It is like looking at a picture of someone you love.

Standing Chinese Buddha.

LINDA SAXTON

The picture itself arouses the emotions you feel toward them. There is nothing magical about it. The difference is that you are doing it consciously to contact a higher energy which naturally flows in the saint or the art work. Once the contact is made, you just have to open to it and absorb it in your own system. I have been doing it for years. Why don't you try it now."

I sat in front of the Buddha. To my surprise, as soon as I began to relax, it started to look back at me. I had to remind myself that it was made of wood.

"Don't worry about what you experience," said Rudi. "It is your energy bringing it to life. It's like priming a pump. Once it starts going, it can serve you."

A few days later, Rudi unexpectedly said to me, "I would like to work with you in a different way."

I didn't know what he had in mind, but how could I refuse? We were alone on the first floor of Rudi's apartment surrounded by a partially unpacked shipment.

"Come and sit facing me. I am going to work with you very directly. Try and absorb it as you usually do, but also take in energy through every cell of your body as if you were a great sponge."

I sat as he asked, directly in front of him, almost touching. It was slightly awkward at first; his eyes were only inches from mine, boring through me. I could feel great heat coming from him. After about ten minutes, Rudi got up.

"It must have worked," he said. "My whole spine hurts."

I didn't know how I felt. I was still slightly in shock.

"In a few minutes," said Rudi, "you should feel great."

And in a few minutes, I did. My whole body began to radiate.

"What we did was a much more intense way to transfer energy, but I rarely do it. I knew you would accept it,

though, because you have enough faith in me to try anything I suggest."

"That's true," I said. "Everything you've done with me
in the past has always worked."

. . .

In the next few months Rudi slowly clarified the basic
outline of his teaching. He did not present it all at once,
but continued to develop the details for many years. His
basic conception was that there existed a psychic digestive
system within the human organism. Its function was to directly transform internal and external energies into
nourishment for higher human and spiritual functions,
which were usually dormant due to lack of proper fuel.
This conception is not unknown; it exists in various forms
of yoga philosophy, for instance. But the specifics were different and Rudi's approach as a teacher was unique.

In one talk Rudi gave after class during this period, he
told us, "The third eye is the mouth of the psychic digestive system. From there, energy comes straight down the
center line of the body, into the throat and then into the
heart center, in the middle of the chest. Once you can
identify this experience of energy flow in yourself, you
consciously work to circulate the force, drawing it all the
way down to the sex organs and from there backwards to
the base of the spine. Then it rises through the spinal cord
and ultimately emerges in the top and back of the head.
That is the complete circuit of the psychic digestive system.

"It really is very simple. But few people ever experience
it as a completed cycle because the various centers and
their connections are not open. They generally do not
open except under the influence of strong emotion or special
circumstances, and then they quickly close again. Unlike

the physical digestive system, which works almost totally by instinct, the psychic system works only through conscious effort.

"What I have just given you is a very simple description. A person develops by transforming the level of the energies that are working within him. Every situation we have ever had is potential food. When the psychic system begins to open, we can digest situations more fully and begin to work backwards on the junk accumulated in our unconscious. It is all fuel. We burn what can be burned and eliminate the rest.

"Religious belief has nothing to do with it. The psychic digestive system is not the possession of Hindus, Buddhists, Christians, or Jews. Anyone can verify its existence through his own experience, if he is willing to do the work involved over a long enough period.

"Under every system I know, the student is basically on his own. He may be taught how to breathe, or what to focus his mind on, or how to surrender, but the student has to do the work. There is no way to avoid it — you are responsible for doing your own work.

"I make it much easier. I give a higher energy directly to you. The first or second time that I open to a new student, a spiritual energy flows from both of us and comes together as in a complete embrace. There is nothing sexual about it. The meeting occurs in another dimension. But it symbolizes the beginning of a real relationship between us. Once this connection is established, you have only to absorb the energy that comes from me like water from a faucet. This is much easier than having to extract energy out of the atmosphere through your own efforts. But it is still work.

"There is a wonderful little Chinese book called *The Secret of the Golden Flower*. In it, they speak of 'circulating the light' and 'reversing the flow.' If you read the book, you will see that they are describing essentially what I have said, but from the book alone you would never understand it. 'Circulating the light' is digesting energy by bringing it through the psychic centers. 'Reversing the flow' describes the direction. Instead of the energy rising up and going out to other people as is usually the case, it is drawn down and back. Behind these poetic Chinese phrases lies a very practical understanding of inner development.

"When you start this work, it's a little like starting to fix up an abandoned house. Everything has to be fixed; each section of the heating, electrical, and plumbing systems has to be tested and repaired, even replaced if it is not working correctly. In a material sense, this requires the services of a skilled technician who can diagnose the situation and make the correct adjustments.

"For most people, the psychic system is weak and clogged through lack of use. If something has degenerated or broken, generally you are just out of luck. The ordinary teacher cannot begin to handle this kind of difficulty because it requires psychic surgery."

Rudi didn't talk about it often, but he could manipulate the psychic system, as a doctor might work on the arteries, muscles, and organs of the physical body. He aligned parts, replaced worn-out mechanisms, and opened up clogged passageways. If a new part was needed, he had to create it and then graft it into the individual. Over the years, I was one of the main recipients of such surgical efforts. Evidently I required them. Also, they were successful, which justified the effort as far as Rudi was concerned.

When he performed a psychic operation, it cost him a great deal internally. He was usually exhausted and often in pain afterwards, but he did not mind if the result was good.

Each step involved in the opening of the psychic system, whether produced naturally or through direct intervention, was crucial since it constituted a link in a chain of connections. The turning point in the process was the awakening of the kundalini force at the base of the spine. Much has been written about this force, most of it fanciful, misguided, and completely misleading. It has been described as everything from the basic creative force in the universe to an evil influence that feeds illusions and imagination. Equally fanciful are the means utilized to awaken kundalini. Characteristically, Rudi approached this highly charged step in a very practical manner. I quote from another talk he gave after class:

"The highest force that normally exists in the human mechanism lies asleep in a psychic center at the base of the spine. The only natural way to release this force is to give this center the nourishment it needs. Then it begins to open and the force is free to rise. Unfortunately, this nourishment doesn't normally exist in the human mechanism. It can, however, be created. One way is by transmuting sexual energy. Everything we do in the preliminary phases of this work is geared to making such a transformation possible. By absorbing the cosmic force in the atmosphere and bringing it down through the various centers, the original energy is progressively altered. When it reaches the sex center, a chemical reaction occurs. More accurately, it is an alchemical reaction. The base metal of natural sex energy is changed into the gold of transmuted sex energy. This refined product is the natural stimulus for releasing the kundalini force.

"This is why the suppression of sex or the denial of its relationship to inner work successfully castrates your possibility for growth. It is true that sex, in the ordinary sense, leads nowhere except to its own satisfaction and possibly to children, which is all that nature intended. Sexual relations that result in the birth of a child are the closest most people get to being creative. It's their bid for immortality. Of course, it usually backfires — the children want independence; they refuse to fulfill their parents' dreams. But from our viewpoint, the crucial aspect of sexuality is that a small amount can be transformed and fed into the base of the spine. Gradually, this arouses the serpent force held there in an enchanted sleep, and this force rises up a passageway in the center of the spine. Until this begins to happen, everything is preparation. When this process is activated, real inner growth becomes a possibility."

4

A Summer of Opportunity

AS THE SCOPE OF HIS WORK grew, Rudi decided to buy a house in the country. He had bought a house on Hudson Street in the City several years before. Now he was ready to expand again. In 1964, he started to explore the areas surrounding New York on Sunday afternoons, but for a while nothing materialized.

Then one day he returned from his search full of enthusiasm. He had found some marvelous property in a completely isolated pine forest near Woodstock, New York. It had been built by Alexander Archipenko, a famous modern sculptor who had recently died.

"The whole ground floor is one great room built on solid rock," Rudi described. "I think it was an old stone quarry. The cement walls were poured right on the stone."

A few weeks later, I set out for the house guided only by the vague set of directions Rudi had given.

The first part was easy enough: "Go to Woodstock." From there, it became increasingly obscure. "Turn left at a deserted gas station; follow the road until it shifts from asphalt to dirt; look on the right for a track going through an open field into the forest." It was the latter that was particularly puzzling. There are a lot of tracks going through open fields when you start to look for them.

I saw one that appealed to me because it didn't look too treacherous. I made my way slowly over the bumpy field and into the woods where the semblance of a road returned.

I drove for another half mile with growing insecurity until I saw several familiar cars parked in a small clearing. I had made it! And so had everyone else, which was amazing, given the ambiguity of the directions.

Rudi was eagerly waiting to take us on a guided tour of the forest and the house. The woods were great. The house was rather crude for my taste, but no one was asking what I thought, so I relaxed.

It was late spring. The air was warm and the countryside in full bloom. Rudi was ready to move in immediately. As with every move that Rudi made, the result was the same — work! Every weekend we drove up and painted, cleaned, repaired, and removed accumulated junk. We paused only for classes.

Though it wasn't immediately obvious, the productivity of our efforts was totally dependent on Rudi's presence. It wasn't as if Rudi did all the work, but he supervised the entire process and kept it moving.

One day, I noticed what happened when Rudi went away for about four hours. I watched with helpless fascination as things began to decay. People who had been working quietly began to drift off. Others who had their own ideas about what to do, but who stayed quiet in Rudi's presence, began giving orders. Little was accomplished, and most of that was sloppy and incorrect. The wall that was supposed to be orange was painted blue. Machinery that should have been protected by a dropcloth got spattered with paint.

When Rudi got back he took stock of the situation, and in ten minutes had everything straightened out. I never forgot the implication of what I had watched. Remove Rudi from the situation and decay sets in almost immediately. He understood what he was dealing with and knew how to keep otherwise stupid or difficult people moving along the right lines.

A few days later, during a pause in the work, Rudi called me to join him. He was sitting on a partially decayed log. At first he was quiet.

"I could hardly believe what was happening while you were gone the other day," I said, to fill the silence. "Everything began to disintegrate."

"I know," said Rudi. "But no one else noticed the difference."

"How could they not see it?" I said.

"Just ask them. You'll find out they thought it was fine. The fact that everything we are trying to build was being undone escaped them. You saw it because you know something about working from the years you spent in the Gurdjieff system. But you were probably happy that I was away, too."

"Sure," I said. "It was much more relaxing."

"At least you're honest. I don't enjoy yelling at people and pushing them in a direction that's good for them. It isn't my nature. If it were up to me, I would be lying on the beach at Fire Island. I need a place in the country like I need a hole in the head."

"Then why are we here?" I asked.

"Because," said Rudi, "we are interested in growing, not vegetating. You can't just do what you want. Growth always occurs against resistance. The seed breaks out of its husk even though it would rather stay a seed.

"It's just as hard for me as it is for you to take a step and experience the inner changes it produces. In fact, it's harder for me, because I am much more aware of my condition. You are still partially anesthetized. But don't worry. I can feel for you and keep you moving in the right direction. But who is going to do that for me? I have to be sensitive to myself or I'm in trouble. Your only protection is your inaccessibility. And that is what you are working to destroy.

"I don't mean to sound down on you, John. Actually everyone else is worse. Think of Alice. She is a good friend, but she has no burning desire to change her life. She is fascinated by my potential, but that is not the same thing. And even she does odd things. She slaps me on the head for no apparent reason just when I am in a very delicate condition. It really drives me crazy. She mumbles something about a mosquito, but that doesn't justify her action. I know why she does it. She is threatened by my growth. It is her way of interfering with my development. But understanding the situation doesn't make it any easier for me to take. Roy has a wonderful potential for spiritual development, but I have no illusions. He is just as likely to drop the whole thing in the pursuit of his career. There is really no one to whom I can give in depth, because no one wants it enough to make the effort. If I could just cast it away like a farmer scatters seeds, I would. But it isn't possible. Unless the other person has worked very hard, and for a certain time, there is no place in him for it to go. The ground isn't prepared. And even if it were, the person wouldn't have the discipline and responsibility to care for the seedlings when they sprout. They would die and it would all be for nothing."

"Why are you telling me all this?" I asked.

"Because, John, with all your inner deadness, you are still the only one who might have a chance to receive some of what I have to give."

I was silent, trying to absorb what he had said. It was flattering, but also sobering. The amount of work that might be required gave me pause. I was already working hard enough as far as I was concerned. I didn't know if I was supposed to respond. I didn't know how I wanted to respond. Was Rudi just expressing a mood of discouragement with his students, or was something deeper surfacing at an unexpected moment? Was this an opportunity I must grasp now or lose?

"Do you want me to say something?" I asked.

"If you have something to say," Rudi was looking off into the distance.

"I am persistent," I said, "but that is not enough."

"It isn't really anything," said Rudi. "It just gives you a certain opportunity." He stirred restlessly. I felt compelled to say more.

"Are you talking because of a passing mood or not?"

"What do you think?" he asked.

"I think not."

"You're right. Just because I seem very involved with certain people doesn't mean I lack objectivity when I need it. I see them for what they are."

"I know, I know," I said. "It's just hard for me to accept the possibility that I might be the only one to whom you could give more."

"I'm not flattering you. Who else is there? You show me. It is really up to you, John. If you can work harder, much, much harder, then I can fulfill my promise. If not — there is nothing to say."

We parted in silence. I went back to painting. Rudi walked off into the woods. I do not look back on that day with pride. I know that Rudi spoke the truth, and I know that I did not take advantage of the offer he made. Maybe I was incapable of making the effort at that time — there are many explanations and some of them are true. But there is no way to eliminate the ache of lost opportunity.

.   .   .

Each weekend that summer we poured in more time, materials, and energy. The house was cleaned up and painted, and minor repairs were made. There was little opportunity for relaxation beyond an occasional Saturday night movie or swimming in a nearby river once or twice. Water was a scarce commodity in the Catskills and the river shrank as the summer progressed. On the few times we went swimming, the cold water covered only about half our bodies. Rudi relaxed, but that seemed only to increase the intensity of the energy in him. We splashed and laughed, but it was hard to be casual next to an atomic pile.

As the season drew to a close, we went up to Woodstock for a final weekend. The work we had done was immediately obvious: cleared land, cut brush, and painted buildings. It was satisfying to view the results of our efforts, particularly when there was no immediate prospect for having to do more. I took one last walk in the pine woods. They were always my favorite part of the property, completely private, whispering, and primeval. I said goodbye to them quietly and then returned to look for the others.

We departed as we had come three months before: through the woods, across the bumpy field, and onto the main road. The summer disappeared behind us.

Three weeks later, I walked into the store, and Rudi greeted me with a sigh, "It's hard to believe, but it didn't go through."

"What didn't go through?"

"The house in Woodstock. The title was defective; I can't get title insurance."

"Are you going to buy it anyway?"

"No."

"But all that work. . ."

"So what?"

"Well, I guess if it doesn't bother you, it doesn't bother me," I said.

"It served its purpose. I would have been happy to have the house, but I'm just as happy not to have it. Maybe next year I can go to Fire Island and lie on the beach."

"Are you going to look for another country place soon?"

"Not just yet. There really is no need. That is one of the things this summer taught me."

It was almost five years before Rudi looked again.

5

A Gift

IN JULY 1965, when I turned thirty-seven, I stopped at
Rudi's store. Rudi usually gave students a special class on
their birthday, but this time he invited me to lunch.

"Do you feel like some fish?" he asked.

"Sure," I said. Anything would have been fine.

We left the store and walked down Greenwich Avenue.
I loved walking with Rudi; he made New York City seem
like a small town. On every block he stopped to talk with
someone he knew. If there was no one on the street, he
wandered into neighborhood stores.

At the restaurant, I got right down to the business of ordering and eating because I knew Rudi would want to get
back to the store. But he didn't eat much. After a few minutes I noticed that the atmosphere was unusual. I
stopped eating and immediately felt dizzy and slightly
nauseated. Rudi had grown quite withdrawn.

"Is something happening?" I asked.

"Just be quiet and surrender inside," Rudi said in an unfamiliar voice. Gradually the intensity around us di-
minished.

"What happened?" I ventured again.

"You were being programmed for your next year."

"I don't understand."

"On a person's birthday, the pattern of their next year is
projected. It's like a computer program. But unless you're
sensitive to the process, it'll go right by and you'll never

know the difference. It can only settle in you if you open to it."

"Did it take?" I asked, still bewildered.

"Yes. I was here to make sure it did. Why do you think I invited you to lunch?"

"I thought it was a treat."

"Not to me; I couldn't touch my food," he said.

"But nobody knows anything about this possibility."

"Like many things, you have to be told first. Now you know. Next year you may have to open on your own."

"How should I go about it?"

"For the moment just be quiet and absorb what has happened. But when the time comes, you have to be very sensitive to your inner condition. At the slightest unusual sign, drop everything and open for all you are worth. It's like being prepared for a knock on the door. If you are waiting, it is easy to hear it. But you have to answer quickly or the visitor may be gone." Rudi paid the check and returned to the store in silence.

Later that afternoon, Rudi surprised me again: "I definitely feel that you can write."

"That makes one of us," I said, shaking my head. "I don't mind writing professional papers, but I do it just to get ahead in my work."

"I'm not talking about that."

"But you never seem interested in what people write. I've never seen you read anything but mystery stories. Why do you want to push me into something you don't believe in yourself?"

"The one thing has nothing to do with the other. If you have the potential, you should develop it. There may not be any immediate reason, it may be ten years before you need it. But if you don't want me to talk about it, I'll save my breath."

"Just give me time," I said. "I never react well to new ideas. The idea of writing just doesn't fit my own self-image."

"That's the best thing about it," Rudi grinned.

"But what do you actually have in mind?" I asked.

"You should write a book."

"About what?" I was completely at sea.

"What do you know most about?"

"Psychology — Social Psychology."

"That's a popular subject; you ought to be able to develop something."

"But who's going to publish it? I've never written a book; I don't want to compose an exercise in futility. There is too much work involved."

"I have an idea."

"About the amount of work?"

"No. About how to get it published. I have a friend who is a science editor."

"He may be your friend, but he's not going to give a contract to an unknown writer."

"That's true," said Rudi. "But trust me. I'll figure something out. The main thing is, are you willing to do the work?"

"I guess so," I said. "What's your plan?"

"You think of the book. I'll take care of the plan," said Rudi, ending the conversation.

I didn't know how seriously to take the whole conversation, but I decided that I could write a book about various frontier areas in psychology. I had already met Harold, the editor Rudi was referring to. He was an interesting but demanding character. Rudi felt he had a touch of genius; I couldn't really judge, since when I was around, he seemed primarily concerned with the misdeeds of his landlord with whom he carried on a chronic cold war.

The next time I saw Rudi he seemed pleased with himself. "Harold is coming over to the house for supper tonight. Can you make it?"

"Sure. How am I supposed to act?"

"Do you have a book in mind?"

"Sort of. Why?"

"Because if you don't, I won't bring up the subject."

"Don't you think it would help if I knew what you were going to do?"

"No."

"All right," I said, accepting the inevitable.

That night, Harold appeared at the house and we all had a relaxed meal. During a pause in the conversation, Rudi said innocently, "Harold, I'd like your advice on something. John has an idea for a book. It sounds pretty interesting to me, but I'm not a professional. Would you mind giving him your opinion?"

"All right," said Harold. "Do you have anything on paper?"

I shuddered inwardly as I said, "Not with me. But the basic idea is very simple. Many people are interested in psychology, but the latest developments are hidden away in professional journals. I would like to write a book called *Frontiers of Psychology*, or something like that, to summarize these developments in understandable language for the layman."

"Give me a few examples," said Harold.

"Things like studies of creativity, the implications of space medicine, behavior change, computer applications," I replied making it up as I went along. "There must be at least twelve to fifteen topics of that nature that I could cover."

Harold thought for half a minute, then he said, "It might be interesting. It depends on how you handle it. I can't really say without a detailed outline. Did you say you had one at home?"

"Not really, just some notes."

"It might be worth developing," he advised. Then the conversation went on to other things, including Harold's continuing battle with his landlord. After a few minutes, I noticed Rudi giving me the high sign to disappear. I took my leave, thinking that the whole affair had been pretty pointless.

The next day, I discovered that at least one concrete result had emerged from the evening; Harold was moving into the currently unoccupied third floor of Rudi's house.

"What about the book?" I asked, more out of morbid curiosity than genuine interest.

"There should be more chance to talk about it with him living in the house," Rudi answered.

"But how do you feel about it?" I persisted. "I know that he's your friend, but being his landlord is something else again. He sounds like a pretty difficult tenant."

"You're right about that," Rudi laughed wryly.

A few weeks later, I happened to see Harold at the store. He was very friendly. "Have you done any more with the book?" he asked.

"I've been compiling some notes," I lied.

"Why don't you prepare a brief outline and send it to me. Then we can make an appointment to talk it over in my office."

I nodded, too surprised to say anything at all. A few weeks later the meeting occurred. Rudi told me before I left, "Do whatever he asks, even if you don't see the point." So when Harold outlined some questions he wanted answered, I agreed to reply in writing. A few weeks later, we arranged a lunch at which final details were clarified. Somehow or other, to my complete amazement, the project was materializing.

When I reported my success to Rudi, he was pleased, but not particularly surprised. "Just make it a good book," he said.

"I'll try."

"Do more than *try*, John. Harold and I made a deal. When he moved into the house, it was on condition that he give you a contract."

"Are you kidding?" I said totally surprised.

"Not at all. The book had better be good; Harold is a wonderful guy, very brilliant, but he's a tough tenant."

"I just don't get it. Why did you do it?"

"Look, I knew he wanted to move in, and it was the best way to get you the contract. Otherwise, he wouldn't have bothered with you."

"I'm amazed!"

"Are you? Well, don't be. Just write a good book so I don't regret doing it."

"I just can't believe you'd do such a thing for me."

"What's so surprising about it, John? Every time I teach, I give my life's blood. This is a much more external thing — I want you to have a chance to develop your abilities."

"I'm grateful," I said, "even though I'm not crazy to write the book."

"Just drum up some enthusiasm and get on with it," Rudi concluded with his characteristic directness.

That was the first of ten books I was to write in the next decade. *

---

* See list of titles on page 343.

6

Raising the Serpent Power

FOR SIX YEARS the possible arousal of kundalini was something I had to take on faith. When I was particularly open and relaxed, I could feel something stirring at the base of my spine. But there was nothing I could describe as a living flow. During all that time I waited patiently, but when the kundalini was finally aroused, it was not an anticlimax.

I was teaching a seminar in group relations at New York University, when the lights suddenly went out. I opened the door. The hall and surrounding rooms were also dark. I assumed there was some trouble with the wiring and returned to the class; I lectured in the dark for a few minutes and then dismissed everyone.

The elevator wasn't working either, so we stumbled our way down the pitch dark stairs, laughing nervously. When we stepped outside, the sight was awesome. There were no lights anywhere and night was falling. People were wandering in the streets; everyone was off-balance, disoriented — what was happening? From overheard snatches of conversation, I slowly realized that all of lower New York was without electricity — it was the Great Blackout of 1965. I didn't have a car, and the subway and electric trains were disabled, so I couldn't get home. I looked at my wristwatch; it was 6:30. I set out across town to see if Rudi was still in his store. He usually stayed open until seven. Cars began to cruise slowly, their lights the only illumination. A slightly tense holiday atmosphere prevailed. People streamed out of their apartments and walked along the sidewalks uncertainly. I walked, too, enjoying the situation and not feeling terribly involved in it.

When I reached the store, the door was locked. Rudi was gone. Of course! Why would he stay open without lights? But suddenly the situation was no longer enjoyable. I felt very, very lonely. What was I going to do? The electric train to my home wouldn't be running. The subway to my parents, ten miles away, would be out of commission. I couldn't think of anywhere else to go.

I started over toward Hudson Street to see if Rudi had gone home. I walked quickly and with increasing insecurity. From a distance I could see that his house was dark, and I started to get more anxious, when I remembered that *everything* was dark — there was no electricity! I ran up the stairs and pushed the bell. There was no answer, but maybe it wasn't working. I knocked. Nothing happened. I knocked louder. Nothing. I was really worried now. I banged for twenty seconds. No answer, but a neighbor looked out his window. I stopped knocking and moved away. Maybe Rudi was back at the store by now, but that was unlikely. He could be anywhere.

I walked aimlessly, feeling alone and without direction. The moon was up and it was bright and clear, but the thin moonlight gave things a slightly haunted appearance. Streams of people were moving around; most seemed as aimless as I felt. Where was Rudi when I really needed him? It was almost as if he had never existed. I overheard more snatches of conversation and gathered that the blackout covered most of the East Coast. I felt very strange.

I found myself back at the store, but of course it was still locked. What had I expected? I walked uptown, with no destination, just walking. Suddenly a hand reached out of the gloom and grabbed my arm; my whole body tensed.

"John!" a familiar voice said. It was Rudi. I had walked right past him, but he had found me. "Let's go to the house," he said.

I followed along, my sense of relief growing with each step. It was almost 8:00 p.m. by then, the time Rudi regularly met with students. I asked half seriously, "Are you going to have a class tonight?"

"Why not?"

"I may be the only one there."

"It doesn't matter. There is something I wanted to do with you anyway. This would be a good time."

"What?"

"It's better that you don't know in advance," he said.

We walked silently the rest of the way to the house. It took Rudi a minute or two to get the front door unlocked in the dark, then we groped up the stairs to the kitchen. We found some candles, and soon the living room was filled with warm, flickering light. It was slightly after eight when someone banged on the door. I couldn't believe it. People were showing up for class. I asked Rudi if he would still do what he had alluded to earlier if other people were there.

"Don't worry," said Rudi. "If the entire East Coast is blacked out, the least I can do is see if I can light you up."

I answered the door. Two people were waiting outside. We waited for ten more minutes, but no one else came. Finally, Rudi said, "I am going to give a special class tonight for John. The rest of you can act as witnesses." He motioned for me to sit directly in front of him on the floor, then he said quietly, "Kundalini rises gradually if it awakens at all. It is also possible to activate it directly. That is what I am going to do tonight."

When I heard that, I was thankful he hadn't told me anything beforehand.

"You have worked for a long time, John, and been extremely patient," Rudi continued. "I feel very right about doing this for you."

I sat still, trying to relax.

"Begin," said Rudi, "by asking from deep in your heart to be able to open to whatever is about to happen to you. Remember all the efforts you have made in the past and ask to receive the result now. Then let go of everything. There is nothing else for you to do but work in the usual way. Absorb the force in the atmosphere. If I touch you, absorb the force in my hands. Otherwise let me do the work."

Rudi looked at me, the candlelight reflected in his eyes. I could sense that he was making an effort, but I had no idea what he was doing. I concentrated on following his instructions. I kept asking inside and then surrendering. I wasn't aware of anything happening, but I didn't dare stop long enough to judge.

I felt like I was crossing a woven suspension bridge across an abyss. I could only walk forward and keep my eyes on the further edge.

Five minutes passed, then Rudi paused and said, "The opening in your spine is much smaller than I expected. It's hard for the kundalini to emerge."

He got up and appeared to look through me for a moment. Then he touched the base of my spine, pressing in. The sense of pressure built as he stepped away. I just kept trying to surrender. Then, without warning my back began to arch and I went into a spasm. I was frightened, but I tried not to interfere. The next spasm carried me to the floor. I lay there feeling energy moving through me in waves as it was released from within me. I lost track of time and of my surroundings.

When the physical impact started to subside, I sat up, slowly and hesitantly. The room and the candlelight came back into focus. Rudi was sitting in front of me smiling happily. "You just had your first real spiritual experience," he said. "How did you like it?"

"I don't know yet."

"Why don't you go inside and rest for a few minutes," Rudi patted my shoulder. "Give the energy a chance to settle."

I went into the bedroom and was happy to collapse. As I lay there, I realized that for the first time a warm current was flowing in my spine. There was no mistaking the experience. It felt wonderful. After a few minutes, Rudi called to me from the other room, "You can come back now."

I got up reluctantly and went into the living room. Rudi must have been talking to the other two people there, because they smiled and nodded and looked at me as if I were some kind of wonderful freak. They obviously wanted to ask me questions, but restrained themselves. Rudi looked at me proudly but with a slightly pained smile. "You must feel great, because I feel terrible," he said. "For a while there I didn't know if you were going to make it."

"Suppose I hadn't," I asked, getting a little alarmed.

"But you did. Why speculate? I never lose a patient," Rudi chuckled.

I sat quietly for a minute, feeling the force rising in waves up my spine.

"I've never seen you look better," he said.

"I've never felt better."

"I'm glad that it worked, John. I don't know anyone who can raise kundalini directly."

"Is that really true?" Now I was really overwhelmed.

"Yeah, it's true. Traditionally, the kundalini starts to flow only because of the student's effort over time combined with the fact that it is already released in the teacher. But to reach inside and start it going is psychic surgery. I've never seen it done or even heard of it."

"I don't know what to say."

"There is nothing to say. Just appreciate what happened and use it well. That's all I ask. Now, if you don't mind, I'm going to collapse for the night. I don't feel very well. Just make yourself at home on the couch, and I'll see you in the morning."

The other students said goodnight and went home with only the moonlight to guide them. I was left alone again in a darkness that covered the East Coast. Outside there was no heat, no electric lights; subways had stalled and elevators had stopped between floors. But within me a current of fire was flowing and a light I had never seen before had been released.

PART TWO

Influences
of
India

BARRY KAPLAN

"He worked late into the night, strengthening the force within him..."

7

Rudi: The Student

RUDI MADE TWO TO THREE trips to the East each year for spiritual and business purposes. The business aspect was always a tireless treasure hunt for art throughout the Orient. His spiritual quest took him specifically to India.

Rudi never left until he felt thoroughly prepared. Six weeks before the trip, he began to accelerate the intensity of his inner effort. He worked late into the night strengthening the force within him, breaking down whatever resistances existed, raising himself to a pitch of inner preparation as an athlete might train for an Olympic event.

A few days before a trip I once said to him, "You look like a wrestler about to go into the ring."

"That is exactly what I am," he said, "a spiritual wrestler struggling with powers that try to stop me."

"I would hate to be in your way," I said.

"There is nothing I wouldn't do when it comes to my spiritual growth. That is the source of my strength. Everything else comes with time, but without that resolve, there is no cement to hold it all together.

"You look at me and think I am completely beyond your own experience, but I have been working inwardly since the age of six. When I was young I was completely innocent. I was open to everyone unless they tried to attack me. I lived in a very tough neighborhood in Brooklyn. I remember one day a gang cornered me on the steps of my house. They were going to beat me up. I didn't know what to do. Suddenly I had an inspiration. I pulled down my pants and peed on them. They were utterly flabbergasted. By the time they recovered, I was gone. Another time, when one of my brothers was tormenting me, I decided to refuse to accept it. He was much bigger than I was and five years older, but that didn't stop me. In the middle of the night I took a baseball bat and hit him with it. When he woke up screaming, I told him, 'If you don't stop picking on me, the next time I will kill you.' There was no more trouble after that. I just wouldn't allow for the possibility inside myself, so no more could occur.

"But most of the time I loved everyone and was perfectly happy just to be alive, even though we were very poor.

"One day I was playing in the park when two strange figures came out of a tree and approached me. I was too naive to be afraid when they told me that they represented the Heads of the Yellow and Red Hat sects of Tibetan Buddhism, and that they were going to place within me all of their energy and spiritual understanding. I accepted it like an exotic Christmas present. Some large jars appeared next to them and they put them into me, in a space between my belly button and my bowels. They said that when I reached the age of thirty-one, the jars would begin to open and gradually reveal their contents through my own inner efforts, starting a process of assimilation that would continue for the rest of my life. That was the beginning of my spiritual work.

"The first time I went to India, many people referred to my Tibetan aspect. One psychic said that he saw strange books and broken pieces of pottery inside me.

"When I was eleven years old, I began to have a recurring dream. It must have happened almost a hundred times. In the dream I was quite old, maybe seventy or eighty, but I looked wonderful. I was standing on a great box, about four stories high, dressed in a white gown. I raised my arms to the sky and noticed I was surrounded by thousands of people with beautiful faces. I took a great breath and slowly began to rise into the air. When I got about a thousand feet up, great flames began to spurt from my lower body. I sped upwards faster and faster until suddenly I exploded into dust which spread out across the sky and became a rainbow. It was this vision that enabled me to survive the predictions made by the Gurdjieff people of my death at thirty-one.

"But the experience that had the greatest effect on me occurred when I was eleven and a half. During that period my body and spirit began to separate. I would wake up in the middle of the night, and be able to look down at myself asleep in bed. I assumed it happened to everyone.

Then one day I felt very strange. I had a headache and felt nauseated. This kind of discomfort was often a symptom of a coming spiritual experience. My chemistry was preparing itself. That night I awoke to find myself detached from my body, as usual, but when I looked down to see my sleeping self, there was nothing there. I wasn't afraid because I didn't know how strange that was. I just tried to relate to my physical self even though I couldn't see it. At that point I entered another dimension. I saw vast stone doors that were incredibly magnificent. I sensed, rather than saw, a great mountain disappearing in the clouds. I realized that it was not a mountain, but a foot and part of a leg.

"A great booming voice, which I instinctively felt belonged to God, began to lecture me. It said:

"'Everyone who has ever grown spiritually and started to teach stopped growing. They sold out because they thought they were there to serve the world and not me. They got caught up by their position and their external duties.

"'Promise me that no matter what happens, you will never stop working!'

"I promised innocently, like the small child I was. I did not understand what was being asked until many years later.

"After I had committed myself, the voice continued;

"'You will have everything you want except a permanent relationship with another human being. By staying free, you can serve others and serve me. If you do this, you will have everything, but you will not be attached to any of it. Every experience will become nourishment for your own growth.'

"And that is what has happened. As I have grown, the fiery stream inside me has grown, too, and consumes everything it touches."

"It is a great gift," I said.

"It is a great something," said Rudi. "It drove me crazy for years. There is nothing as nice as a pure fountain, forever flowing, but nothing as repulsive as a polluted one. For years I was a polluted fountain. It's hard for you to believe because you didn't know me then. But it was true. I had no choice but to destroy the flow or work to purify it.

"The energy drove me wild. Sometimes I had to walk the streets all night just to wear myself out. When I wasn't walking the streets, I used to go to all-night parties. I knew lots of theater people. They found me very entertaining, but I was going crazy inside.

"For a time before you met me, I was living with a friend who worked with me in the antique business. One night I was awakened by the sound of my own voice screaming. I could not remember anything about my dream, but I was frightened by my state. My friend had naturally woken up also. I asked him, 'Has this happened before?'

"'It has happened,' he said, 'about once a week for the last six months.'

"That was one of the most shocking statements I had ever heard.

"After that it got much worse. I began to have terrible headaches and started to hemorrhage from my nose and ears.

"The energy made me work, and the work dug up more garbage which had to be dumped. I fell behind in the garbage removal. I was choking on the results of my own efforts and didn't know it. The more congested my system became, the harder I worked, and the more garbage I produced.

"At the time, I had an image of a great train that would pull inside me every morning. At night, it would pull away carrying nothing but garbage in every car. This went on day after day for years.

"I might have died in the end, but I met the Shankaracharya* and he saved my life." Rudi paused and seemed to go backwards in time. His eyes grew softer as he continued. "He was an old, old man when he came to America. He was very high in the Hindu hierarchy, something like the Pope. I was with him for three months and all that time almost no one asked him a real question. Slowly it dawned on me that he had come to America for me. If he hadn't come, I would have gone out of my mind. I couldn't control the energy in me and I was choking on the waste products my inner work was creating.

"Whenever the need is great enough, it draws a response. My need drew him, even though I didn't know he

---

* His Holiness, Jagadguru Shankaracharya Sri Bharati Krishna Tirtha, ecclesiastical head of the Govardhana Monastery in Puri, the apostolic successor of Shankara who founded the Vedantic order in the ninth century, lived from 1880 to 1960. His visit to the United States in 1958 was the first time any leader of his order had ever ventured to the West. He was known as a saint, a scholar of vast learning, a brilliant mathematician, and a gifted speaker committed to world peace and the unity of all religions.

existed until I saw him get off the plane with a great shining halo around his head.

"I remember once he asked me what I wanted in life. I said, 'To work and to suffer.'

"'No, no,' he said. 'That is wrong. You should wish to work and be happy.'

"'Unfortunately,' he continued, 'you still have fifteen more years of hell to go through, but at the end of that time you will begin to experience a flowering of overwhelming happiness and love.'

"'How did I get into this situation?' I asked him.

"'You were conceived by two people who hated each other. Your soul was pure but immediately at conception it was surrounded by a hard core of bitterness and misunderstanding that expressed your parents' relationship. That is the hell you have to work out of in order to find your way to the light. It is not your own nature that surrounds you, but the conditions of your birth.'

"Then I asked him a remarkable question. I said, 'When I have completed my work, why should I continue doing it?' There I was, a kid in torment, asking about a time twenty years in the future.

"His answer, which I certainly didn't understand at the time was, 'You work to keep the wheel turning.'

"Later I came to realize that growth is its own reward. What starts as a needed discipline can turn into a mindless tyranny. What is felt as the flowering of an inner experience, may turn into a spiritual hedonism that retreats when resistance is met. There are natural departure points where a person can leave. But fundamentally, if you want to fulfill your potential, there is no end of working. It is for the rest of your life.

"I always felt warm in the Shankaracharya's presence, but one day as I walked through the doorway to his room,

The Shankaracharya of Puri.

I began to burn. It was extremely painful. I couldn't understand what was happening. I had to force myself through
the doorway inch by inch. The only thing that made me
do it was my faith in him. I couldn't believe that anything
associated with his presence could really hurt me. When I
was finally in the room, my whole body caught fire. That is
the only way I can describe it. This process went on for two
years and destroyed all the garbage. You were lucky you
didn't know me then."

"I doubt it," I said.

"I wouldn't have been of much help to you. I was like a
crazed idiot dancing on the flames. Anyway, the best proof
is that even though we were both in the Gurdjieff work at
the time, we never met."

I couldn't say anything to that.

.   .   .

Rudi left on his trips as quietly as possible. One or two
people would drive him to the airport and would pick him
up when he returned. He never wanted a fuss. He was con-
centrating on the inner level he had attained and wanted
to stabilize it. I rarely saw him on the day of his departure.
But once when I did, he looked like a totally different person: vast and invincible.

Invariably, before he left it would rain. It always rained
at significant times in his life. Only once in all his trips did
the sun refuse to be dimmed. Rudi recalled it on his return.

"I was riding out to the plane with Alice and Donald.
We were talking about trivial things. But inwardly I felt
some concern. There had been no rain. Was that a bad
sign? Should the trip be postponed? I didn't think so. I am
not superstitious, but I certainly watch for signs. I tried to
surrender the whole thing but it remained in the back of

my mind. As we neared the airport, I made a casual remark to Alice.

"'It seems like this is a first,' I said.

"'Yes,' she said. 'No rain!'

"And at that moment we drove through a great puddle which completely spattered the windshield. Donald had to use the wipers. We all laughed. I felt better."

Rudi always went to the East during the winter if he could possibly arrange it. I used to kid him about getting away to the tropics while the snow fell in New York. As usual, he turned the situation around on me.

"I double my growing season," he explained. "The natural cycle is to die in the winter and be reborn in the spring. By going to the tropics in the winter, I have two seasons of rebirth."

Rudi usually returned from his trips exhausted, but he was also burning inside with the impressions and energies he had absorbed in the Far East. I always tried to see him as soon as possible, to get the full impact of the experience.

On his first trip to India he had known no one. Every contact was yet to be established. He went with money for the ticket and a small additional amount for buying art. From that meager and lonely beginning, he had assembled, disbanded, and reassembled a network of dealers, collectors, and shippers, who worked all year to prepare for his coming. I heard about these people only indirectly. They remained exotic strangers made familiar only through Rudi's colorful recollections of his latest dealings with them. I never met them unless they came to America.

The man who could have most easily made the trip, Beebee, the multi-millionaire who had introduced Rudi to Nityananda, came only once. We visited him in his room at the Waldorf Astoria. When we entered, he was watching cartoons on television. While we were there, he continued watching. As we left, he was still absorbed. That is my memory of the fabulously wealthy Indian aristocrat. I think he was laughing at Donald Duck as we closed the door.

Everything that happened to Rudi while he was away came to me in bits and pieces through his own words. He told me most of it shortly after his return as we sat in the store or stood on the sidewalk, but additional nuggets would surface at unexpected moments. Sometimes the pattern would only emerge much later.

For example, in 1962, a year after Nityananda's death, Rudi took Swami Muktananda as his teacher. It was only during the following decade that the reasons for this decision slowly became evident.

Rudi's relationship with Muktananda always varied, but his approach was very practical.

"Swami Muktananda is always after me to learn Hindi because he doesn't know English. But I put him off. It would only be a distraction for me to know everything he says. Let other people get absorbed in his words; I go for the essence of the man. But fundamentally he can demand whatever he wants. There is nothing for me to do but give what he wants or leave. What does it matter? If he expects devotion, I provide it."

"How do you create a feeling you don't have without his sensing it?" I asked.

"There is only one possible way," said Rudi. "It has to be real. I work on myself before I enter his ashram until I get into a condition that makes it real. If I don't feel it, I wait. If you had to do the same thing before stepping through the door of this store, I wouldn't see much of you. Maybe I should start a new policy."

I said nothing, trusting that he was kidding. Rudi smiled and went on.

"I work myself into a condition where I feel he is the key to everything I want, the embodiment of God in human form, my spiritual father. It is more of a test than anything else. Swami Muktananda probably doesn't really care what anyone thinks of him.

"Then there is the other side of it. Each time I go to the East, I get slaughtered. In a way, it is one of the reasons I go. It helps me grow stronger. But I am human. Before I go I try to figure out how to protect myself. Nothing I ever think of works for more than a day. It's childish on my part to try to outwit him. In any case, that is the way he teaches. He creates difficult and painful situations that I have to transcend."

"It sounds more like a military school than an ashram," I said.

"It's all a question of what you want," said Rudi. "For most people who go there, it's a place to follow their dreams. They simply exist in the environment. They never open themselves to a depth where the energy of Swami Muktananda, or whoever the guru may be, can affect them profoundly. They go to be part of the atmosphere, and to have the illusion that they are pursuing a spiritual life. Most gurus don't care. A person can sit around half a lifetime and no one will say anything to them, as long as they do the required work and don't cause trouble. They don't have to grow.

"Personally, I think that whole attitude stinks. It encourages fantasy and weakens the atmosphere. But in India they aren't interested in creating the best conditions. They are much more creative about placing obstacles in your way than removing them. That is how they teach. You must wait and wait, overcome and overcome. If you survive the treatment, you grow very strong. For the most part, people settle for some comfortable level and only struggle to remain there.

"I will never forget the time I visited Ananda Moyee Ma, a very famous woman saint. I had been waiting for about an hour for her appearance. Finally, the door opened and she entered. At the same moment, the musicians who had been idly tuning up, began to perform. Shortly thereafter, temple dancers began a sacred dance. It was enchanting until it struck me that everyone was listening to the music and watching the dance. No one was paying any attention to the saint. It had obviously been planned that way. Once I understood the situation, I completely ignored the show and concentrated on her, opening to receive the inner energy of her being. But I doubt if anyone else in the room was even aware of her presence. Maybe they would get around to it when the music stopped. I wondered about that.

"When the music did stop, she quietly arose and excused herself. The opportunity to receive her energy had passed. They had probably all missed it, with only a momentary sense of regret."

"I am used to being tested in this way, but I would never do it to any of you. It isn't necessary. Life provides enough tests. The teacher doesn't have to create new ones. But I never had any choice in my own studies in the East. I am not complaining. It has forced me to cultivate various psychic abilities that I might have otherwise ignored. But I still hate it.

"They never really teach you anything in India. You almost have to steal it. Last week in class I gave a new kind of breathing exercise to increase the flow of kundalini in the spine. I'll tell you how I got that. I was sitting with Swami

Muktananda and I noticed that he made a strange snorting sound. No one else noticed it. If they had, they might have thought he had a cold. My assumption was that he does nothing by accident. He didn't have a cold. There must have been a conscious reason for that noise. So I imitated it. I had no idea what to expect. I tried it a few times as quietly as I could and found out what it could do. I didn't say anything. I didn't even ask him about it. He used it for himself, but because I was awake, I reached out and made it part of my own work. How many of you would be capable of such a simple thing? How many of the people who surround him would do it unless he specifically told them to?

"Of course, it's different when you come halfway around the earth. I would not accept the possibility of returning empty-handed. That's my underlying attitude. It is part of the inner conditioning that I go through. My preparation causes him to prepare also. He doesn't admit it in words, but I can feel it happening at a distance.

"Most saints that I know have worked tremendously hard. By the time I meet them, they have stabilized at a level that is acceptable to them and idealized by their students. They stay at that level unless they force themselves or are forced by circumstance to change. The major change that usually occurs is an expansion of their work on the physical level. Their time becomes more in demand. This can prove useful if the teacher makes a greater effort so that more of his being is available to go around, or it may simply dilute what is available.

"Occasionally, however, the teacher attracts a great student. When this happens, it may force them both to work beyond themselves. This may be done in a partly competitive spirit or more ideally, as an expression of their mutual devotion to God. But the dynamics of the situation contain

85

tremendous potential for growth, if the teacher accepts the challenge and the student refuses to be limited. Often in such situations, the teacher consciously or unconsciously seeks to weaken the student so that he is easier to control. If that doesn't work, they may come into open conflict and the student may be forced to leave. Either way, it is a terrible waste.

"You have to respect the essential quality of a teacher if you are going to open to him. Otherwise, it is a foolhardy act. Most people find it so difficult to open to anything that they feel it is an achievement when it happens. Unfortunately, we open most easily to people and situations that are bad for us. You cannot trust your instincts at such a time. I don't trust mine. When I go to a party and look around the room, I am inevitably attracted to someone who, sooner or later, (usually sooner) proves himself to be the worst possible person for me to know. Either he brings out a quality in me that I am struggling to overcome, or he offers nothing but the illusion of enchantment.

"If that is what happens to me, and I am a fairly shrewd judge of character, what chance do other people have? We are usually drawn by death in human form. It is the most powerful attraction that exists for most people. If you offer life, almost no one will take it, once they realize that the responsibility to preserve it goes along with the gift. You don't have to take care of death. It takes care of you.

"When I am with Swami Muktananda, it is a struggle between two spiritual heavyweights. It is a battle of energies. I assume that what he is doing is for my own good. I don't know what he assumes. It doesn't matter because the results are good for me. Through this process I have gradually come to realize that he is a great magician."

"What do you mean?" I asked, slightly horrified.

"He uses his will to change the world. He's an illusionist."

"Is that what you want?"

"No. It's the last thing I want," said Rudi. "But the great spiritual beings are gone in India. There was a final generation of giant God-men. They all died within a few years of each other. Bhagavan Nityananda was one of them. And who is left to take their place? Either kind, devoted swamis who lack the power and grandeur of the men who taught them, or great magicians. A nice little old man can't do much for me. A great magician can make me strong. I have to grow to contend with him. He has to keep growing to be ready for me. We both need each other.

"And then Muktananda is the partial inheritor of Nityananda's spiritual force. His ashram is in the town Nityananda created. There is a psychic connection between them which I can experience and use. And I also have my own contact with Nityananda.

"In most ashrams in the East, the guru doesn't pass on his power and position until death intervenes. As he leaves the earth, the energy with which he has worked is freed to be used by others. One may have to wait half a lifetime for this opportunity to occur. Then, and only then, the designated man, or the man who arises to fill the vacuum left by his passing, can receive the inner mantle of the teacher.

"I don't believe in doing it that way. There is no reason that death has to be the source of the gift. I intend to pass on my own capacities during my lifetime. I am glad to do it and in this way free myself to go on to other levels of development.

"The major teachers I have known died shortly after I met them. It was wonderful for me. It gave me a great opportunity for absorbing what was released at their death. The initial contact was enough to create the possibility. It happened with the Shankaracharya.

"The three months I spent with him were enough. On my next trip to India I was within miles of Puri, but I didn't visit him. It didn't seem necessary. Later I heard that he had died. But I didn't feel bad, the inner contact was still there. He is a living force to me. The same thing is happening in relation to Nityananda.

"But you must be able to assimilate the guru's inner content when it is available. Then their essential quality is inside you, and can continue to attract the energy they leave behind. That sounds easy, but you can't assume that people will understand it.

"When I stopped at the Divine Light Mission at Rishikesh on my last trip, they took me to the room where the late Swami Shivananda used to live. He was one of the great saints of Nityananda's generation. The whole ashram was recovering from his death six months before. They were sad. The whole place looked deserted and run down. It was depressing, until I walked into his room. He was still there! His force was shining and ringing, but nobody else seemed to notice it. I asked to stay in the room for a few minutes. They left me alone, and I worked deeply to absorb this marvelous energy. I emerged in ten minutes filled with radiance and overflowing with joy. They were still sad. It was ridiculous! The essence of their teacher was with them, but they could not open to accept the possibility. For them he was dead. For me he is alive!"

"Is it going to stay that way?" I asked.

"Who can say? I expect that in time his presence will fade. Why should he stay there with the vastness of the universe to inhabit? No one of a higher order will stay connected with a particular location for long if their presence is not utilized.

"It's a different story with Swami Nityananda. Partly through Swami Muktananda's presence on the scene, a beautiful marble temple is being built to house Nityananda's remains. It is becoming a place of spiritual pilgrimage. As long as seekers and holy men go there with an open heart looking for nourishment, there is no reason that the energy should not remain and even grow stronger. But there is nothing inevitable about it. The only thing one can assume about higher energy is that it will disappear quickly unless it is consciously appreciated. One reason it takes so long to grow inwardly is that no matter what energy level you contact, it won't do any good unless you can absorb it deeply before it evaporates. It is like rain in the desert; wonderful, unexpected, rare, and almost before you know it, gone; a little into the earth, most of it back to the sky. It is almost totally useless except for highly specialized organisms such as cacti that are built to absorb and hold every drop available.

"The ordinary person is full of leaks. Every tension is a leak. Every strongly held belief is a leak. Every relationship into which we pour energy is a leak. What makes the situation more difficult is that the first thing we lose through these leaks is the higher energy, because it is the most volatile. We are not used to working with anything so refined. It is almost inevitable that the first few times, perhaps the first hundred times that we make the necessary effort to accumulate a little of this rare energy within us, we lose it almost immediately. It is only based on the frustration and futility of such an experience that we begin to see the need for plugging our leaks and for allowing nothing to rob us of this rare element that can only be gathered consciously from a source that has it to give.

"Timing is crucial. When you have received a gift of inner spiritual force, you must remain open and quiet for about half an hour to allow it to penetrate more deeply into your system. Anything that disturbs you will impede or abort the process. It is vital to take this extra time or all your efforts, whatever they may have been, will be partially or totally in vain.

"Growth is gradual and basically natural. The life a person has attracted around him when he starts to work is the best possible life for him. It contains all the elements which represent him in an external form. If he casts that life away, how will he ever understand why he attracted it in the first place? The way to change is to absorb what surrounds you, digest it, and grow beyond it. Some of it will naturally and inevitably fall away, like the lower leaves of a plant. Everything is connected. You cannot change one part without producing unintended consequences.

"That is the problem with breathing exercises in Pranayama Yoga. Breathing is very important. You cannot absorb prana from the air without the right kind of breathing. But, at the same time, many of those exercises place an arbitrary scheme on the normal pattern of breath. It doesn't make too much difference unless one takes these methods seriously. But if they are done with sufficient intensity, they begin to take over and the body loses its understanding of how to breathe. This in turn sets off reactions in the nervous system that were unintended and may be harmful.

"Left alone, our body understands the need for breath. But instinctively, it absorbs only a small part of the energy in the air. We can increase the amount through our own conscious desire. We have to breathe from a place within us that wants to be nourished, and that is much simpler than it sounds. If you walk along the sea shore or in a pine forest, what is the natural thing to do? You take a slow, deep breath and savor the odors of nature as you absorb them. That is the beginning of conscious breathing. Then, if you take in something you value and enjoy, such as fine wine, what is the next natural thing to do? You hold it on your palate and let the sensation spread through you. In the same way, after you have breathed in slowly and with awareness, you hold your breath and allow the energy you have received to expand in your system.

"Finally, in the last phase, when you breathe out, you can let go of all kinds of tensions; physical, emotional, and psychic. If you slowly absorb energy when you breathe in, allow it to go deeper while you hold it inside you, and consciously allow tensions to flow from you when you breathe out, each completed breath is a unit of work. And when the energy absorbed by this type of breathing is fed into the psychic digestive system, it vitalizes the whole transformation process.

"The problem with more arbitrary breathing exercises is that we have insufficient understanding of the inner functioning of the person who is using them, and consequently we cannot anticipate all of the effects these exercises may produce.

"A teacher has his own experience to guide him, and he accumulates the experiences of his students who are passing the same way he has already traveled. But each individual is somewhat different. Inner growth is not like following a recipe. It is more of a treasure hunt, the clues to which are all buried in the present. Or rather, they lie in eternity and flash through the present when we least expect them. They are usually lost as fast as they appear because the person doesn't see them.

"Time is not an iron band or a straight line that grows from the past into the future. It is elastic and can disappear altogether as one's consciousness varies. You have been sitting in the store with me all day. Does it seem long or short to you?"

"Sometimes very short," I said. "At other times like weeks. But right now it seems as if I have been here for ever. I feel as if I were a deep-sea fish swimming to the surface of the ocean. When I break through into the sunlight, my whole perspective changes. All the earlier time seems confused and meaningless. It is only now that anything seems real."

"It is, John. The hardest thing to imagine is a level of consciousness that we have not attained. No matter how vivid our fantasy, the next level is always the one we cannot imagine. It is the same with most of the problems we have. The one solution we never think of, no matter how obvious, is the right one. We really can't resolve most of our problems because all our thoughts occur in a certain context that we take for granted.

"There are two directions we can pursue in resolving any situation. We can attempt to think it through or we can try to go to a place where the powers of understanding are greater. That is why I have to go halfway around the earth to pursue my own development. In India these powers still exist, though they are dying out. And the irony of the situation is that when one contacts them, it's on a different dimension. They aren't on the earth at all."

8

Rudi: The Teacher

RUDI GENERATED STRONG emotional reactions in the people around him. It was therefore remarkable that there was relatively little jealousy among them. It was also fortunate, because there was constant shifting between people and situations as Rudi himself grew and the quality of his being attracted some and repelled others.

"When someone new becomes close to you," I said one day, after some recent changes, "it doesn't seem to bother me."

"Ordinarily it would," replied Rudi. "People get really upset when anyone with whom they're involved forms a new relationship."

"So why don't I feel that way?" I asked.

"Because when I meet a new person it in no way threatens our connection. Most people can't stretch themselves to encompass new situations without letting go of the old. I don't permit that to happen inside myself. If someone leaves, I can't stop them, but as long as they remain and preserve a certain vitality in their effort, I work to stay open to them.

"But there is another side to the situation. There is nothing you or anyone else could do if I decided to cut the connection between us. The student is at the mercy of the teacher in that respect. A true teacher is a servant, not so much of the student, but of the force that comes through him. When he works, his personality is suspended. It is the higher force that directs his actions. If that is not entirely the case, the student is partially at the mercy of the ego of the teacher. There is nothing the student can do but go along with the situation in order to get what he wants, the higher force. He must work to find this kind of humility inside himself. It may not seem fair, but if you want something that someone else has to give, you play the game according to his rules.

"I make it very, very easy for people. The only thing they have to do is put up with the impact of the changes in my internal chemistry produced by my own growth. There isn't much I can do to shield them from that. But otherwise I expect almost nothing. Probably I make it too easy. If people don't pay enormously for what they get, they don't value it. It's too bad."

"But why should it be that way?" I asked.

"I don't really know. If people felt more worthy," said Rudi, "they would take the energy in a quiet and grateful way, understanding that there was nothing they could really give in return. That's the simple truth. No matter how long you continue to know me, John, and it will probably be for a long time, there will never be anything you can do for me that I really need. All you can do is receive from me the nourishment you require, take it in, digest it, and use it well. That is all I ask of anyone, but how many can accept something that simple?

"You have to study in the East to appreciate what I'm offering. Most people think of holy men and saints as quietly smiling, highly moral individuals who freely give their help and blessings. It isn't true. The saints I have met were a strange group of characters. Sainthood has to do with level of being, not personality. A saint can be a son of a bitch. There is nothing you can do about it if he is, except surrender or leave. You look doubtful, John."

"It's just so different from what I thought."

"I'm a good human being because I want to be," said Rudi. "But if I weren't, what could you do about it? If I were mean and sarcastic, would you leave?"

"No."

"If I lied to you, would you leave?"

"No."

"Why not?"

"Because it wouldn't matter. I would still need what you have to give."

"That's true, although most people wouldn't be able to look at it that way," said Rudi. "You wouldn't have any choice. That's what I face in India. I constantly have to prove myself, and at the same time accept whatever is in front of me. Most Indians don't believe an American can be spiritual; if you weren't born an Indian, you've had it as far as they're concerned. But even if I were an Indian, I would still have to accept whatever the guru did. He makes the rules. If he expects to be loved, you love him. If he wants to be served, you serve him. Sometimes it's easy, usually it's not, but either way you have to find it in yourself to do what is required or you can't possibly get anything from him. And the guru can make it very difficult."

Rudi stopped to dust off some statues on his desk. Then he continued, "When I am at Swami Muktananda's ashram, hardly anyone accepts me. I am generally either ignored or being tested. I don't feel sorry for myself. I am not going all that way just to be loved. But it is still hard. I get along best with the children in the town. When they see me coming, they drop whatever they are doing and start to jump up and down with excitement. We roll down the hills together. I chase them around, throw them up in the air, catch them, and blow on their bellies. It isn't just a way for me to let off steam. I desperately need the sense of love that I get from them. Otherwise, the whole situation gets too grim. It's like climbing rock cliffs eighteen hours a day.

"I have one friend, Chakrapani. He is a wonderful psychic. If it weren't for his sense of my future, I would find it pretty difficult to keep going. He works for me out of love. The rest of the people leave me alone because of their fear and prejudice.

"In the end, it doesn't really matter. I come to receive what I need for my growth or to be examined on what I have attained. And then I leave. I don't stay an hour longer than I have to. Often Muktananda urges me to stay a few days more. I have to plan my retreat without offending him. It's a question of very careful timing.

"When I first arrive, we are both totally involved in the encounter. Any mention of leaving, on my part, would cause him to insist that I stay for at least three weeks. So I keep my peace and wait. I know that nothing ever interests him for more than a few days. I bide my time until the fourth day. Then I say casually, 'I must be leaving the day after tomorrow because I have heard of a collection I should see.' He expresses great regret, but he allows it to happen. I promise to stay for an extended period the next time. He makes a few remarks about my business activities and my spiritual life interfering with each other. But I counter by asking, 'Do you think that I should give up my business?' He would rather have me successful than permanently around him. He accepts the inevitable.

"On the final day, we go through an elaborate farewell, with expression of regret and love on my part. He responds accordingly, but I can see that he has already lost interest and is just as happy that I am going."

"Doesn't he really care about you?" I asked.

"That isn't the point. You can only go so far in any direction at a given time. Once that has happened, why drag it out? It is always better to leave too soon than to outstay your welcome. That way, your next visit will be anticipated."

"Nityananda is as real to me as Muktananda," said Rudi on another day. "One is physically dead, the other alive. It makes no difference. In many ways, Nityananda is easier to deal with. Swami Muktananda can make me wait for days in agony before he does anything about it. He may have someone say something against me just to see how I will react, or he might even use magic against me to see if I can overcome it. But understand one thing, John. I complain about him when I am in New York. That is my privilege. But God help anyone else who ever does that in my presence. He is my teacher. If you respect me, you must also respect him. Do you understand that?"

"I have never said anything against him, have I?"

"That isn't the point. In accepting me, you must accept him. Otherwise, you would have to assume that while I am fine for you, I don't know what is right for me. It can't be. If I don't understand myself, how can I understand you? Swami Muktananda can be very difficult. He doesn't really care about other people. It is part of his detachment. But I am learning and growing through my contact with him. I need the challenge he presents. It would be more pleasant for me if he were sweeter, but I wouldn't grow as fast. If you or anyone else were to go to him at this point, you would get nothing, because he's too difficult to understand. He would distract you with some little trick, ignore you, or perhaps cast a spell of some kind on you which you wouldn't even suspect.

"I don't care what he does as long as I grow. If he wants to enchant me to test whether I am conscious enough to realize what has happened, and strong enough to get out of it, I accept his right to do it. But don't look so sick. I'm not going to do anything like that to you."

"Could you if you wanted to?" I asked uneasily. I had never looked at Rudi in that light before.

"I could find out how to do it in a hurry if I needed to. But all life is a magic spell. Why add to the weight of it? I don't want to use my own will against other people. How can they grow that way? I have never made anyone go through tests which I have devised. That has been done so often to me that I hate it. Life is difficult enough.

"If Nityananda had lived, he might have been as hard for me to get along with as Muktananda. When Nityananda didn't like someone's inner state, he was liable to pick up a stick and start to beat them. When he was younger, he used to live in a tree. If anyone came near, he threw stones at them. He had renounced the world and didn't want to be disturbed. But if children came, he threw flower petals.

"Since he died, I don't have to contend with his personality, for which I am grateful. The cosmic part of him is still there. I see him, talk to him, and have the same basic experience as I would have if he were alive. I can't really expect you to believe that, but I'm not talking to make you believe anything."

"So why are you talking?"

"It is necessary," Rudi said. "It helps me get perspective on my own experiences. It is one thing to go through them alone. It is another to listen to myself as I tell someone else about them. Then I begin to understand what I couldn't see at the time and also sense whether it feels real to me as I recall it. I have many reasons.

"The first time I went back to Ganeshpuri after Nityananda had died, I was still numb from the experience of meeting him a few months before. It was too soon for me to feel any sense of personal loss. I didn't honestly think he was that important to me. But when I entered the room

that held his remains, I immediately realized that the presence of the man was there just as real as before. There
could be no doubt about it."

"Would I feel it if I went there?" I asked.

"Yes. You would feel it in the same way that you feel my
presence. You might not know exactly where it came
from, but you would experience it like the force that works
when I give a class.

"Nityananda didn't teach people through giving them
his energy. He worked and worked to transform the energy
he drew into himself. Because of the magnitude of his effort, there was a continual overflow. In that way, he enriched the atmosphere and permanently polarized the area
around him so that it continued to attract higher forces.
There is really no loss involved in his death if you understand how to relate to the energy that remains."

"The sun shines. It doesn't spend its time determining
how worthy each person is to receive its light. In the same
way, Nityananda never worried about how his soul force
would be used. It poured out of him. If no one used it at all,
it would still have overflowed as long as he opened, circu-
lated, and surrendered to God.

"I have had many encounters with Nityananda when
I've been in Ganeshpuri. I never know what to expect. I
may see his figure pointing to the hot springs near his
tomb. He wants me to bathe and purify myself. I take off
my clothes and sink into the wonderful warm sparkling
waters. After a few minutes he motions again. I am to follow
him. I emerge, get dressed, and go where he has indicated.
It may be his samadhi temple where his body is enshrined,
or the room where he slept and held audience. And there,
with or without words, he works with me. He is as real to
me at those times as you are now. But you have to understand one thing. This isn't everyone's experience. He can

work with me and through me because I am willing to open myself to him. Otherwise, nothing would happen."

"Would he work with me if I were there?" I asked.

"He is already working with you, but you are too insensitive to know it."

"What good is it then?"

"Only a limited good. But you are looking at the whole thing in the wrong way. It isn't a question of whether you would have my experiences. Why should you? But it is crucial that you are nourished by Nityananda's energy. That is already occurring. Through my inner contact with him, his energy reaches you. This is the significance of the lines of work that are emphasized in all spiritual teaching. When you open to a teacher, you open to everyone with whom he is connected. He is simply the last link in a chain that extends backward in time. It is a lack of concept and scope that prevents people from opening to what is in front of them, and using it as a doorway into eternity."

"I never thought of it like that," I said, feeling stupid.

"That is your limitation," said Rudi. "What I have told you can give you, if you use it properly, a direct contact with Nityananda and the line of teachers that he represents. Even without understanding the possibility, you still have the contact. His energy is one of the main currents that flows through me when I work. You have been receiving it all this time without understanding what it is."

"Is it really the same as if I'd met him while he was alive?"

"Not exactly. When I work, all the energies that I can attract flow together in a great stream. There may be five or ten small streams that combine for this flow. They may come from various cultures and different historical periods. This work is not originally Indian or Tibetan. It was developed in Atlantis. But once the streams merge, it's impossible to separate them for analysis, any more than you can isolate the ingredients of bread once it has been baked. But there are times when Nityananda manifests particularly strongly. If you could see psychically at that moment, you would see his presence in me; or rather you would see me disappear and him appear. But don't worry about that, John. Psychic sight can be a great distraction. Anything you see is only the manifestation of higher energy hitting a lower level. The important thing is how much of it you can absorb and use for your own growth.

"In my last trip to Ganeshpuri, I saw and felt the whole experience I had at the age of six, with the two Tibetan monks, repeat itself. Then I experienced them releasing energy and knowledge they had put into me so many years ago. If I thought too much about the reality of it all I would probably drive myself crazy. But I know that in the end, everything comes down to work. And the more you work, the more you become aware of your own nothingness. That is the antidote.

"A teacher is really a servant — something many teachers would rather forget. In some Buddhist scripture it says, 'The Buddha is a shit stick.' It can't be put more graphically than that. Just because a higher force flows in a genuine teacher, does not mean he is to be worshipped. His function is to serve the student's potential. Most teachers demand a great deal of respect, which is correct, if it is the cosmic force that is respected. But it too easily shifts into honoring the personality of the teacher. It requires a willingness on the teacher's part to surrender the subtle advantages of his role, for the relationship to remain mutually productive.

"No situation, no matter how satisfactory, is an end in itself. It is all material for surrender. You build to give away. Otherwise, what starts as a creation ends as a prison you have constructed for yourself.

"There can be nothing permanent if you wish to grow. Anything you hold onto will, in the end, turn out to be precisely what you have to surrender. It is not cruelty on anyone else's part, but an inevitable aspect of growth."

"That sounds reasonable," I said, "but I don't see where it applies to me particularly."

"You are a somewhat different case," said Rudi. "You don't care enough about anything to make it worth sacrificing. What do you have, except the art you bought from me, that you wouldn't happily give away?"

"The problem is the other way around," I said.

"Exactly. With you, it is a question of growing strong enough to attract a real situation that you would want to hold. Then you will have something to sacrifice."

"I would rather not know about it in advance," I said.

"Don't worry," said Rudi. "You will forget the whole conversation by tomorrow, but in the years to come, when the situation finally arises for you, think back to what I have said today.

"And by the way," said Rudi, suddenly shifting the subject again, "do you need any incense? I just got a shipment. It always arrives just when I am running out or when I'm going through a difficult period and need direct contact with India."

"You get the best incense I have ever been able to find," I said.

"That's because it is completely fresh," Rudi replied, lighting a stick. "They air mail it to me from the factory."

I helped myself to one package of each scent. Rudi never charged his students for the incense. Occasionally he charged a customer, though he was reluctant to sell it to anyone not working with him.

There was another pause. Then Rudi said, "Would you go to the deli around the corner and get me two franks with mustard and sauerkraut and a dill pickle on the side?"

"Sure!" I said, happy for the diversion. Rudi didn't offer to buy, which was unusual. But I was glad to pay. There was little enough I could do for him.

Leaving the store was always a shock. I never knew how deeply I had been affected by its atmosphere until I was out of it. I could feel the energy I had absorbed glowing within me. I walked along the street breathing deeply and feeling wonderful. I ordered the franks and returned carrying a warm bag filled with delicious-smelling food. Rudi undid the foil that surrounded each frankfurter and ate them quickly.

"Most people eat slowly and breathe quickly. I breathe slowly and eat quickly," he said.

There was a contented silence. Then Rudi asked innocently, "Isn't there anything you would particularly like to have, John?"

I hesitated. "I'm afraid to make a wish. I'm never sure of the implications."

"Very wise," he said. "Nevertheless you can always add, 'don't give it to me unless it will help me grow.'"

"I suppose," I said. There was nothing casual about the conversation. I knew I was being given an opportunity.

"What should I wish for?" I asked.

"That's up to you," he said.

I had the sense that there was more involved in buying the frankfurters than fulfilling his request. They were a gift that had to be given so that he could offer something in return.

Rudi seemed to enjoy the situation. "Just sitting there, John, isn't going to get you anywhere, if you don't know what you want."

"I hate to be asked what I want," I said. "They did that once to me in the Gurdjieff work when I went to live on their farm. The first night three of them sat me down and asked me why I was there. It really irritated me. All I could

say was, 'If I truly knew what I wanted, I wouldn't be here!'
I thought that was a really good answer. But it didn't im-
press them much. I knew what they wanted to hear, but I
had many different feelings, some of them directly op-
posed to each other. So if I gave them the right answer, it
would have been a partial lie."

"I understand all that," said Rudi. "But I don't care
what you say, or whether you say anything. It's an invitation, not a command."

"That doesn't make it any easier," I said.

"Then sweat a little," said Rudi. He got up from his
chair and moved outside. I continued to sit in the store.
There was no use following him outside. He wasn't going
to be any help.

I continued to sit. I felt a sense of waste and anxiety. I
was afraid that someone would come along and distract
Rudi before I had a chance to act.

I looked out the door. He was talking to someone from
the neighborhood, but he saw me looking at him and
waved casually. That didn't make me feel any better.

After five long minutes, he came back in the store.

"Well!" he said.

"I can't think of anything."

"That's not good enough, John."

"You don't have to tell me. I feel like an idiot."

"There isn't a child who walks past the store who
doesn't know what he wants," Rudi said. "It's still not
too late."

"But I don't know what to ask for."

"It isn't that."

"What is it, then?" I asked with mounting frustration.

"Do you really want to know?"

"Yes!" I said.

"You could think of at least ten different things to ask for," said Rudi. "You don't ask because you don't want the responsibility that goes along with the fulfillment of the wish. That is my gift to you. The truth. You can sit here with me for years until I go away or finally throw you out. You will grow. But only to a certain point. Other people come and go. They don't persist. Your longevity is a virtue, but not if it is mindless. A couple of years have passed since you first asked if you might ever become a teacher. That is the real symbol of responsibility. You don't ask me about that any more. You sit and wait."

"I felt you would tell me if I was ready."

"You can't wait for me. You have to make a move in yourself. It's true that right now there is no particular need for anyone else to teach. Nor are you ready. But you don't really care. You are just as happy to let it drag and leave it all in my hands."

"What can I do to change?" I asked.

"You can begin to ask from deep inside your heart center."

"But for what?"

"To want to accept responsibility for your own growth. To mature. If you don't want it, I can't inflict it on you."

"And all this from two lousy frankfurters with mustard and sauerkraut," I said.

"Do you want me to leave you alone?" Rudi persisted.

"No. I don't want that. Don't pay any attention to me. I'm glad you put me on the spot," I said.

"I'm not doing it because I enjoy it. It's easier for me to let things go. But I can't afford it. In India they say, 'God is patient. He can wait many lifetimes. But the guru is impatient. He wants the student enlightened in this very life.'

"You are my limitation. If I let you hang on indefinitely, it will slow me down. So I am warning you. Passive working and waiting is not enough. There is a natural period for everything. You need a long time to grow. I accept that. But a long time is not forever. If the day comes that you run out of time before taking the next major step, I won't hesitate to throw you out. It may not seem just when it happens. And it could come with as little warning as today. Everyone gets many chances, they just don't happen to know when the last one is coming up. They kid themselves into thinking that new opportunities will always develop. They only learn the truth when it is too late.

"Every year there is a new crop of students. Others from previous years leave. You may not have noticed, but the ones who come are generally of better quality than the ones who go. We are working with a refining energy. It attracts students at a higher level. This makes it more and more difficult for those who started earlier. There is nothing I can do about it. There is nothing I would want to do about it."

"You are succeeding in scaring me," I said.

"It's about time. What is the good of all of the effort and time you have put in, John, if it doesn't lead you somewhere in the end? I don't want you to be a sacrifice to the ascending level of the work. You have to dig deeper to find a place inside yourself that hates your inertia and stupidity."

"I know all that," I said. "You don't have to convince me."

"But it doesn't do you any real good to know it!"

"No. Not really. But why not?"

"Because there is only one little place in you where the truth is kept. It has to spread all through you like ink in a blotter. It has to keep you up nights and haunt the ease of your life. Stop living off your relationship with me. What would you do if I disappeared?"

"I don't know."

"You'd better think about it. There isn't that much

keeping me here. I stay in New York because it is the most difficult place on the earth to work. I grow very strong overcoming the tension of the city. Buried far under the ground is a dragon. It lives on the negative energy released by the millions of people. It sucks them dry. This is what I must transcend in order to grow. When I get to the point where I don't require that kind of resistance, I will leave. Nothing will keep me. I am not going to sacrifice my own existence to your inadequacy. I pay a hundred times more than you do for what is received. I have the right to choose what is done with it, and ultimately, where I go when I work my way out of this situation. It won't happen tomorrow or even five years from now. But I am absolutely certain it will happen. And maybe it will be tomorrow."

"I wouldn't blame you for leaving if you could," I said.

"That's all very well," said Rudi. "But what would you do then? I know what's going to happen to me. I know the basic outline of the rest of my life. I even know how I am going to die."

"How?" I couldn't help asking.

"I'm going to explode and burn alive. But that isn't the point. Stop living in my drama. Face the fact that you don't really expect a life of your own, John. That is your basic problem. I have told you before, you really weren't meant to have one. But you will, if you start really working. You don't know the meaning of the word yet, even after all these years."

"I don't understand," I said. My feelings were hurt.

"You don't know the meaning of work. You don't want to know, so you don't know. The last time I went to India, I started to get ready way in advance. Immediately before I left, I stayed up the whole night, just to be sure I was prepared. Hour after hour I surrendered every thought and tension that might stand in the way. I built up the flow of energy within me until it turned from a quiet stream into a vast river. You didn't know it. I didn't talk about it. Even when I felt I was ready, I didn't stop. I over-prepared.

"The moment I got off the plane in India and started for Ganeshpuri I began to burn. It went on continuously, but Swami Muktananda ignored me. I was making a real effort but he said nothing, he gave me no sign of recognition. I went on and on for three endless days like some crazed traveler in the desert. I didn't dare stop. On the fourth day, I decided that something must happen to break the torment. I would grab hold of Swami Muktananda physically if I had to, until he released me from the terrible tension of my state. That didn't prove necessary. After several hours of waiting, he gestured for me to approach. He put his hand on my head. It was a small action, but it was enough to trigger the tremendous charge I had built up within me. The next thing I knew, I was on the floor, being shaken by great electric currents. Then there were flashing lights. People were taking pictures. I got very angry. What was I, some side-show exhibit? I wanted to get up and smash their cameras. But I caught myself. 'Stupid' I said to myself. 'Is this what you have worked for? What difference does it make what they do? Let go!' In the background, I heard Swami Muktananda commenting on what I was going through as if I were a scientific phenomenon. I didn't go for that very much either. But I surrendered: him, the people in the ashram, my own life. After about an hour the intensity of the experience began to subside, and I discovered that I was back in my room. They must have carried me there. I felt that I had done as much as humanly possible. I started to relax. And then a great voice spoke to me. I will never forget what it said as long as I live." He paused, lost in recollection.

"What did it say?" I finally asked.

"It said, 'This is how you should always be working.' I didn't know whether to laugh or cry. I turned over and fell asleep. But when I woke up the next morning the voice was still there. It said, 'Now you can begin to understand what it means to work.' Believe me, John, I didn't want to hear that voice. It meant only endless effort. For what? For whom? Hadn't I done enough? Certainly I had already worked harder than anyone I had ever met. But the voice just laughed at me and said, 'This is your reward for the effort you have made.'

"There is very little competition for such rewards. No one wants the burden. I don't want it either, but I can accept it as necessary. Many years ago, I had a vision of myself as an ox going round and round, running a grain mill. It's a very accurate picture. The energy is thrown into the mill. I go around endlessly grinding it down finer and finer.

"On another trip when Swami Muktananda was making things as difficult as possible, I began to get to the point where I thought I would go crazy. I couldn't give up and I couldn't go on.

"Finally I decided to continue working until something gave way or I dropped dead. And then suddenly I had a vision of a great dragon that extended a half mile along the ocean floor. It had endless strength and was completely untouched by anything that was happening to me. I realized abruptly that the dragon was my inner nature. All the torment I was experiencing was on the surface of the ocean. It was just the play of the waves. It had no reality. I was free! Do you understand what I am saying?"

"I understand how it applies to you," I said.

"It isn't your experience," said Rudi. "But it should help you begin to realize the limitation you put on your own work. You cannot coast on what was done last year. There is only one way to coast, downhill. Everyone wants to be comfortable. Rats, birds, people — but that is the addiction which stops any creative growth. You have to make a choice, to pursue your own destiny wherever it leads or make the best of a bad bargain. But by far the worst thing that can happen to anyone is to get caught in the middle. Don't let that happen to you! The door is open. You can leave any time. But if you stay it won't be out of habit or the lack of any real alternative. I don't want you as a booby prize."

"I understand," I said. "But if I told you I was going to work ten times harder, it wouldn't be true and you wouldn't believe it. So what can I do?"

"You can work," said Rudi, "to find a new depth in yourself, and from that place you can make a new commitment to your own growth. This is essential for you to do at this time. Otherwise, you will get left behind. I don't want that to happen, but I can accept it if it does. Others will come to fill the vacuum. But for you, it would be the end of your opportunity for this life. And I don't intend to be around for the next one."

"All right," I said. "You're finally getting to me."

"All these years," said Rudi, "that you have been with me, you hardly touched the surface of what might be possible. The hardest thing I have to bear is that no one really can begin to take from me what I have to give. That is the reason, more than any other, that I will have to leave here. It isn't my personal preference. I eventually must go where people have the capacity and the need to take from me very deeply. Now go take a walk around the block and let it all sink in."

I left reluctantly. I should have been happy to get away from the battering I was taking. But I was afraid that if I walked through the door, it might disappear behind me. I had felt that only once before: the first time that I met Rudi.

9

Growth

"THE AMOUNT OF EFFORT required to teach is unbelievable," said Rudi as we sat outside the store one cloudy day
in the spring of 1966. "If there were any other way for me
to grow, I would take it. But there isn't. In fact, if all my
students disappeared, I would line up six chimpanzees and
work with them. I don't know if it would help them any,
but it would sure be good for me."

"Growth is always gradual. Feeding should be gradual
too. It takes a lot of strength to be able to absorb a concentrated dose of energy. That is basically why I take four to
six weeks to prepare internally before I go to India. When
I am there, I absorb tremendously. Some of what I absorb
is in the atmosphere, most of it I get from contact with
saints. The preparation that I require is to make room inside myself to receive what they have to give.

"Most people go tilt when they are subjected to strong,
higher forces. They lose consciousness or go into shock. If
that doesn't happen, their capacity to absorb is quickly ex-
ceeded, and the excess flows over and is lost. There is no
point to it. The psychic system is no different from any
muscular system. It develops its strength through gradual
and consistent use. There is nothing passive about it. You
have to stretch, surrender, and if necessary, break through
endless resistances which you uncover only as you get to
them. Hatha yoga is helpful on the physical level and

represents, in a visible sense, what you must do on the psychic level to grow. But nobody is really willing to make that effort."

"It doesn't sound so difficult," I said.

"It isn't," said Rudi. "It is like deciding to hold your breath for one second longer each day until you get to three minutes. It is simple enough, once you get into the habit. But everyone is very quick to feel that they have done enough. It's not that human beings aren't capable of remarkable efforts, but mostly they do it for unreal or insane reasons. A person will devote himself to revenge, to competition, to achieving his version of security or fame. He can accomplish incredible feats of endurance in wartime. But the last thing people are willing to struggle for is their own inner development. They are satisfied with what they are, unless it is really terrible. Even then, they often tolerate it. Only when other people also find it terrible do they begin to react. If we could put the same energy and intensity into our inner work that a child puts into getting a candy from an adult, there would be no problem. But the unfortunate truth is that perhaps only two percent of a person wants to grow. The rest doesn't care or else actively opposes it."

"Those aren't very good odds," I said, feeling vaguely uneasy.

"No, but every other alternative is worse, though nobody wants to believe it. That is why people are so easily led astray. They get interested in their own development, like they get interested in anything else that catches their fancy. They move in that direction until they hit their first major source of resistance. Then they pause. Next they begin to move sideways, still thinking they are going forward. Then they begin to look for reasons why they should stop. They are not getting results: the methods are wrong, the teacher is imperfect. Then they move into something else or back to their old life which, though imperfect, is at least familiar.

"There is only one antidote when this begins to happen. A person has to have made the same mistake so often that he begins to realize inwardly that it must stop. That is the function of life, to learn that one fact. Then when the ship begins to flounder, the individual understands from his past experience that there is no alternative but to stay with the ship, make necessary repairs, and continue on the assigned course.

"Nothing else matters. The inner direction is either the central fact of one's existence or a person is a conditioned robot governed by society and his own compulsions. And knowing the truth of what I am saying makes no difference. You know lots of things from your work with the Gurdjieff people and your own reading of mystical literature, but what real good did any of it ever do you?"

"It helped me to understand my predicament," I said.

"And what good did that do?"

"It gave me motivation."

"Maybe a little," said Rudi. "But I doubt that you had to read in a book that you were in a bad way to know it. Just living your life with a minimum of awareness would tell you that hundreds of times a day." Rudi got up to wait on a customer, and I left the store to walk through Greenwich Village and absorb what he had said.

During this period, I continued my work at the college, I taught my classes, had office hours, and then departed, leaving it all behind. But as I was in the graduate school, there was no escape from serving on an occasional doctoral oral examination. At such times, I was forced to marvel and shudder at the lives of my colleagues. I did not think myself better, but I could never get used to the importance they attached to minute distinctions of analysis, and the way they masked their egos in displays of rationality.

One day I came directly from an oral examination to the store.

"I'm still shaking inwardly," I said after I settled down.

"Academic people are very frightened of the world," said Rudi.

"I guess that's it. They attach such importance to minutiae. But I can't say it's nothing to them. So I don't say anything."

"I'm glad you have learned to keep your mouth shut," said Rudi. "College is a game for grown-up children. If you play it well, you get a reward. But all life is like that. Only, college people hardly ever touch real life inside their insulated walls.

"Intelligence is wonderful thing, John, but there is nothing cheaper. It is a futile ability unless one also knows how things work. A man of power buys and sells people who can think. The average intellectual is helpless when removed from his environment, whereas he should be like a cat, landing on all fours wherever he is thrown. But the one thing you must never do with any of your colleagues is to threaten their security, unless you are prepared to replace it with something better. They will never forgive you, and it is an irresponsible act."

"I don't. I haven't," I said.

"I know, but you might get brave some time and decide to tell them all what you think of them," said Rudi.

"I don't think anything bad. Most of them are nice as individuals. And besides, there is nothing better for me to do right now than teach!"

"It is a good place for you," said Rudi. "It is near my store. It is relatively easy. It has prestige, and you are invisible. If you weren't studying with me, it might be different. Another kind of daily work that was more demanding might be useful. But this way you make the money you need to support your family, and still have ninety percent of your energy to plow back into your own growth. You are very fortunate in that respect. But in another sense you require that kind of situation for growth to be possible at all. I hope you realize that."

"I guess so, but doesn't everybody?"

"Not at all. I used to work at two full-time jobs. It wasn't just for the money. I had to break down my internal chemistry that way. If I had one easy job, it would have been terrible for me. But you need a gradual approach. If it couldn't be that way, it wouldn't work for you. At the same time, your greatest obstacle is that your life is too easy. It has always been too easy. You have never had to struggle for anything. But don't worry. I know that is only external. Inside, it is very difficult. That is why I accept the outside.

"When I was in college," continued Rudi in one of his startling shifts of emphasis, "I studied engineering."

"You've got to be kidding," I said. Rudi disliked and avoided anything connected with too much rationality.

"I didn't say I was a natural, but I did the work."

"Why?" I was really puzzled.

"Just because it was unnatural for me. I figured if I could do that, I could do anything. I hadn't even been to high school, but I wanted to go to college so much that I convinced the admissions officer to take a chance on me. I'm sure he must have been amazed by his own actions, but there was nothing in me that would accept any other possibility."

"How did you do?" I asked, amazed at this latest bit of information.

"I wasn't at the top of my class, but I passed all right. That was when I learned to cook."

"I don't see the connection."

"I had to support myself, so I got a job as a short-order cook. I didn't know anything about it, but I sure learned how in a hurry."

"I'm glad you didn't become an engineer," I said, a little breathless from all this information.

"I don't think I could have stood it. But, in a way, some of what I do now is psychic engineering."

"In what sense?" I asked. "I thought you were giving spiritual nourishment."

"When I activated the kundalini force through touch and energy transfer, that was psychic engineering," he replied. "And there is another, more important type that has no physical aspect.

"The last time I stopped in Japan I was feeling rather strange. It was at the end of my trip and I had absorbed all I could take. When I was falling asleep, I smelled something like chloroform. It was so real that I got up to look around, but there was no obvious source. So I returned to bed. During the night I was bothered by clicking sounds in the air, but I was very tired and always went back to sleep.

"Sometime in the early morning, I awoke in a detached state. My body was beneath me. It was in an operating theater. There were some strange beings working on my head. The clicks I had heard were the sounds of the instruments. If I hadn't been through such experiences before, I might have panicked. But once I got the picture, I even managed to go back to sleep. The next morning I had a terrible headache, and the next night they went back to work on me. You look shocked."

"How do such things come about?"

"You earn them. It is not so much what you do that is important. It is the capacity to work enough to get to the point where the force finally begins to work on you. When it takes over, then things begin to happen. That is when you have to surrender everything and have faith.

"When I was in college," Rudi continued, shifting backwards in time, "I stayed for the summer with a very rich family in Oregon. It was wonderful. I loved them. They loved me. They wanted to adopt me, but I couldn't stay. It would have undermined my whole development. In the end, I had to force myself to return to an uncertain, brutal existence. I did it for the sake of my own growth."

"It seems a little extreme to me," I said.

"John, you don't know what I am being prepared for. I can't afford to take the easy way out. It will catch up with me later when I really need the strength. At this point, it may not be necessary, but I am not just living for today. I am living for what may be required ten years from today.

"Many people in spiritual work live a rarefied existence. They eat only certain foods, see only certain people. I do just the opposite. I train myself to be able to eat anything, relate to anyone.

"The whole conception of a holy man being too spiritual to touch is unreal. The Shankaracharya of Puri was an old and delicate man when I met him. He was one of the highest dignitaries in the Hindu religion. He fit my stereotype of a saintly man — refined, dignified, and holy.

"One night I accompanied him on an overnight train trip. He had a berth, and I slept sitting up in the next car. At about five-thirty in the morning I was horrified to hear what sounded like a water buffalo in the area where his holiness was sleeping. I jumped up to silence the offender, but was puzzled to find no source for the noise. Then I realized with a shock that what I had heard was the Shankaracharya stretching as he woke up. He was totally uninhibited. I never looked on him as unapproachable again. He might be holy, but he was very real."

The next day I asked Rudi another question about psychic engineering. "I don't know what you mean," he said, to my surprise.

I wasn't sure whether to believe him, since we had just talked about it the day before, so I asked the question again.

"I no longer remember anything about it," he said, sensing my uncertainty. "When we were talking yesterday, it filled my attention. As soon as we finished, I dropped the whole thing."

"How could you do that? Do you suppress your thoughts?"

"No. I let them go. They are like water drops over the waterfall."

"That is a lovely image," I said.

"You think it is poetic because of the difference in our states. Understand it is literally true. It gives me tremendous room for expansion. I am not haunted by the past."

"I should think that would be extremely disorienting."

"If you are in a state of surrender," said Rudi, "you are not concerned with being oriented. As long as you think you should know where you are and what you are doing, then you need to be oriented. I don't care where I am. I don't know what will happen next. When I am in this state, my own words are more of a surprise to me than yours. I listen to myself as if I were hearing someone else speaking."

"But you always know the price of every item in the store," I said, trying to pin him down.

"I need to know. But I don't learn it by heart. I absorb it. The object and its price are part of me. I know the cost like I know how many fingers I have. It is there. I just look inside."

"Why can't I do that?" I asked.

"Because you can't surrender your thoughts for more than a few seconds at a time. You feel the need to be oriented. It would frighten you to cease to remember. It takes great inner strength and a very firm sense of reality to let go of thinking.

"One of my favorite Hindu sayings is, 'The mind is the slayer of the soul.' You can't understand the depth of those words until your mind surrenders in the midst of action. Then you realize that nothing is lost except a screen which dims and distorts your perception of reality. You don't have to think about anything to sense the inner state of another human being. You don't have to think to have a spiritual experience. Thinking is designed to steal reality from us. It is tremendously overvalued in this society. But don't misunderstand. The mind can be a useful instrument. It can help to keep things moving in a direction we consciously desire. It performs simple calculations. But it does not create. It cannot really choose. For that, we have much subtler mechanisms.

"How many people do you know who think themselves out of their personal problems? Usually they think themselves more deeply into them. Thought is a tool, not a solution. Scientists do not follow the scientific method. Read some autobiographies. Hunch and intuition play an enormous role, and this is usually ignored in the official accounts of scientific discoveries. A hack uses his mind. A really talented man uses intuition. Later, of course, he subjects his conclusions to a common-sense process of testing.

"Over the years I have developed an intuitive inner computer that feeds me answers. I don't really understand how it works, but the results are usually excellent. I don't mind applying the answers to myself, but when I am told something inwardly that concerns someone else, I have some bad moments before I force myself to act on it.

"A few weeks ago, a man I know came to the store with the strangest girl you could imagine. She looked and acted like she had been raised by wolves in the forest. To get the full picture, you have to know this fellow. He is a rather delicate, rich, spoiled man who is not particularly interested in women. It was one of the most bizarre combinations I had ever seen.

"In the midst of talking with him, I heard this inner voice saying to me, 'They should get married.' I was horrified. She could eat him alive before breakfast. But the message came through loud and clear.

"I didn't have enough faith to act on it immediately. Anyway, no one was asking me for my opinion. They had met only a short time before. But two weeks later he was back, wanting to know what I thought of her. I couldn't very well ignore the question, so I said, half jokingly, 'Why? Are you thinking of marrying her?'

"'It's kind of sudden,' he said, 'but I might be. Do you think it would be a good idea?'

"'As a matter of fact,' I said, 'I think you should.'

"He looked at me vaguely shocked, but didn't ask me why I thought so, which was lucky because I don't know what I would have said."

"What's going to happen now?" I asked.

"I have fulfilled my part of the story," said Rudi. "He needed to know what I thought. I had been told what to think. If it turns out to be a horrible abortion, I will know the next time not to believe that voice. But I have heard it many times in the past and it is almost always right.

"When I was a kid, I used to do palm reading and fortune telling. I was very good. Nobody taught me how. I hadn't read any books. But I knew. The capacity was born in me, and the challenge of the situation brought it out."

"You keep that side of you hidden," I said.

"I didn't want to be a freak, so I stopped displaying psychic gifts. Sometimes I will look at a person's palm to get a quick impression or to clarify a particular point. I occasionally go to astrologers and psychics. I use them to get a fix on the future. I take what three or four of them say and see how their predictions overlap. It helps me get a sense of perspective. But it is so easy to use a gift as a substitute for growth. I didn't want to be a psychic. I wanted to be a human being. I let the one go for the other. Now I hardly need anything like that. I feel my way directly into a person to find out what is there. And also it is written on the forehead if you know how to read it."

"What are you talking about?" I asked.

"Exactly what I say. As you grow, different signs and symbols appear on the forehead."

"Are you talking about using psychic vision?" I asked.

"Some of it is psychic. Some of it is physical, available to anyone. You may notice that I glance in the mirror when I go to the bathroom. I'm not admiring my beautiful profile. I'm checking my forehead."

"That's kind of hard for me to accept."

"That's what I mean by thoughts being the enemy. You have ideas on the subject. Your ideas don't agree with what I am saying. You begin to feel threatened and tense. It's absurd. There is nothing to think about. It is either true or not. Look and see. Don't think about it!"

"I'm looking. I don't see anything. What am I supposed to see?"

"If a little man popped out and said 'hello' in Tibetan you wouldn't see anything. Come over here!" He went over to the mirror and examined his reflection.

"Here," he said, outlining an area with his finger. "Can you see the circle inside the cube?"

"Aren't those just lines on your forehead?" I asked obstinately.

"How many circles have you seen on anyone's head lately?"

"I don't know. I haven't looked."

"Well, next time you see me, look again. The circle will probably be gone," said Rudi.

"But how can you expect me to accept such a thing?" I persisted.

"If it's true, you will have to accept it. The hardest thing to understand is that the laws on different levels of experience are not the same. On the strictly physical level, we have some idea of how the body functions and the interrelationship of the various vital systems. But the psychic system is on another level. We have very little understanding of how it acts. If this were a scene in a science fiction story or part of a dream, you wouldn't be surprised if symbols appeared on someone's forehead. Perhaps approaching it that way will make it easier for you. But however you look at it, eventually you will have to look for yourself. And then you will begin to see."

"Does everybody have these symbols?"

"No. Hardly anybody. But you can read a lot from the shape of someone's head. It is the simplest guide to the extent of their development, if you know what to look for."

"It's hard for me to accept that," I muttered doubtfully.

"I can sympathize with your reaction," he said. "I live my life among statues and paintings of Eastern gods and saints. I am saturated with them. As you must have noticed, they have some pretty strange features; bumps on their heads, halos, snakes coming out of the backs of their necks, little men on their foreheads, rods going through their brains. There are endless variations, all having one thing in common. No ordinary person ever looks like that. I assumed, as you would, that these features were strictly stylistic and symbolic. It couldn't be further from the truth. They are literal representations of experiences that occur at specific stages of growth. I have had this demonstrated in my own work hundreds of times, but it still comes as a surprise to me. You don't have to believe it. It isn't a question of faith. The experiences spring on you when you least expect them.

"It's hard for me to talk to you about these things because you don't see manifestations in class. But by now you must have some confidence that they occur."

"Yes," I said. "The first time I really believed it was when I walked into the warehouse the other day to help you with a shipment. I could feel a strange sense of pressure right in the center of my forehead. You took one look at me and said, 'Well, John, I see that you're really learning how to take my energy.'

"And when I asked why, you said, 'Because there is a clear white light coming out of the center of your forehead.' And then you touched my head exactly where the pressure was. I couldn't doubt that."

Rudi smiled and said, "Last night when I was teaching the class, the force suddenly became very strong and I levitated. I was several inches off the ground. You couldn't see it, but Alan saw it. I thought his eyes were going to fall out. It is all part of an unknown world. You haven't even touched the outer surface."

"That's great, after more than seven years of work," I said.

"You have the rest of your life. The longer it takes, the better it will be in the end."

10

Becoming a Little Teacher

"THE GREATEST MISTAKE you can make is to sit and wait like a bump on a log," Rudi said as he talked during an evening class in the spring of 1966. "All that will ever overtake you is old age or death. It is one thing to surrender. It is another thing to be passive. Surrender is active and difficult if you are attached to what you are trying to surrender or afraid of the unknown. Passivity may be good for meditation in the mind, but it will never get you anywhere in this work. If there is something you want, you have to reach for it. You have to ask from your heart. You have to demand that it happen.

"When I really want something, I go straight up to heaven and start banging on the gate. I keep praying and sending messages and requests until they get so annoyed with me they take action just to get a little peace.

"But most of you just sit there, absorbing a little of the force and thinking that your life will come marching through the door to find you. Maybe a little will happen that way, but not much. You have to be waiting for it, watching for it, longing for it. I am giving you notice. If it doesn't come and you don't ask inwardly or talk to me about it, you can only blame yourselves."

I couldn't ignore that. At the next opportunity, I spoke to Rudi. "I've been thinking about what you said."

"What was that?"

"About not just sitting and waiting, but needing to ask."

"So?" He was not going to make it easy.

"So I want to ask about teaching."

"What about teaching?" he said obstinately.

"Not about teaching, about *my* teaching. It's been a long time since my thirty-third birthday."

"That's true, John. What have you been waiting for?"

"I guess some indication from you."

"What is it you really want?"

"I want to be able to begin teaching."

"You could have begun several years ago. But nothing in you cared enough to ask for it. You just waited. Basically, you didn't want the responsibility. To become a teacher is to take on some of the karma of your students. It isn't glamorous. It doesn't satisfy your ego. You can't do it for any reason like that. You have wasted a lot of time."

"I admit all that," I said, "but I can't spend the rest of my life regretting the past. What should I do at this point?"

"You should go home and work on your wish. Be sure that you still want it and are willing to sustain the effort. It is better to wait than to start prematurely. Beginning to teach is like opening Pandora's box. You never know what will come out."

"All right. I'll do that," I said. "But I'm sure right now. I'm only ashamed about all the time that has gone by."

Rudi said nothing more, so I left. During the next two days, I asked myself, when I worked, whether I was really sincere and prepared to carry through wherever teaching might lead me in the future.

The general answer I got was that I would never be entirely sure, but that time was running out for me. I had to make my move or forget about it. I decided I would pay the price, whatever it was.

That autumn the eight acres around my house in the country had one quantity in excess: leaves. They covered the grass in thick layers. Even under good conditions, it was a major operation to burn them.

But this year, most of the leaves were wet. They wouldn't burn. I decided on desperate measures. I began to gather the leaves on the gravel driveway in front of my house. For several hours, I did nothing but collect leaves. The pile reached six or seven feet high and was very wide around. My plan was to pour gasoline on it, stand back, and throw in a match. The theory was that the flames would get hot enough to dry the leaves so they would burn.

I poured on plenty of gasoline, stood back about eight feet, lit a match, and threw it toward the leaf mountain. The next thing I knew, a great fire ball exploded. I could feel my eyebrows being singed, and instinctively I put my hands up to protect my face. I staggered back more shocked than injured, though the left side of my face was very red. The leaves burned merrily.

The next day I looked like a war hero halfway through plastic surgery. I went to the city because my work required it. I didn't feel too bad, but I looked terrible. People stopped on the street to stare. My colleagues were full of curiosity and sympathy. Finally, I concluded my business and went to Rudi's store.

Rudi made no comment on my appearance. I was vaguely irritated. At least he could have asked what happened.

Finally, after ten minutes, I couldn't resist bringing up the subject, "I did something really stupid."

"What was that?" he asked casually.

"I ignited a whole pile of wet leaves soaked with gasoline. It set off a huge explosion."

"Was anyone injured?" Rudi asked. It seemed a pretty stupid question under the circumstances.

"No," I said, "just me."

"I think it's great," Rudi said.

"What's great?" I asked, sincerely puzzled.

"What happened to you. You got a real answer to your question. Do you accept it?"

"I'm not going to ask whether you're serious because I know that you are, but Jesus!"

"Listen, John. When you left here last time, you were going to decide whether you wanted to become a teacher, regardless of the price. I assume that the answer was yes."

I nodded in agreement.

"So the explosion was the next thing that happened. It was your 'baptism of fire.' I think the symbolism is wonderful." He began to laugh.

I decided if there was a joke, it wasn't on me, so I laughed too. And, at the same moment, I recaptured the feeling that I had had during and immediately preceding the explosion. Something in me had known what was going to happen. If I had been consciously aware of what I was about to set off, I wouldn't have had the courage to do it. But something had known. It had the fatality of a ritual.

"Well?" I asked. "What should I do now?"

"Find a student and start teaching."

"But how?"

"Finding the student is up to you. As far as teaching, just start! It will come to you. If you have any questions, ask me. There is a great deal of material stored up in you from all the years we have been together and from the efforts you made before that in other kinds of work. It will all return as you need it."

"But give me some concrete idea of what to do," I pleaded.

"I'm giving you the right to begin. The rest is up to you."

As I left the store, my mind was occupied with the question of finding a student. I went through the catalogue of possibilities, and being of a courageous nature, I decided that a good friend of mine, Janis, would be the least threatening person I knew. I called her up, explained the situation, and invited her to come to New York for the next weekend. She was delighted.

My first class, which was the culmination of eight years of work with Rudi, was given in a small rented room. The only decoration was a sculpture of a serpent, which seemed like a good omen at the time.

Janis sat in a chair and I sat on the edge of the bed. There were several delays, but finally, I took a deep breath and began. At exactly the same moment a one-man band started to play in the next room. There were drums, cymbals, a harmonica, and other diverse instruments. I began to crack up, but I realized that I couldn't afford to let anything stop me.

Janis took her cue from me. We worked for perhaps fifteen minutes. When the moment came that I decided I'd worked long enough, the band instantly stopped. The timing was unbelievable, but it didn't seem funny any longer.

There are some things that remain of lasting significance, regardless of their particular quality, just because they happened at all. The first class I had with Rudi was such an event. It opened the door to my life. The class that I gave to Janis that night was the same. If I could go back and see myself as I was then, I would probably find the whole effort somewhat ridiculous. But it was a beginning — one from which I have detoured, but never lost the way.

11

Swami Rudrananda

"MY TEACHER HAS GIVEN me the title Swami Rudrananda," said Rudi on returning from his trip to India in 1966.

"I hope I can still call you Rudi," I said, not certain how to take the announcement. We were sitting in the store together for the first time since his return.

"Sure. It's going to take me a while to get used to the title. But whether I use it or not, don't take it casually. It would never have happened at all if I hadn't refused any other alternative. I have paid for it in blood. You meet some white people who are swamis, but it doesn't mean much because they receive the title from a very minor person. But I have been playing with the big boys. Bhagavan Nityananda is worshipped as a living god by his followers. Swami Muktananda is considered to be a great saint. When he travels, people wait all night just to see his railroad car pass in the moonlight. They hope to receive a blessing from his presence. They are both, in different ways, at the top of the echelon of Hindu religious life, though they represent very different quantities.

"I resolved to achieve a certain recognition, to symbolize the whole process of growth that I had achieved during the last decade. I went to India with the objective of becoming a swami. Muktananda hasn't initiated anyone as a swami. He does not give anything easily. He must have sensed my objective, because from the moment I arrived, he kept a certain distance between us. I made a special effort to bridge the gap, digging more deeply into my heart to find a greater sense of love for the man. I also expressed my desire to become a swami to others knowing he would hear it through ashram gossip channels.

"He smiled at my efforts, but it was like squirting perfume on a sheet of glass. Nothing was getting through. On the occasions when his guard was down, there was always an interruption: a visiting saint, an immediate minor emergency about which he had to be consulted. I watched all this with a mixture of amusement and desperation. The charade was diverting, but I was never going to become a swami if I went along with it.

"To make matters worse, most of the attention in the ashram was devoted to a rejuvenation experiment. Swami Muktananda was testing an ancient scripture that described how an old man could be made younger if he was put into total isolation and fed a special diet. A house had been prepared, and an old man had been placed in it for several months on the prescribed diet. He was supposed to emerge in a week. Everyone was excitedly awaiting the results. Personally I couldn't have cared less about the whole thing. It just created one more diversion for me to overcome.

"There is only one answer for a situation like that: put your life on the line and refuse to take no for an answer. I started digging inside myself until I came to a rock foundation that I knew nothing could alter. Then I began to work outward. I had only a day and a half left of my stay. I asked Swami Muktananda for the opportunity to speak with him. He begged to be excused. He was ill. A recurrent fever had reappeared. He needed to rest.

"It was true. He did not look his usual self. I sympathized, but persisted. 'Baba,' I said. ('Baba' means 'father' in Hindi. It's a familiar form of address, like calling me 'Rudi.') 'I will be leaving tomorrow. Let me only sit near the doorway of your room. I feel myself in a very crucial condition. I need the power of your spirit to help me!'

"It was true enough. I had been working with mounting intensity for over a week. I felt both strangely dissociated and burning with fever. Something had to be resolved.

"He looked annoyed, but did not refuse. 'I cannot go away in this state,' I continued relentlessly. 'I'll wait until you are asleep and then sit quietly near you, if you will permit it.'

"He looked at me keenly for a moment and motioned me closer. I approached, with more arguments ready. He shrugged his shoulders and said, 'You're dumb like I'm dumb!' Then he touched my forehead. I was in a very finely balanced condition. The force that had been building in me like a static charge in a huge transformer, broke loose. I was overwhelmed with it, and I fell to the ground.

"For the next hour I was wracked by spasms and surrounded by strange visions. I felt unknown areas opening within me and was completely disoriented.

"I recovered slowly to find myself back in my room. Just then someone came in and motioned for me to follow. Evidently Swami Muktananda wanted to see me.

"I stumbled into the dim light of his quarters. He was entertaining a visiting saint.

"'How is our new swami?' he said jovially. I was shocked. I had achieved my objective. 'I have been thinking of your new name,' he continued. 'Do you know the god, Rudra?'

"'Not exactly,' I replied, still in a daze.

"'He was a primeval form of Shiva, a wild man.' Baba broke into laughter and slapped his knee. The thought seemed to appeal to him.' So you are now Swami Rudrananda; the bliss of Rudra.'

"It all felt like a scene out of an exotic children's party. Everyone was festive, as if an idiot son had just made good in grade school. I was happy, too, but I did not forget what all this cost me or take any of it for granted.

"I left the next day with many expressions of gratitude and friendship. Swami's last words to me were, 'Now you are really going to be an independent person.'

"As I got away from the ashram, I began to understand the significance of his last words. There was no doubt in my mind that Baba had withheld the title as long, or longer, than humanly possible. I didn't mind that as long as I was growing. But how long can you keep an infant in a crib? When he gets beyond a certain size, it's ridiculous. Now that I had been certified, there was no telling what I might do.

"Before I left the ashram, I asked to know more about the nature of the god, Rudra. I was told that Shiva stands on a dwarf, but Rudra is surrounded by thousands of people. I was also told that the next nine months would be very painful for me. Many people and situations to which I was attached would be torn away as a major transition occurred in my life. I can feel it starting already.

"I don't know what is coming next, but I have the increasing conviction that my studies in India have concluded. The energy of that tradition is all inside me now. I do not know how it will manifest. I sometimes think that enlightenment in Hinduism is a single flower on the top of a great tree. It is an imposing and wonderful event, but I don't want to settle for just one flower. In Islam they produce a low bush with many blossoms. I would like to graft the bush onto the tree and have the best of both cultures.

"If that is what God wants, it will happen. Whatever I want I will have to surrender anyway to allow the future to emerge from the depth of my own being. So that is what I am doing," Rudi said as he rose from his chair to wait on a customer.

12

The Nature of Kundalini Yoga

RUDI'S WHOLE LIFE WAS a continuous ferment of forced growth. He would not accept anything less. In a talk for an evening class, he said:

"We always think of growth as something pleasant and light, like a flower petal unfurling in the sun. That is just the final stage. How does the seed feel when it is buried alive in the dirt? What are its sensations as something begins to stir within its being? Probably uncertainty, fear, maybe even panic. That is growth!

"Even if it sends out a root and begins to germinate, how would it be after getting used to the warmth, closeness, and safety of the ground to have to face the prospect of breaking through the surface of the ground into a totally unfamiliar realm: the vulnerability of moving into the open, exposure to the elements, the blinding light. The seedling doesn't know what is happening. It grows unconsciously but also on faith; otherwise it would wither away very quickly.

"All of this is exactly paralleled by what occurs inside an evolving person. The only difference is that inner growth can only proceed through conscious suffering. It never occurs otherwise.

"When I rented my first store, which was made of pieces of tin nailed together, I was running wild. I sat myself down in the store and consciously decided to use it to tame my inner nature. I chose to have no heat. I got so chilled that it took until mid-summer before I began to feel warm. There was no bathroom. I peed in a pot which I emptied in the street. I could have afforded a heater and a bathroom, but I vowed to sit in that store day by day until I either broke down or gained control over myself. It was strong medicine and I had to take it for two years, but it worked.

"I couldn't protest about it or feel sorry for myself. I wanted it that way, but anyone going through such experiences has the right to complain occasionally. It's like being a recruit in the Army. You can bellyache about the long marches, the food, and the officers, as long as you do what you are told."

"It is hard for me to relate to such experiences," I interrupted. "I don't feel that I suffer all that much."

Rudi nodded. "You don't, not consciously and not yet. You are still very dead to your own inner state. But there is suffering within you. What else keeps you working? The sense of emptiness that haunts you is suffering. You don't experience it as a physical pain because you keep it at a distance. But you can't escape it either.

"For most people, inner work is like a paraplegic learning to walk again. Each step takes a great deal of conscious effort and must go against the physical pain and emotional discouragement that he feels. But we are not trying to restore a function which was destroyed through a physical injury. We are trying to reactivate a capacity that most have forgotten and everyone has lost.

"When something dead, diseased, or nonfunctioning is being brought to life, it hurts physically. It is disturbing psychically. It is threatening emotionally. How can it be otherwise? Enlightenment is not sitting under a banana tree waiting for a fruit to fall into your mouth. It only comes after working and working and working to gather enough energy to break through the walls that surround you. As this happens, the energy bound up in these walls is released in a sudden surge that carries you to a new level and gives you the experience of enlightenment.

"The classic picture of meditation is the Buddha quietly sitting under the Bo tree. But remember what he went through during the years in the forest, the constant obstacles that finally culminated in his refusal to rise again until he had achieved his goal. And even after that, he was subjected to every temptation that could be thrown against him. All of this before the dawn of understanding began to break. That is the way it happens. You cannot imitate his life. The culture of which it was a part has vanished. The Buddha even said that his influence would diminish a century after his death and that what remained would be a relic, rather than a living force. The past can be a footstool. It is certainly nothing to idolize. You absorb it and move on. Christians who make a God of Christ only put an obstacle in their own way. It is much easier to do that than recognize Christ represents a level of attainment, not the ultimate level, but the ultimate at that time: a man born into the world already in a totally cleansed state.

"The basic reason that real growth does not occur is that no one wants to feel pain. We are animals in that respect, conditioned to seek out things that bring us pleasure, and to avoid those which hurt. Pain must occur in the growth process. When we avoid pain, we avoid growth. That is what stops ninety percent of the people dead in their tracks.

"Then there is a more subtle obstacle for those who remain. Some of them are willing to sacrifice their time, security, and relationships for one overriding goal in their life. Unfortunately, they reserve the right to pick this goal, thereby removing most of the value such dedication might have. No one is in a position to understand what is really good for them when they start to pursue their own fulfillment. They are flying blind. The major contribution a teacher can make is that, having survived much of what the student must live through, he can put his own experience, understanding, and sympathy at their disposal. He can act as a guide to the farther shore. But a guide is useless if you don't listen to him. And it is the major characteristic of a fanatic that they will listen to no one. They have the determination, but not the humility to succeed in inner work. You can learn a lot from such a person, but you would not want to follow where he goes. His success is ultimately a prison from which he has neither the flexibility nor the inclination to free himself.

"Anything which is built on one level of experience may have to be torn down again in order to enter another. It is easy to accept something like that in principle, when you don't have much to lose. But as you begin to grow more rapidly, you will attract people and situations that you will not want to surrender. At that time, only the action of an impartial force that wishes for your growth more than you wish it for yourself can intervene and save you from what you have attracted. And as you already know, I don't hesitate to do that."

· · ·

Though Rudi occasionally glanced through magazines and mystery stories during the long hours he spent in the store, he avoided reading anything about spiritual subjects. When a new student asked for something mystical to read, he recommended Agatha Christie. That usually ended the conversation. But once a very puzzled young man returned two hours later to say, "I went to the biggest bookstore in the city and looked through every spiritual book on the shelves. There wasn't anything by Agatha Christie."

Rudi nodded and handed him a copy of her latest mystery that he happened to have on his desk. "When you have a teacher," he said, "you don't need any books."

For the first five years that he taught, Rudi didn't give a name to the kind of work he was doing. Finally he indicated that it might be called Shakti Yoga. Shakti is the name given to the creative energy of the Universe. She is a Hindu goddess. Several years later, he mentioned in an off moment that we were doing Kundalini Yoga. These were evidently equivalent efforts, though the Kundalini Yoga appeared to be a more advanced version. The nature of the difference, however, was never entirely clear. Rudi himself had little interest in either the distinction or the name.

"I have left copies of *The Serpent Power* all over India," he said. "It is the classic text on Kundalini Yoga and people keep giving it to me, thinking they are doing me a favor. As far as I am concerned, it can only get in my way. All books on spiritual subjects either lie intentionally — the author pretends to knowledge he does not really possess through his own experience — or they lie unconsciously, by giving the impression that the experiences recorded are either easily come by or almost impossible, neither of which is likely to be the case.

"Spiritual books generally feed the illusions of the people concerned. So, for me, they are obstacles. I don't want to know other people's experiences until I have my own with which to compare them. If I know what is supposed to happen at a certain stage, it will make me try to force the result to that pattern. It can't possibly help. That's why I limit my serious reading to mystery stories.

"For a long time I never even knew that what I was doing had any relation to kundalini, the serpent power. One day, when I was at the ashram at Ganeshpuri, someone made a remark in English about serpents that I happened to overhear. I didn't know exactly what they were talking about. Maybe someone had seen a serpent around the garden or maybe they were referring to the kundalini power. I still don't know. But five minutes later, one serpent after another started to run up my spine. Then I didn't need to read any books or listen to anyone else to believe in the reality of the force. I knew it was there and why they called it the serpent power. It was the serpent power!"

One day Rudi received a short article written by Swami Muktananda on "the chakras."* To my knowledge, it was the first time Rudi had read anything on the subject, though he had been working through certain chakras for many years. Perhaps he read the article because it was written by his teacher. Perhaps it was something he needed to know at the time. In any case, it immediately influenced his basic description of the work he was teaching.

"Most people absorb about five percent of what they read," he said. "In a few months they forget even that. I don't read much, but what I read I absorb totally. I keep working and working on it, almost extracting more meaning than was ever there. I don't stop until I have connected it with everything I already knew so that it is completely assimilated."

Before this time, Rudi had emphasized the need to absorb force by drawing it in with the breath, and feeling it come down the center line of the body, shifting backwards

---

* Sanskrit for wheel, refers to energy centers which are, to some extent, contiguous with the physical body and form the channel that kundalini energy follows in an individual.

to the base of the spine, eventually awakening the kundalini, which then began to flow upward through a channel
in the center of the spine, finally reaching the back and
top of the head. Now the description became more elaborate, as his own experience with the separate chakras
clarified the process for him. He described it in a series of
talks early in 1968:

"The basic process involved in doing inner work is one
of absorbing and refining the nourishment needed for
growth. Ordinary life feeds the personality. Higher energy
is required to nourish the inner being.

"Just as there is a physical digestive system for taking in,
breaking down, and absorbing the energy of food, there is
a psychic digestive system that attracts, transforms, and
absorbs higher energies directly in a nonphysical form.
There have been various descriptions of this system. All of
them are, to my knowledge, partially incorrect or incomplete. Either the writers didn't know what they were writing about, or they were consciously making it difficult for
the reader to apply what they were describing. This was
certainly done in various Tibetan writings where gaps were
left that could only be filled in orally by a teacher. This
helped to preserve the purity of the line of teaching, and
served to prevent the student from attempting advanced
work before the proper foundation had been laid.

"Beyond all this, you have to understand one basic principle of spiritual work. The process of putting a method on
paper makes it accessible beyond any immediate point in
space and time, but the energy that is required to start the
process cannot be transmitted by printed words. One must
receive instruction from someone in whom the process is
already functioning. There is no way to steal it. Someone
else must give it of his own free will. You can read books,
listen to lectures, and share opinions with your friends.

None of this can lead to any real result. It may, in fact, serve to confuse your mind with misguided expectations.

"One of the things that has always disgusted me in the various ashrams that I have visited — and there have been many — is the tendency of people to sit around comparing experiences. It encourages a subtle form of competition that is extremely undesirable. People do not, and should not, have the same experiences. There is no one to compete with except your own best effort in the past. But even worse, people lose the energy of their experiences by gossiping about them. That is the greatest stupidity. Experiences should be discussed only with your teacher, and then only if you have a real question about them. Otherwise, they should be absorbed and forgotten.

"In fact every experience you have ever had, or will ever have, should likewise be absorbed and forgotten. This is the only path that leads to inner freedom. Otherwise you may become a living memorial to some past enlightenment.

"All of these things I have said before in various forms, and I will undoubtedly have to say them again. It takes hundreds of repetitions for certain things to sink in. But today I particularly want to describe the working of the psychic system as I am coming to understand it. This is not to alter what I have said before, but to fill in certain gaps. What we were using in the past was a crude sketch. It was sufficient for the purpose, but incomplete.

"The simplest picture of the psychic digestive system is a line drawn from the point slightly above the eyebrows down the center of the body, ending in the region of the sex organs. Located along this line are a series of psychic centers or chakras. The center line itself is a natural stream bed for the flow of psychic and spiritual force. The chakras are like flowers along the stream bed. When they are open, they permit energy to pass through, drawing from it the nourishment they need and working on it as the digestive juices work on physical food to change its original character. All of this takes place naturally *when the chakras are open*. But, under normal conditions, the chakras are closed. They almost never open spontaneously. It must be done through one's own conscious efforts. Even when they do open, they quickly close when the conscious effort ceases. There is no way for the spiritual force to circulate when the chakras are closed. In parallel, one must look into the connections between the chakras. These connections are like the plumbing in a long-deserted house. There is no telling about its condition until you begin to run water into it again. There may be leaks and obstructions. Parts of the pipe may be rotted away. All of this must be corrected before the system can function again.

"For the force to enter into one chakra and to pass all the way down the front center line of the body, the pathway and all intervening chakras must be open. This may happen quickly and naturally as energy is fed in and brought down the pathway, or it may occur gradually, depending on the individual's inner condition when he starts to work. But this process is only the first phase of the digestive process, even though it may involve great patience and persistence to activate it. It has no significance in and of itself, though each chakra is associated with its own function that emerges when the chakra opens. The total purpose of this phase of the work is to absorb cosmic energy from the surrounding atmosphere, progressively refine it, and draw it down until it strikes the chakra in the sex center. There a transformation occurs which has been described in alchemy as changing lead to gold.

"The highest, most vital energy ordinarily available in the human organism is sex energy. When cosmic energy is related to sex energy in the manner I have described, a transmutation of the sex energy occurs. It is very real. You can feel it as a gentle warmth and tingling of champagne bubbles in the sex center. It produces a force within the human organism that is never present under ordinary circumstances. This force is the normal stimulant for the higher creative energy that lies dormant at the base of the spine. Nothing else will activate it in a natural manner.

"When the transformation process has started and the attention is then shifted to the base of the spine, the higher sex force is brought to the site of the kundalini energy, which does, in fact, lie curled around the lowest vertebrae like a sleeping princess waiting for the kiss of the transformed sex energy to awaken her. As this happens, the second major part of the total cycle begins. It usually takes place gradually and gently, though occasionally someone may feel the kundalini activated strongly and quickly. Such people are objectively lucky, but they are usually more frightened than appreciative and fail to do the necessary work to stabilize the inner process that has begun in them. But, for most of you, it has been or will be slow.

"You can think of the spine as a thermometer, open at the very top. As the energy is directed from the sex center to the base of the thermometer, the fluid in the tube slowly warms and rises. Any obstacle it encounters will, of course, interfere with the process, but gradually these blocks are removed. At a certain point, the energy fluid reaches the top of the tube and overflows. It is normally stored in the thousand-petalled lotus chakra that corresponds to the bump on the back of the Buddha's head. This is not a natural bump. It develops only through inner work. As the energy of the kundalini force is raised and overflows, the chakra in which it is stored ripens and expands. It is like a bud. After many years, it begins to open naturally in the form of a great flower. It is then that the thousand-petalled lotus earns its name. The higher energy that is released in the process is of a level and quality that the inner being has not known before. It flows into the brain, fertilizing and nourishing the higher spiritual mechanisms. Then it circulates through the psychic digestive system so that it can touch each chakra in turn and provide it with concentrated nourishment. It is at this point that each human function begins to work at a new and almost totally unknown level. But there is no need to go into that now.

"Different mystical systems describe various numbers of chakras. For our purpose, we will deal with eight of them, though there are additional chakras in the hands and feet, as well as in the head and beyond the head.

"The first chakra is the third eye. Its basic function is to act as a psychic mouth. When it is open, it is the natural entrance point for energy from outside, particularly as you receive it from me in a class. When Christ said, "If thine eye be single thy whole body will be filled with light," he meant that when the third eye opens, you can absorb energy directly.

"The second chakra is in the base of the throat. The third is in the center of the chest. It is the heart chakra. The physical heart is on the left side, but the heart center is in the middle. Below that, though usually ignored, is the solar plexus. Further down is the center emphasized in Zen Buddhism, located about two inches below the navel. All the way down and slightly under is the sex center. The seventh chakra is located at the tip of the spine and the eighth at the top and back of the head.

"The total digestive process involves taking energy in through the third eye, bringing it down the front through each chakra in turn, like stringing a necklace, and then backward to the base of the spine, upward along the central canal of the spine until it reaches the top of the head. The only significance of the total process is when the energy reaches the top of the head. Until that point, everything is preparation. It does no permanent good. But when the total system functions in a complete manner, the higher energy that is required for the conception and nourishment of your own rebirth begins to be manufactured and accumulated.

"There are a variety of technical means for opening the chakras. Some of them have been mentioned before and I will certainly go over them again, because people have an incredible capacity to misinterpret the simplest explanation when it applies to their own inner functioning. These methods include such techniques as directing attention, conscious breathing, visualization, inner asking, supplying energy to a particular chakra through the use of touch. But there are also a variety of specific actions that are helpful in opening particular places in the psychic digestive system. For example, the best way to open the throat chakra is simply to swallow. The most effective means I know for opening the heart and lower belly chakras is the double breath. I'll go over that again in case you haven't received it before.

"You breathe into your heart to the count of ten. Hold for the count of ten, begin to breathe out, but immediately shift your attention to the lower belly and after having expelled a small amount of air, begin to breathe in again for the count of ten; hold for ten and out for ten. That is the double breath. It takes a while to get used to, but the results can be quite remarkable. However, you shouldn't try it often, because it supercharges the system. Once or twice every ten minutes is enough.

"There are many further examples. It helps to rotate slightly on the base of the spine to release the kundalini energy. The head may twist back and forth as the energy reaches the level of the neck. There are an endless number of such techniques and manifestations with which you must become familiar. They are really priceless gifts, but only of value if you are doing the work.

"You might prefer that there be another internal arrangement, or believe that there is. But the question is not one of belief, but of reality. You cannot eat food through your nose or digest it in your lungs. Your physical mechanism doesn't work that way. The psychic mechanism is really no different. Each part is designed to perform an assigned function in a certain order. The problem is to learn what they are and apply this knowledge to your own shifting sensations of the inner environment in which you live. Gradually, you can learn to relate an idea you may hear to an experience you actually have. But it usually doesn't happen quickly. We are clogged, not only with garbage, but with wrong ideas that we will not surrender. We cling to these because they make us comfortable or glorify our condition.

"The truth is all too simple. We are all of us trade-ins on a colossal used car lot called the earth. We are here because we have damaged chakras. We do inner work in order to be reconditioned. The earth is not a good place for living. The vibrations here are heavy and negative. Higher forces from the cosmos can barely penetrate the gloom. A fool tries to fix up his cave to make it more livable. A wise man will find a way out into the light. That is the purpose of all spiritual systems. Each of them is a partial answer. All of them serve as vehicles when they are at their zenith, and all become rigid and dogmatic in time, more a prison than a refuge.

"I would not be saying all these things if I did not feel that some of you were ready to receive them. I can't wait for everybody, or I would never speak. You must understand that what I say is not, in any sense, intellectual. I don't pass on ideas. I try to give you the raw flesh of my own experience. It may be slightly messy at times, but the blood is still warm. It is not for you to evaluate what I say or to write a critique. I can't stop you if that's how you want to use it. But it is not why I talk to you. I am trying to open a doorway to the unknown. It is your response to the situation which will determine, not only what you receive now, but what you will receive in the future.

"Higher energy is the most precious commodity in the world. It is the basis of all inner development. Accurate teaching on how to obtain it is almost unknown at the present time. We often think that the East is the place to go for instruction on inner work. But its spirituality is fading. The East has lived on its inheritance for fifteen hundred years.

"The people of the United States may lack cultural sophistication, but there is more freedom in this country than anywhere in the world. And the human soil is richer, it is not spoiled by centuries of abuse. It is here that the greatest development can occur.

"Two hundred years from now spiritual techniques may be taught in kindergartens. That doesn't matter. The period of the pioneer is the most wonderful time to be alive. The challenge is the greatest and the discoveries that wait to be made are the most fundamental. I would not have wished to be born at any other moment but the dawn of a new age."

13

Death and Rebirth

RUDI WORKED CONTINUOUSLY in every situation that he found himself. Only the intensity of his effort varied. He also talked a tremendous amount, and loved to be surrounded by people. He had been born with an open heart. The words that he spoke, however casual, usually had a purpose which emerged if one stayed around long enough to see the pattern. It is difficult to determine, in retrospect, when certain ideas first emerged, nor does it really matter. Rudi seemed to express what was occurring in him as it happened, more or less to whomever would listen. It seemed to me, watching this endless overflow, that either his experience was so continuous that talking about it did not diminish its content, or that he could not control this tendency in himself and so decided to make the best of it. His friends and customers grew to expect it. And by giving them direct access to his latest experience he was allowing them to make contact with the possibility of joining his work.

It was only after more than a decade that I realized there were certain aspects of his experiences that he rarely mentioned to anyone. This threw his apparent expressiveness into quite a different light. He was doing what he consciously intended. There was nothing compulsive about it.

Although Rudi was interested in the inner experiences of his students, he did not encourage them to talk with him about them unless they had a particular question. In any case, he had a pretty good idea of where they were. He could follow the flow of the force within them, and see various psychic manifestations functioning through them when they worked in class. It was harder for him to see them in himself. He did not particularly want to know too much about what was working through him because he didn't want to identify with it.

Once, at about the time I first met him, he was observed by members of a spiritual group. They described to him what they saw: the people who appeared, the strange creatures that manifested, the lights, colors, and so on. It was all very dramatic. He was interested, but he didn't look for such information again for a long time, for fear the knowledge would cause patterns and expectations to develop in his work. He wanted his work to be spontaneous. Whatever appeared did so as a function of his surrender. It was not him, but that which worked through him. There was no reason to record it or analyze it as far as he was concerned.

I was not distracted by these manifestations because I could not see them. But I gradually admitted to myself that they must exist. I had to believe it when Rudi would describe an experience that had occurred to him in class only to have someone else, who had been in class but who had not heard him mention it, describe the same thing later.

It is hard to single out a particular manifestation to describe. They were continuous. Each one set the stage for the next. If Rudi had worked less hard, the time between experiences would have lengthened considerably. But he was always building toward the next breakthrough.

Though he rarely spent much time discussing these occurrences, on one occasion late in 1967, Rudi described odd stirrings in his brain. Occasionally, he felt as if feet were scratching his head, but that seemed so strange that he ignored it. In one particular class, however, the sensation just kept growing. It finally came to a climax when a bird emerged from his forehead. It stood there for a time, took a few steps, and started to fly around the room. Afterwards Rudi said, "It was all I could do to keep the class going. I just wanted to stop and watch the bird."

Other people described it also, both in the same conversation and independently. I had to assume it had really happened. Rudi spoke of the bird afterwards:

"What I saw was a phoenix. I never get used to the strangeness of such manifestations. They obey a logic of their own. Most people never have such experiences because they are threatened by them. They can accept exotic birds as poetic or unconscious expressions of universal desires, but not as reality. No one has ever seen a phoenix flying in the sky, but it exists in the astral realm. Its significance is exactly what it is supposed to be: death and rebirth.

"That was exactly what I felt. When the bird appeared, something in me died. After the class, I felt terribly empty. I didn't understand what had happened until a few days later, when life began to return to me, like green shoots appearing in the early spring.

"Everyone dies once, in a physical sense. But the most remarkable thing about a human being is that he can die many times before his physical death. Such psychological and psychic deaths must occur before any rebirth experience is possible. You are all very naive. You assume that circulating and transforming this force will bring you enlightenment. There is not time enough in eternity for that to occur. The only hope of getting out of the web you have created around yourself is to die to the level of experience you have known.

"When I look back on my life I see a string of corpses trailing behind me. They are all different aspects of myself that I have shed. I have never found dying to be enjoyable. But by now I recognize the symptoms and know how to react. Whenever I sense a great withdrawal, as if the tide were going out, never to return, I begin to suspect the process has started. Everything that seemed full of significance is hollow. The objectives I had seem pointless. The relationships closest to me have no meaning. I feel surrounded by an endless fog. Voices call out to me. Temptations appear to attract my energy just when I need it most. A person is very vulnerable at such a moment.

"The most crucial thing is that he sees the process through, and that others around him understand what is happening so that they can support him. Unfortunately, that rarely occurs.

"You have to understand the subtle dilemma involved to appreciate the difficulty of successfully dying. First of all, the person himself either grows afraid of his condition or ceases to care about anything. Second, those who are closest to him will either be anxious about his state or feel rejected by him and reject him in turn. This is terribly unfortunate. A person needs to be helped through his inner death with understanding and love. All of his energy is absorbed by the inner process. He cannot communicate. Unless this is understood and accepted, those around him can't respond properly.

"As a result, the chances of dying successfully are not good. Usually the process aborts. Then the person feels better. Others feel better. None of them know that the fruits of his inner labors have just been totally lost. It is really tragic.

"Spiritual work can only be done by healthy human beings. Such natural development is a relatively rare attainment even though it has nothing to do with spiritual growth. But when it occurs, then it becomes meaningful to work for rebirth, that is, the conception and development of a completely new level of being.

"Conception occurs in the seeds of your potential. It can only be fertilized by a higher energy. This happens more often than you think. I have had students who left after working for only a week contact me nine months later to report that they were feeling very strange. I can't tell them they've been spiritually knocked up, but that is what has happened. The power of the initial contact fertilized something in them. It follows the physical parallel closely. Nine months later they can't help feeling the effects, even though they haven't worked at all since that time. If I told them that, though, they either wouldn't believe it or it would make them feel bad. So I just tell them not to worry, the sensations will vanish in a few days. And they do. A psychic miscarriage occurs. And the person never knows what he has lost.

"But if you are properly prepared, you can create your own inner climate for the development of the seed that has been fertilized. That is the purpose of our work. A higher level of being requires higher energy for its nourishment. By activating your psychic digestive mechanism you are doing the one essential thing, creating the food for the spiritual embryo within you.

"I'm not being fanciful. It is a concrete process that takes a long time. That is why no one should enter this work unless they can make a commitment toward the longevity of their effort.

"If the conditions are right and the inner embryo is created within the physical adult, it goes through the various stages of maturing like a normal child. During all of this period our ordinary self must act as the parent. Beyond

the responsibility involved, the process is complicated by
the fact that the child who is growing is on a different level
of being than the adult who is taking care of him. The
adult must serve the child like a steward, as suggested by
the parables in the New Testament. Over and over the
steward is placed in charge until the master returns.
Where is the master? In one sense, hidden and buried in
the depths of the creative unconscious. In another sense,
elsewhere in the cosmos. But in the present sense, he is
not yet there because he is still growing up. He is at our
mercy until he comes into his maturity and takes on his
inheritance.

"It is a demanding task that we undertake when we experience rebirth. We never really understand who is reborn and at what cost, until it begins to happen. As we
are, we cannot be reborn. Our personalities are the husk
from which the seed breaks. If we are attached to the husk,
the suffering involved is greatly increased and we fight rebirth rather than help it. It will seem to us as if an alien
being is absorbing our consciousness. This is extremely
threatening if you have the illusion that you know who
you are. But none of you even know who you *were*. Your
only real opportunity for growth lies in the fact that you
cannot know who you will be. When you feel this as
clearly as the taste of a fresh lemon, then you will be in a
position to surrender in the right way. It is very threatening from one viewpoint and a great adventure from
another. No one has the right to ask or expect another
human being to undertake such a transformation for any
external reason, including the preservation of an existing
relationship. Seeking this kind of inner growth is too con-
suming and subtle to be based on anything external. It
does not justify giving up one's external responsibilities,

but these responsibilities cannot form the foundation upon which the inner effort is built.

"A slow-moving stream is easily polluted. A rapid stream, with a broader bed, sweeps away anything that enters it almost instantly. In the human being, it is more like a stream of fire. At first, it is easily extinguished. But as the stream grows and the temperature rises, it burns whatever it contacts. In the end even metals will be vaporized. Then no protection is necessary from the situations we attract. It is the other people who will need protection from us. They will instinctively stay away from the heat, unless they are reaching out for the energy it contains.

"It is good that our culture has become more open to experiences that would have been denied or condemned without understanding a decade ago. But experience itself cannot be the motive. Pleasure maintains the bondage. It does not erase it. We are no different from the rat in the maze in that respect. It is the capacity to accept pain, to persist in spite of results, not because of them, that is necessary in order to achieve anything permanent. We must move with growing awareness toward a goal that others can't see or find meaningless. And the achievement will be our own partial destruction so that someone much greater than we are today can appear.

"Whatever you wish to accomplish, whatever direction you want to go, you will need to be strengthened inwardly. Otherwise, even if you get there, it will be a twisted, dwarfed being that receives the reward. He will not know what to do with it and his success will be hollow. This work can strengthen and complete your inner development. That is the first major phase in which we are engaged. It is a big effort, and most people are deluded into thinking it is not necessary.

"When a person has reached the first level of attainment it doesn't bother me if he moves away. But he must earn the right to do it or there is no freedom in his choice. Roy worked for a time, developed certain inner gifts, and finally attracted an opportunity on the earth level that interested him, so he left. He didn't have to leave. He was just beginning. But I wasn't surprised when it happened. His need for growth was not great. It came too easily for him to fully appreciate the opportunity he had.

"I had another student who left recently. He worked hard, both in his business and in spiritual work. His wife owned some property down south in the middle of nowhere. A major corporation decided that they wanted to build in precisely that spot. It was incredible. Suddenly he was rich. He had never had money in his life. He left the work in order to enjoy it. Getting rich is no reason to leave. It could free a person to work more. But it was sufficient for him. It was a reward for his efforts which he could accept. Personally, there is no material payoff in this world that would tempt me. But I don't expect other people to have my fanatical viewpoint. I respected him for his honesty when he left.

"Unfortunately, most people leave too soon. They have achieved nothing that can permanently enrich their lives on a level that is real and important to them. They leave for many reasons, and with many rationalizations. Usually, they don't really know why. The work is too difficult. The rewards are too distant. They must face something in themselves they have always tried to deny. What does it matter? There are thousands of reasons for not doing. Only one for doing. To grow! To transform! To die and be reborn! It is a stern, vast, and unknown realm of experience. But it is very real.

"For me it has been wonderful, painful, and very lonely at times. It has wrenched every bone, muscle, and nerve in my body. There are many paths, each for different types of people. Most of them wind gently around the foothills of the mountains. Some of them end on the edge of a cliff on a dark night with beautiful music urging you on. A few are for those who wish to climb mountains. And one or two are for those who want to use the mountain top as a launching pad into the cosmos.

"What we are doing has no end. Total enlightenment is the illusion and limitation of people who have gone before. They had a remarkable experience and did not wish to work anymore, so they called it ultimate and settled down on that level of attainment.

"People talk of 'God' with the illusion that by using the term they are somehow raising the level of their own existence. In older times, men were wiser. They treated the spoken or written symbol for God with reverence and fear. If nothing is sacred to us, how can something that is of a totally different nature enter our experience? We would not let it. It is precisely what our whole personality is designed to prevent. Contact with a higher being tears us apart because we fight it; or it reaches us only very gradually as we learn to tolerate it, like fish learning to crawl on land.

"The sign of God's love is often pain, not rose petals and soft music. How could the love of something infinite be soft and sweet to a finite, fearful little being with millions of stupid illusions? It is the nature of light to reveal the truth. On the physical level, the truth is bound up in various tensions. On the psychological level, the truth is an existential hopelessness for people who have the misfortune to understand without being able to act, or the illusion of attainment by those who can do but do not see the effects of their actions. Even if God approaches quietly as a good parent in the night, the effects are bound to be devastating.

"When I was younger, before any of you knew me, I felt the need for a sign. I asked and asked for a few days. Then I got an answer. The left side of my body was suddenly paralyzed. It took several months for me to get back to normal. I could hardly walk, but I continued my business. And during all that time, when any normal person would have been frightened and overwhelmed, I felt happy. This was a sign I could recognize. I experienced it with every step I took.

"The purpose of work is not to feel pain, but to be free. You work to experience a higher level of reality, the flowering of the chakras, the opening of unknown spiritual mechanisms moving into greater simplicity, abstraction, and fulfillment. All of this brings happiness that is real, not just the overflow of a good day, but the dawning of a new era in your existence.

"I have worked too long to be surrounded by psychic malcontents, psychological cripples, blinded enthusiasts who claim everything is perfect but cannot see the stone in front of their way. I want simplicity, dignity, respect, and finally love as the flowering of maturity. Perhaps it is too soon for it to come, but bliss is not something abstract. It must begin to be available now. Open your hearts. Feel gratitude for the opportunity to work and to serve a cause that is unknown to you, but in which you nevertheless enlist through your own efforts to grow. And then ask to taste a drop of bliss. Feel it on your tongue or in your heart. You have the right to the experience. It is only a foretaste of the future."

PART THREE

The American Practice

Rudi in his new store.

BARRY KAPLAN

14

Expansion

ALL OF THE EVENTS that I have described occurred when Rudi lived and had his business in West Greenwich Village. During that period, he traveled widely, maintaining a large number of contacts with people around the world, but his home base was the west side of lower Manhattan.

I had been working with Rudi for nine years. During that time, my own process of inner transformation had gradually begun. There had been many delays and detours, inside myself and in others around me. But I knew that all of this was somehow necessary. If I had thought there were any other practical alternatives, my attitude might have been different. There weren't! I had read books, visited various groups, and invested eight years of work in other approaches before meeting Rudi. Though I had attained few positive results, at least those years of exploration had helped me to understand my own situation realistically and had given me the capacity to endure.

The energy I steadily received during the long hours at the store and from the classes was going into a deep, almost bottomless pit. I was not discouraged, nor was Rudi.

"It took a very long time, John, before anything began to happen to me," he said in a moment of empathy. "All I could see inside myself was inky blackness. When I first noticed a tinge of dark grey it was a turning point in my life. People grow at different rates. The longer it takes to begin to break through to the light, the deeper your foundation in the earth will be rooted."

•   •   •

In 1968, when Rudi shifted the center of his operation to the east side of Manhattan, a new and expanding period in his life began. The immediate impulse for the move was his growing business and the need for a larger meeting place for his classes.

As this occurred, the landmarks with which I was most familiar were removed. Rudi changed the location of his store and his house, and the scale of his business and spiritual efforts. The new store was at least five times as big as the old, the new house twice as large. Starting at first with a small group of students that later expanded, he formed a household around him. The group lived together and for the most part worked together, either in Rudi's art business or in other businesses that he sponsored. They constituted the beginning of the first ashram.

I was not a part of this inner group. It was not practical, since I had a home in Peekskill and a job at New York University. But, otherwise, things followed their familiar pattern. There were generally five kundalini classes a week. I attended the classes and sat in the store often, but not as often as before.

Every Saturday morning all available students spent a few hours cleaning the three floors of the brownstone building where classes were held. The first floor was the meditation room. The second floor was an extended living room and bedroom for those who lived in the house. The third floor was Rudi's bedroom. Because the house was saturated with art, the cleaning had to be done carefully. It was supervised by one of Rudi's older students, Jack, who had a real sense of identity with dust or dirt, wherever it might be hiding. If someone missed any, he would unerringly point it out.

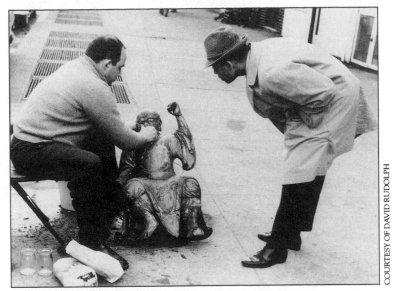

Rudi and a passerby outside his store on the east side of Manhattan.

COURTESY OF DAVID RUDOLPH

. . .

In parallel with all of these developments, the current of activity around Rudi moved more swiftly. The new store attracted a greater variety and quantity of people. For the first time there was enough space to begin to see the art in a proper setting. Rudi laid flagstone on the floor and put in an extensive lighting system. He was not after an uptown decorating effect, but the store was impressive and beautiful in its own way. It was at that point the largest Eastern art gallery on the East Coast. In the next few years, it became one of the largest in the world. As the supply of the goods dwindled for others, Rudi accelerated the pace of his buying. He was able to get items that no one else could bring out of Asia. It was a constant source of amazement to other art dealers who came to the store when a shipment arrived to buy from him what they could not buy directly for themselves.

It also surprised them to discover that Rudi usually didn't know or care that much about the history of the art works that he sold. He didn't have the time or inclination to carefully research them. Over the years, he learned enough to identify the period and type, mainly as a basis for pricing. There his interest ended. If he wanted to know more, he entered into the piece by working with it as he did with a student. He never studied oriental art in any formal sense. Occasionally this led him to undervalue a piece. But more often he would find a special value amidst a shipment of varied quality that the seller had himself overlooked. The two tendencies balanced out over time.

"Even though I began many years ago," Rudi said, "I came in at the end of the business. It was the same in my spiritual life. It is the twilight of everything that existed during the last age.

"All sources of great Eastern art are drying up. It becomes more and more difficult to bring art out of these countries, even when it is available. In many areas, it is simply all gone or the cost is so prohibitive it might as well be gone. Most dealers go on a trip to look for a few pieces of a specific type and period with a special customer in mind. That's one reason their prices are so high. If you select just one thing you pay a premium. I would rather buy a whole warehouse.

"A decade ago the countries in the Far East didn't appreciate their own art. It was only after westerners began to import it in quantity that they began to change their minds. Even then, it was more from a sense of nationalism than any aesthetic appreciation. If you walked into the house of a rich Indian, you would be shocked. They would just as soon have a plastic Shiva in a shrine as a twelfth-century masterpiece carved in stone. To them, it is all the same.

"There is one exception and that is the Japanese. They are a nation of collectors. More and more I find they have been there before me, buying up everything they can. Sometimes I could sell my goods at a higher profit in Japan than in this country. But I would be in competition with some of the people from whom I buy in Japan, so I don't do it."

Rudi stopped talking and moved off to work on crating a large and beautiful Japanese figure. It was obviously old, authentic, and valuable. "I'm selling this to the Zen Center in San Francisco," he said with enthusiasm. "It's worth fifty to a hundred times what I am charging them for it."

"Did you get a great bargain?"

"No, I just want them to have it. They need it right now."

"I don't understand," I said, puzzled.

"Their Zen master has died. A younger man, an American, is taking his place. I'm sending this piece to him as an expression of my love. It's my way of telling him that I believe in his capacity to carry on."

"But their work is so different from ours."

"Sure, it's different," said Rudi, "but it's real in its own terms, and I respect that. Most spiritual work is fantasy. People kid themselves and each other into thinking that they are really trying to grow. Even when they make a serious effort, they are usually doing what they think is right, not what they should do. There is a big difference; you can't just listen to your own ideas and expect to get anywhere."

He finished packing in silence.

The next time I visited the store, I saw a huge stone statue of Vishnu reclining on the cosmic sea. I was silent as I looked at it, but Rudi smiled at the speculation in my eyes.

LINDA SAXTON

"The next time I visited the store, I saw a huge stone statue of Vishnu reclining on the cosmic sea."

"Forget about it, John. It's a gift from the finest Eastern art dealer in the city. I am really amazed that he gave it to me, especially since there is nothing I can do for him in return. He never gives anything to anyone, he's not the type. I'm going to put it in the courtyard behind the house and build a Japanese rock garden around it. Stones grow better than plants in New York City."

As Rudi gradually settled into his new existence, my life took an unexpected turn. I was offered the chairmanship of the Sociology Department of the State University college at Geneseo, near Rochester, New York. I immediately discussed it with Rudi. My main concern was the distance that the job would take me from him.

"It's a natural progression," he said. "Don't worry. You can come down for weekends. It's not the amount of time you are here that matters, it's the intensity of your effort. I'm at the ashram in India for only a week to ten days in the whole year. But I spend the rest of the year either digesting the results or preparing for the new trip. You should definitely take the job; it will be a chance for you to expand yourself and try out some of your ideas. You can start a

Kundalini Yoga group up there; it can be your spiritual kindergarten."

With the ending of summer, I made the move to Geneseo and started a new life upstate.

When I returned to the city on one of my early visits, Rudi spoke at an evening class about the necessary conditions for inner development:

"If a person is growing, everything is relative to that. There are no universal principles. At one phase, he may need a lot of meat, at another none at all. The essential thing is to cultivate a sensitivity to your own inner condition, particularly to the changes that are occurring. You must learn to evaluate each situation by the effect it has on you inwardly, and be guided accordingly. This is not easy. There may be certain obvious actions to take, such as getting enough sleep or avoiding places with heavy negative vibrations. But there are always exceptions. There are times when you really need to stay up all night to break through a crucial resistance.

"When we were painting the front of the new store, I had the men work through the whole night. The job had dragged on long enough. It was really necessary to finish. So we rigged spotlights and worked nonstop. Anyone who didn't like it had to overcome his resistance. If he said 'the hell with it' and quit, he would just have had to deal with that resistance in some form a little later. Better to get it over with now.

"But beyond such simple acts is a world of subtleties. We have to examine each experience to learn how it affects us. Many people have the illusion they are having a meaningful and nourishing relationship because they feel a strong flow between themselves and another person. What they don't know is that the flow may be one way, in which case they are losing energy. One way to discover the truth is by sensing how you feel after leaving the other person. Are you tired or invigorated? If you are usually tired, the conclusion is inescapable. You are being drained. Such situations are dangerous, particularly if our emotions are strongly involved. In conscious work, love should be mutual. We lose too much otherwise, regardless of what we feel.

"The best guide is simplicity. The fewer our choices, the clearer they become. I don't recommend simplicity for its own sake. I lead a very complicated life, but I understand what I am doing for the most part, so that I can keep the various contradictory elements separate and avoid being caught between them. Most people I meet also lead fairly complicated lives, but they don't know what they are doing or why they are doing it. They seek to reduce their tensions through various partially destructive means that have worked for them occasionally in the past. When they are temporarily at peace, they are satisfied. None of this has anything to do with growth.

"The more aware you are of how the various situations in your life are affecting your efforts to refine your own vitality, the more responsible you become for the proper use of your own energy. Everything real is either a test or a source of nourishment. We overcome the test and absorb the nourishment. The more we do it, the more we have at stake. The reward of work is more work.

"Even when a person achieves a state of being that is illuminated in comparison to the level on which he began, it is not freedom or the expression of freedom. After a while he grows attached to that level and it becomes only a more beautiful prison than the one he left.

"I am not working to go to heaven. I would be bored out of my mind. Most people's vision of paradise is some glorified suburban country club with wings. I can't stand the suburbs; middle-class people drive me up the wall. They are almost totally dead and completely sure that they have it made. There is nothing you can do with such an attitude. It is hopeless.

"So, to retire to a glorified old folks home run by angels is not my ideal. I want to get beyond it to the next frontier. No artist ever paints his last picture, no artist paints for the applause of the critics. His work is a projection of an inner need. It is the same with our work. The satisfaction of growing through the work is its own reward.

"But none of you have begun to understand the amount of effort involved. You all take it very easy on yourselves. You don't want to know how to work five and ten times harder because then you will have to do it. That is why everything takes so long.

"On the other hand, the level of the work can only rise as the expression of the continuous refinement of energy that is consciously occurring within me. Those who start now meet a different force than those who started five years ago. Their diet is richer so they can grow faster. This may not seem just to those of you who have been here a longer time, but how can it be any other way? Nothing stands still. There is only one choice: grow or leave. There is only one kind of competition: with yourself. I do not compare you to each other. That is meaningless. Each of you comes from a different situation, and with a totally different series of past lives. These things cannot be equalized. Even if I could do it, it would be a waste of time. Everything from the past is either a source of nourishment or a burden that needs to be dropped. Breathe it in or let it go.

"Each phase of the work has its own dynamics. There is a time when a new wave of people are attracted. There is a time for these people to develop. And there is a time of harvest when the wheat is separated from the chaff.

"When I look backwards, I see countless numbers of people who have come close to me and left for various reasons at different times. I loved many of them. I did not want them to go. But there was nothing I could do. It is the force working within me that attracted them in the first place. It is the acceleration and refinement that caused them to leave. The power of my own growth began to drive them crazy.

"And so, again and again, I have to surrender someone to whom I was attached. It never ceases to hurt. But I have to learn to accept it. It is only the willingness to detach from every situation that makes growth possible. First the situation develops. It crystallizes into a pattern. After that, it must be melted down and burned away. The image of rebirth is the phoenix, rising from the ashes of its own destruction. This is what we are working for. If it doesn't appeal to you, perhaps you had better reconsider what you are doing here.

"You listen to many of the things I say and think you understand, but there is only one way to really understand: to work until you find yourself in my position. Then these words will take on a different sense and urgency. There is no reason why some of you can't be where I am now in a couple of years. But don't look for me when you get there because I will be gone."

•   •   •

As Rudi settled into this phase of his life, he started to look again for a house in the country. There was no immediate need for such a place. He had more than enough space for his teaching and his business, but he continually projected a year, two years, or a decade into the future.

In the fall of 1968 he began to spend his Sundays searching in rural areas to get a sense of what might be available. By late winter he was growing impatient to have the matter settled. He almost made an offer on a satisfactory place, but a friend who was with him insisted it wasn't good enough. So he continued to look and in this way stumbled onto Big Indian. I heard about his discovery on my next trip to the city. Rudi was overflowing with enthusiasm. I remembered the last country place near Woodstock and reserved my judgment.

"It's just beautiful," he said. "It used to be a small Catskill resort. It's got a completely equipped kitchen, a walk-in freezer that must be fifteen by twelve, endless space, loads of bedrooms. But the most remarkable thing is the setting. It's on a dead-end road enclosed on both sides by mountains, and down the road are only more mountains. There is a stream and a swimming pool fed by the stream. And lots of other smaller buildings. It has a hundred acres and I can get an option on the whole valley."

"How long does it take to get there?" I asked.

"Two and a half to three hours. And you don't even need a car, there's a bus right to the town of Big Indian."

"It sounds great," I said, more or less believing it.

"It is," said Rudi. "It really is."

A few weeks later, Rudi officially acquired the property. He started to spend his weekends there, leaving the city Friday night and returning Sunday night or early Monday.

For most of Rudi's students, Big Indian was a new beginning. The day started at 6:00 a.m. and the physical work the property required was endless. When the work finished, the classes began. Nobody needed to be persuaded to go to bed at night.

COURTESY OF JOHN MANN

"For most of Rudi's students, Big Indian was a new beginning."

The main building needed renovating. The wiring was insufficient, the plumbing quixotic, and every wall needed several coats of fresh paint. The other buildings on the property needed similar attention, since nothing had been done for two years.

There was a separate theater that had been used for dance and music performances when the property had been an active resort. We turned it into a meditation hall.

Our first project on the land was to clear a place for a garden. This meant cutting down trees, excavating the stumps, and then taking out thousands of stones by hand. Anyone who considered himself Rudi's student came and worked. There was no escape.

While the country itself was beautiful, I shuddered whenever I turned into the drive for Big Indian. I didn't want to work that hard, and I never really felt at home. I came alone from the north, while it seemed that everyone else came in groups from the city. Also, as Rudi had predicted, the newer students were better than the old. It made me glad for him, but uneasy about my own future. I had been used to my shadowy existence, sitting in his store and attending classes. But at Big Indian everything was more out in the open and the competition for Rudi's time was continuous.

The first few weekends were memorable. Everyone got sick. Some got headaches and fever. Others threw up. Still others couldn't sleep. And those who escaped these obvious symptoms simply reported a state of total exhaustion.

Rudi clarified our situation one Sunday morning when he asked Stuart, a serious student who had been studying with him for several years, how he was feeling.

"Really terrible!" said Stuart.

"Yes," said Rudi, "I feel awful, too. Everyone is paying a price, but it is very necessary. Whenever you enter a new situation, particularly when you buy a piece of real estate, it saps your vitality. I don't expect anyone to enjoy it, but it is an honor. We are helping to bring Big Indian back to life by feeding it our blood. Once it begins to function, it will feed us. There is a wonderful vitality here. The earth is saturated with energy. That is why I bought the place."

Occasionally everyone would be enlisted in some concentrated effort such as removing rocks from the potential garden. We would form a vast human chain, move the stones to the road, and stack them there. Each rock passed from person to person to person without a break for five hours. It went on all afternoon. The whole world seemed nothing but the accepting and passing of rocks. No one could stop for a moment without disrupting the whole line.

Big Indian was initially hard on most of us, but it was terribly difficult for Rudi. The pain he experienced was both physical and psychic. He did not complain, but when it got too intense he hid in the woods until the worst of it had passed.

. . .

Whenever Rudi made a major change, he extended his situation as much as possible and then dug inside himself to find the energy to sustain it. In this way, he maintained a steady pace of forced growth. I had known very ambitious people who acted like that to attain some goal in the world, but not anyone who did it simply to encourage his own development, irrespective of the practical implications. Rudi didn't really care about anything but growth.

He had lived like this for years. It was the one aspect of his work that people appreciated the least. They were interested in his experiences, but no one wanted to know about the pain. Occasionally, however, he talked about it.

"One day many years ago," Rudi said in a lecture given at the end of the summer, "a woman came into the store. I was in agony at the time. She asked me how I was doing. I told her in graphic detail. She immediately turned to leave.

"'I come here because you are cheerful,' she said as she walked out the door. 'I'm not interested in hearing your problems.'

"At first, I was angry and resentful. Why did I have to put on a show for her sake? But as I thought it over, I decided she was right. She came for some warmth and I gave her shit. No one is making me go through this suffering. There is no reason I should inflict it on innocent bystanders.

"Everyone suffers, even movie stars. The only difference is whether you take it like a dumb animal being led to the marketplace or open to it as the means to attain your objective of inner growth.

"One of the reasons that work takes so long is that people believe there is a loophole. They will do almost anything to avoid suffering, if it holds even the slightest hope of being a way to grow. There is no such way. The obstacles within us must be faced and broken down. This has to be difficult. If it weren't so, the obstacles would not still be there. But no words will convince you. Not even mine, not even after all these years. You will each of you try to outwit yourself until you finally discover you are paying as much as ever and getting nothing for it. Then you may begin to approach your growth with a little maturity, accepting the cost and paying what is due. It is hard, but it is real. In time, you may even begin to respect yourself and then you can grow faster.

"There are only two forces that can motivate a person toward growth. One is to glimpse a higher state. This is a very powerful inducement as long as it lasts, but it doesn't last very long. Normal human consciousness does not have the capacity to remember a state beyond itself.

"The second force is the recognition of our own condition, which must of necessity involve suffering. When the moment of truth occurs, we all think we are uniquely stupid, crazy, and awful. Actually, it is the thing we have in common. We are all in trouble. The earth is more like a hospital than a lost paradise. The only paradise we have lost was on another level of experience, not here.

"You can stall the suffering for years, even for lifetimes, but you can never avoid it. When you have forgotten even its possibility, it will spring on you in an unsuspected form. It is a sign of maturity when a person begins to open to things inside himself that are painful to recognize. It gives him the motivation to work," said Rudi, concluding his talk.

·   ·   ·

The summer had passed. The leaves were falling from the trees, and we resumed our normal schedule in New York City. Rudi continued to visit Big Indian every other weekend. But the people who remained were on their own when the first snowstorm of the season struck. They limited their living space and began a continuous struggle with antiquated plumbing, limited heat, and a temperamental water supply.

A number of these people hardly knew the basic nature of Rudi's work. They had simply appeared at the right time, and he had sent them up to stay the winter at Big Indian. One group had come from Los Angeles, bringing with them a lifestyle more appropriate to California than the Northeast. They settled in and proceeded to survive in their own manner.

Rudi generally ignored the difficulties of the situation when he came to visit and concentrated on giving his energy and inspiration, leaving the students to work out their difficulties with each other. Most of them had little or no money. Rudi personally underwrote the major expenses. Eventually, a small baking business was started to help defray costs, but it remained always a losing proposition.

To save fuel, class was conducted in a small room in the main building. But conditions were impossible. The door to the room squeaked loudly every time it was opened. The fluorescent lights in the room were blinding. Each person who entered either turned them on if they were off, or off if they were on, to the distraction of everyone else. There was no organization, little discipline, and very little heat.

There were only a few cars and many students stayed on the property for months, leaving only to make bread deliveries to New York City.

That winter was unusually cold and snowy. At times, the temperature fell to thirty below. But even though there was a great deal of snow, there was also a lot of sunshine. And even though the main building caught fire from the ancient kerosene furnace, the fire was contained, and all was preserved intact. When early spring came, the survivors congratulated themselves and prepared for the return of the city students, who were completely unaware of the ordeal the winter residents had undergone.

15

Preparing for Muktananda

ONE EVENING IN MARCH, 1970, Rudi made a general announcement to his class in New York City.

"I have invited Swami Muktananda to come to America, and he has accepted!" He paused to let the message sink in, and then he continued, "For years, he has wanted to come, but I always put him off. We were not ready to support the effort it involves. We needed a place like Big Indian for a proper setting. Now he is coming, probably in the early fall. I expect him here for the Labor Day weekend. It's not that any of you are ready for him, but you have six months to prepare."

Rudi paused again.

"The basic difficulty which you will face as a group is that you have not been trained in how to behave with a Hindu saint. I don't know what Baba will expect, but whatever it is he had better receive it. I'm serious! If he gets off the plane and someone looks at him the wrong way, he is perfectly capable of getting right back on the plane and leaving. I have seen him do similar things. It doesn't help to think about what kind of a nut would do something like that. He doesn't need us. We need him! So, whatever he does, whatever he wants — that is right. And if you are not prepared to act that way, then forget about being around when the time comes.

"But all of this is a side issue. The important thing is that he is the real goods, a genuine Indian saint in the ancient tradition. He represents a species that is almost extinct. In meeting him, you will be meeting the whole line of Indian spirituality that he represents. None of you would normally ever get to meet such a person in your lifetime. They almost never leave India. If you went there, you would be ignored or palmed off on some lesser person. But when Baba comes here, he will be available to you, if we treat him right.

"I don't mean to scare you. He may be on his good behavior and make things very easy for all of us. But you have to realize that the guru is the absolute dictator in his domain. His word potentially governs every facet of ashram activities. One either accepts it or leaves. It is hard for an American to understand the mentality involved. It is not like a head of a monastery who is selected for his experience, understanding, and general capacity. The Indian guru is chosen because of his other-worldly attainments. He exists on another level of being and is treated accordingly. You don't have to believe it, but you better be prepared to act as if you do. And you all can start by learning a little manners.

"Americans have the lousiest manners in the world. We are all used to it, so we take it for granted. We even enjoy it. But every gesture we make could offend someone brought up in a more traditional culture. I am no great example in that regard. I don't care very much how some of you look, or dress, or what you say to me. But when Baba is here, you will have to take the attitude that we are entertaining visiting royalty.

"Swami Muktananda is as complex as a three dimensional chess board. He might seem friendly, he might be friendly, but he has more things going on inside him than you could ever imagine. He will appear to you how he wants to appear. If you are taken in by that, it is too bad for you. At the same time, he expects you to accept what he shows and react accordingly. If you don't, there will also be trouble.

"I'm not trying to give you a nervous breakdown in advance, just some sense of perspective. What you are preparing for is a once-in-a-lifetime opportunity. Probably the only reason he is coming is that he trusts me to do right by him, which I certainly will, and also because he is chronically restless.

"He is a caged tiger. Nothing occupies him for very long. He goes through an experience and moves on. Like any creative person, he needs new material. Even when I go to his ashram in Ganeshpuri, and I am probably his best and certainly his most challenging student, the relationship between us begins to bore him after a few days. That doesn't bother me. It's a relief, really, because it makes it possible for me to leave without offending him.

"There are plenty of you. He should not be bored. But even one day or one pointless hour could cause him to take off to California or Texas, if he has been invited. Instead of staying with us a month, it could turn out to be only a week."

When I had the chance, I asked Rudi further about Muktananda's visit.

"He can't wait to come," Rudi told us. "He keeps writing me about it. I think he wants to turn it into a world tour. I'm not a travel agent, though, I just want to get him here and keep him here for as long as possible. But there is one helluva lot of work to be done before that.

"The trouble is, John, that I am the only one who realizes it. If he came next week, you would all get excited and think it was great. He would leave, and you would be satisfied. You would never know that you hadn't even touched the surface. But I would know! I have spent ten, twelve — I can't remember how many years — working with the man."

"The thing that puzzles me," I said, "is that you are building him up so much now. At other times, some of the things you have said certainly weren't so favorable. How can it be both ways?"

"Very easily," Rudi answered. "I contradict myself all the time. Generally, it doesn't bother you, although I'm sure it bothers some people. But often opposites are true. The average person avoids contradicting himself if he can because it doesn't sound logical. I am not very interested in logic. I want results. I am trying to stir people into making an effort, into facing certain sides of themselves they would rather ignore. I am prepared to do anything to accomplish this aim. If it requires love, I'll give love. If it requires strength, I'll give strength. If it requires scourging, I'll scourge. It's all a question of what you want to achieve. Once you know that, you judge everything by whether it helps you attain that goal.

"As an example, the most important aspect of Swami Muktananda's visit isn't anything that will happen while he is here. It is *that* he is here. Once you understand this, it clarifies the whole situation. If he can be persuaded to stay put in Big Indian or New York City for a few weeks, he will inevitably put not only his own energy, but also the energy of the whole line of Indian teachers whom he represents into the atmosphere. No one may be directly aware of this process as it occurs, but the energy will remain behind and continue to enrich the ashram. So the important thing becomes to keep him here for a sufficient time for this magnetizing effect to occur. Anything that aids the process is good. If he wants special foods, we get them. If he wants to give lectures, we listen. If he wants to sing, we will love it. And with all of this, he has to believe that there is a need for him that he is interested in fulfilling. He can't be fooled about that."

That spring, as part of our preparation, Rudi began to allow other people to teach his work in New York City and Big Indian. This action was entirely without precedent. Michael A. was the first, followed a little later by Stuart and Calvin. All of them had been with Rudi for several years. They were very different types. Stuart was quiet, slightly distant, but seemingly gentle. Michael A. had a military style. Calvin was much more ebullient, theatrical. However, none of these personality differences mattered when they taught. The being who emerged was different from the person one had known personally. It was always surprising, like trying to anticipate the color of a butterfly from looking at the caterpillar.

While I accepted this change without any difficulty, I had to speak to Rudi eventually about my own position. I found the opportunity on a quiet moment one Saturday morning.

"I have been teaching yoga at Geneseo for more than a year," I said.

"Sure, so what?" Rudi responded discouragingly.

"I have no illusions about the value of what I am doing, but it must represent something or you wouldn't let me do it."

"True," he said, ready to drop the matter.

"What I want to know is what I have to do to be able to teach down here," I persisted.

Rudi paused as if he had something difficult to say and was not quite sure how to put it. "It is possible that you could start by the end of the summer," he said. "But the problem is, John, that there are certain pieces missing in you. If you can get them, then you can teach."

"How would I do that?" I asked.

"It's basically quite simple. Stuart, Michael, and Calvin each have some of these missing parts. What you have to do is to acquire what you lack from them."

"But how? I don't understand."

"First, spend time with them. Get them to open to you. That shouldn't be too difficult because they are supposed to do that as part of their teaching. But even more important, you have to open completely to them and ask to receive those aspects of their inner nature that you need. If you ask deeply enough, it will occur."

"But how will I know?"

"Maybe you won't know. I will know. That's what counts. But I can't do the work for you. It is part of the price you must pay for the chance to teach. I have replaced psychic parts in you in the past. I won't do that any more for you or anyone else. You have come a long way. But that no longer matters. If you want to teach, you must fill in the gaps by your own effort. You have the rest of the summer in which to do it."

I left, still not sure what Rudi meant, but determined to try. I had the distinct feeling that if I didn't make it this time around, it would be far more difficult in the future.

On my subsequent visits to Big Indian, I concentrated on opening to the teachers. I talked to them, worked with them in the fields; anything that I could think of. It wasn't so bad, but I didn't have the slightest idea whether I was succeeding. At the same time, I had a fateful meeting that enormously complicated the whole process of preparing for the fall. I was just settling down from a divorce the year before.

I walked into my first summer school class in late June. Sitting at the opposite end of the room was a beautiful blonde girl, seemingly intent on blending in with the background. My first thought was, "What is *she* doing in Geneseo?"

I was giving two three-week courses, back to back. She was enrolled in both. Her name was Melanie. During the first three weeks, I fought my attraction to her. I avoided looking at her or talking to her, but I was falling in love with her just the same. She was beautiful, exotic, very intelligent, and had a quality of untouchability that I found totally irresistible.

After the first course was over, I went on a two-week publicity tour in connection with my recently published book, *Encounter*.* In the course of a radio interview, the interviewer asked me what happens if the leader gets involved with a member of his group. I said I would let him know in about six weeks.

I returned to Geneseo to give the second course. Each day that Melanie and I were together became a link in the chain that was being forged between us. Toward the end of the course, I made a move. The group was over for the day. She was walking out of the room. I caught up with her and asked if I could talk with her.

We walked out onto the quadrangle surrounded by most of the college buildings. It was probably the most public spot on the whole campus.

After a preliminary silence, I spoke.

"I have been fighting my feeling for you since I met you," I said.

"I know," she said in a matter of fact, but slightly tense tone. "What made you change your mind now?"

"The group is coming to an end," I said. "You are graduating. It seemed like I should talk to you now or forget about it."

---

* Mann, John. *Encounter: a weekend with intimate strangers*. New York: Grossman, 1970.

"I'm glad you're saying something," she said. "What made you hesitate?"

"I can think of a couple of good reasons. But, anyway, all I want to say is that when you graduate and settle down, I want to see you. How do you feel about that?"

"I want to see you, too," she said.

I smiled and felt very happy. There was nothing more to say. She left shortly thereafter. I felt very much in love.

As the term drew to a close, we decided to take a trip together. This was not an expression of my better judgment, but the course was over and she was about to graduate. I felt like Adam with a ten-day pass to the Garden of Eden.

The trip was set for the following week. The weekend before, I went to Big Indian. On the way there, Dora, an old friend who was driving with me, announced, "I'm going to tell Rudi about what you are doing with Melanie." I was shocked, but I knew there was nothing I could do to stop her.

When we arrived, I decided I had better speak to Rudi first. I found him between the main house and the meditation room.

"Could I talk with you a minute?" I asked hesitantly.

"Sure. What's up?"

"I wouldn't bother you, but I know Dora is going to say something, so I want to give you the background."

"What have you done now?"

"I've fallen in love," I said. "I wanted you to hear it from me first."

Rudi looked at me without expression. I waited. He didn't say anything.

"Is there anything you want to know?"

"No. I'll talk to you after I hear what Dora says."

On those less than reassuring words, I went back to work, removing brush from what was to become an or-

chard by the end of the season. As the hours passed, I became more nervous. The more I thought about it, the less
I liked the situation.

In the afternoon, Rudi came by. He motioned to me to
drop what I was doing. I walked over nervously, like a
school boy caught in the act of cheating on an exam. He
didn't waste any words. "What is wrong with you, John?"

I didn't say anything. One thing I had learned was that
there was no defense. Whatever came, it was my job to
open to it and absorb the impact. Any decisions could
come later.

"First of all," said Rudi, "this girl is a student. How can
you do such an idiotic thing?"

"I haven't done anything yet."

"But you are going to."

There was nothing I could say to that. I was getting the
horrible feeling that I was not going to be visiting the Garden of Eden.

"Don't you have any sense of responsibility?" Rudi was
relentless. "You can't expect to be protected for the rest of
your life. How many times do I have to save you from the
edge of a cliff?"

Finally, I couldn't resist defending myself: "I don't really
see what is so terrible. I love the girl. She is graduating. It
may not be entirely right, but how can it be that wrong?"

"Listen, John. All you see is the beautiful girl in front of
you, a sparkling enchantment. But when it's over, what will
you have? Nothing! A waste of energy. I can understand how
you feel. You have had so little in the way of real human relationships for so many years. But it's still wrong, particularly
since you feel more for her than she does for you. It should be
more equal."

"What am I supposed to do?" I asked, knowing the answer
in advance.

"When you go back, see the girl and tell her it's over. Maybe she'll understand. But whether she does or not, that is what you must do."

I looked at it, hated it, recognized a certain inevitability in the situation and agreed. If I hadn't, there was no hope of my becoming a teacher. I cursed Dora inwardly, though at the same time I felt peculiarly grateful. Her influence might have saved me, if indeed I needed saving.

Finally I said, "After she graduates in September, is it all right then?"

Rudi was silent for a moment and then said, "Even then it would be better if you didn't."

He walked away and I went back to work. I would have fought if that had been possible, but I had too much at stake and I knew that what Rudi said was more or less true.

The next time I returned to Big Indian, Rudi asked if I had ended it.

"I hated doing it," I said, "but I did it."

"Good," he said. "You really had no choice."

"I know," I said.

"It was the effect it would have had on you that was crucial."

"What do you mean?" I asked, not sure I really wanted to know.

"You certainly would not have become a teacher. At another time, perhaps the whole thing wouldn't have made too much difference. Right now, the timing is crucial. If there is a miscarriage, the time and effort you have invested would be largely wasted. Inwardly, I think you knew this. That is why you did what had to be done. I'm sure it was hard for you. Better it should be hard and done, than to lose all you have worked for. It was a test and you passed."

He paused and looked at me speculatively. "Don't feel sorry for yourself. Be glad for the girl's sake."

"That's a hell of a thing to say," I answered, taken aback.

"In a year or two, you would grow tired of her. Then you would move on looking for someone else to repeat the same pattern. Over the years, you would have left a trail of broken situations and lives behind you, and you would be left with nothing. It would have been the end of the work for you." I sat very still, feeling the cold chill of these words.

"Why didn't you tell me this earlier?" I asked.

"You wouldn't have believed it. Enough time has passed for you to be able to see things differently. To enter the Garden of Eden, as you imagined this would be, leads nowhere except to the back exit. You blow a great amount of energy on the illusion of paradise. There is nothing real about it but the emotion you feel at the time. You don't grow in paradise. You can't! If it were only necessary to follow your desires in order to become enlightened, you wouldn't need to be with me today. Nothing is attained without sacrifice. And no one is in a position to know what he should sacrifice until the answer falls on him, usually unexpectedly. God chooses what he wants from you. If you pay, you receive an unknown gift in return. That is where faith is required. It is the bridge between unknowns."

Rudi paused and looked at me and through me, and when he spoke again it was with a different tone. "You are a monster, John. You are a vampire sucking the blood out of situations and then leaving them dead. You have been doing it all your life. For a long time, it didn't matter. You were too dead yourself to have much effect on others, and people instinctively shunned you. But I have been bringing you to life. You are getting to the point where you can attract other people to you. It isn't *you* doing this, it is the force working through you, and that makes it my responsibility."

I was shocked. Rudi had never said anything like this to me before, not in eleven years. What had I done to deserve it? I had given up Melanie. I was working hard.

"If you asked to be my student at this point, I wouldn't take you," Rudi continued relentlessly. "I am not just saying that for effect. It is the simple truth. You are a menace to me and could be a menace to the work unless something is fundamentally changed in you."

"Is this what you have always thought?" I asked as I tried to recover my balance.

"Yes. I always saw these things."

"But for eleven years you never said anything. I can't understand that."

"It would have done no good. You would not have been ready to hear it."

I felt a growing sense of numbness. The implications of Rudi's words spread in all directions, like black ink on a blotter. So many years of experience were being recast in a different light. How could he have felt such things and never said them? I sensed that I had been cut in half with a psychic meat cleaver. It was a clean cut with little blood, but I could imagine the two pieces just falling apart. I couldn't say anything. He was silent. Then he resumed.

"Perhaps you think I don't mean what I am saying or that I am exaggerating it. You couldn't be more mistaken. I haven't made you a teacher here because I dared not turn you loose. You couldn't do much harm up in Geneseo, but unless something changes in you drastically, you will never teach down here. I have nothing personally against you. It is my responsibility to protect others from the result of my own efforts where you are concerned."

I left slowly. It had been relentless torture from the least expected source. I walked up the road, along the brook, past whispering trees. But I was blind to the scene around me. I felt like the picture of Dorian Grey come to life. I had escaped from the mirror and there was nowhere to hide. It was horrible! It had happened in the full light of day, delivered from both barrels by the man on whom my future most depended. If he thought these things, what chance did I have?

But I did not care what he thought at that moment. My own nakedness came before anything else. I sat down on a secluded rock by the stream that bordered the road and began to cry, deep hopeless tears. I cried in the merciless light that shone on me from all directions. It was one of the most awful moments of my life. Every rationalization and excuse had been stripped away. If anyone else had said it to me, I would have doubted the words and so muted the effect. But I had gained an admiration of Rudi's extraordinary ability to see to the center of a situation. I had watched his insight operate on others for over a decade, continually revealing things that were obviously true once pointed out and invisible until then.

Crying brought little relief, but it eventually exhausted me. I walked for a long time. I didn't know where I was. Gradually it grew dark. Whatever had happened seemed to be over. I made my way back feeling exhausted and defenseless. If I had wept my soul out of my eyes, I would not have been surprised.

It was quiet in the main house. I wanted to be inconspicuous. I walked towards the stairs to the upper floor where I was staying. At the base of the stairs, Rudi was deep in a poker game.

I tried to walk by unnoticed. Probably if I had wanted to attract his attention, he would have remained absorbed in the game. So naturally, this time he stopped what he was doing to give me a searching glance.

"You look good, John. Your eyes are clearer."

"I feel totally exhausted and empty," I said, stumbling up the stairs.

That was the beginning of a process that extended through the rest of the summer. Every time I worked deeply it was followed by tears of sadness and remorse. I could not have said why I was crying, other than because of my own inner state and the seeming hopelessness of ever doing anything about it. If it had not changed in all this time, what hope could there be? What I did not know was that the change was occurring as I cried. In every bitter harsh tear, something was leaving me that had been deeply buried under forgotten layers of my experience. I might never understand what I had done in the past, or only after it had ceased to be a problem to me, but the effects that had haunted me were being purged from my system.

When it was necessary, Rudi continued to scourge me. He was utterly merciless. I had always thought of him as relatively easy-going, inclined to think too well of people. I never assumed that again. He saw people for what they were. He focused on their positive aspects by choice, not blindness. He reached for the good because growth and nourishment lay in that direction.

A month later I saw Rudi alone after lunch as everyone left to go back to work. I gathered up my courage and took the opportunity to approach him.

"At the beginning of the summer, I asked you about becoming a teacher at Big Indian. You told me I needed some missing pieces that I could get if I opened to several of the teachers. I have tried. I am going to keep on trying. But time is passing. The summer is more than half over. I want to know how I'm doing."

"You are doing all right," he said.

"That isn't terribly definite."

"At this point, it is up to you. It is possible for you to succeed, but certainly not inevitable. How much do you want it?"

"I want it. I wouldn't have given up Melanie if I didn't want it."

"Have you given her up?"

"Yes."

"Good."

Rudi was quiet for a very long time. Then he broke the silence. "There will be ten teachers produced this year. You have been with me longer than anyone and you certainly deserve a chance. But you have to understand something, John. I am basically detached. Each person who becomes a teacher requires a great effort on my part. It's like having a child. I am willing to make that effort." His eyes took on a stern but distant glimmer that focused beyond me. "It makes no difference to me who the ten people are. They will emerge in terms of their preparation, need, and capacity. I certainly want you to have every opportunity, but at the same time you must realize that if you don't make it, that will be all the same to me. The ten teachers will come through whoever they are. I will have fulfilled my responsibility and my commitment."

I sat there experiencing a cold chill. I knew I was hearing the truth, and it was just. I would not have wanted it any other way.

Rudi saw that I understood and accepted his words. He smiled slightly. "There is no reason why you shouldn't be one of the ten, if you do what you have to do."

"If I should make it, when could I begin?" I asked, wanting to pin him down before the conversation ended.

"On the Labor Day weekend," said Rudi. "Remind me about it if I should forget."

He got up and left. I sat there, stunned. Labor Day weekend! That was when Swami Muktananda was due to arrive. It was the first weekend he would be at Big Indian. It seemed like an incredible time to begin.

One of the major tasks at Big Indian during this period was to finish the outside of all the buildings. This included repairing the roofs and gutters and repainting the house. I was involved in the painting. The main house was three stories high. We had extension ladders, but they were not fully adequate. Standing on the next-to-top rung, I could still reach only within ten feet of the peak of the roof. I worked with another fellow who was afraid of the wasps that had built their nests in the eaves. Slowly we worked our way up. We had to cover a huge area. But inevitably the effort converged on the relatively narrow strip at the top. My partner didn't want anything to do with it because of the wasps. I had always been afraid of heights. One of my nightmare fantasies was to have to cross a fragile hand bridge over a high mountain pass in the Himalayas. As I mounted higher, my legs and shoulders became increasingly tense. I had to come down to rest more often. During one of these periods, Rudi appeared.

"Where are you working?" he asked me.

"Up there." I pointed toward the fully extended ladders.

He nodded and said, "Good."

"What's so good about it?"

He didn't reply.

"If I fell from there," I said, "that would be the end."

"Don't worry about it, John," he said. "You won't fall. You weren't meant to have such an easy way out." And on that note of sympathy, he departed. But I felt much better. He was aware of what I was doing and was unconcerned about it. I felt I would get through somehow without a serious accident.

At the end, I had to stand on the last rung of the fully extended ladder using a paintbrush tied to a long broom handle. Wasps were swarming around me. I didn't mind getting stung, but I was really afraid of falling off the ladder. My legs began to quiver. I was tempted to quit and let someone else worry about the last few feet. It could hardly be noticed from the ground.

I came down the ladder to rest and think it over. My partner, who was supposed to be holding the ladder, had disappeared somewhere without telling me. All my laziness and fear urged me to walk away at least for the time being. But I felt that the situation was not accidental. If I ever wanted to teach, I'd better get my ass up that ladder and finish the job. I reluctantly forced myself to turn back. In the end it wasn't so bad. My partner came back after I had finished. I was tempted to slug him, but my legs were still shaking and I was just thankful that the job was over. The wasps were swarming angrily above.

As work on the ashram proceeded, there was word from India to spur us on. Swami Muktananda was getting excited about the trip.

He wrote that he would like to bring fifteen people with him. Rudi was shocked, since he had accepted responsibility to underwrite the expenses of the trip. He wrote back a tactful but firm letter:

"Dear Baba, We all look forward to your arrival. Excitement is mounting. Fifteen people are out of the question. Much as we would like to have them, the facilities are inadequate and I do not have the money. I am not a millionaire, regardless of what you may think. Please limit the party to three."

"That way," Rudi explained to us, "he will probably limit it to five or six."

For the first time since I had known him, Rudi began to collect money from his students. It was not for the expenses of running the ashram, but to help cover Muktananda's visit. Even then, he was apologetic about it.

"He is really coming for all of you," he said after class. "I can go to India to see him. But very few of you will ever go to the East. And even if you did, you would not have the opportunity that will exist while he is here. Endless stupid obstacles would be placed in your way unless you went with me.

"But this time you will have a remarkable opportunity. He wants to make the trip, so he will make himself available. His own people will not be here to occupy him and insulate him from outsiders. That is the real reason I would not accept his bringing fifteen people. If he did that, he might as well stay home. I don't care about the money. If I really thought it was necessary, I would raise the money for twenty-five people. But the problem with any teacher is that you have to get through his advanced students to get to him. It's like trying to see the head of a corporation. The difficult part is to penetrate the layers of protection that surround him. The man himself is usually accessible if you have a real reason to talk with him."

During the three months before Muktananda's arrival, various new classes were instituted. An American woman who had spent time in Ganeshpuri gave lessons in proper behavior at ceremonial occasions. For the first time, we learned to chant. Rudi had previously discouraged chanting. He felt that it too easily produced a superficial effect that gave people the illusion of working without doing much work. But Muktananda approved of it. So we would chant.

Droupadi, an Indian woman who had been with Baba a long time, came ahead to prepare the way. She was very gentle and inwardly dedicated to her master in a devotional manner I had not seen before. On one occasion, Droupadi was scheduled to give a class. When I arrived, she was alone, although I would have expected twenty-five to thirty people. Later, I learned that Rudi had started to talk in the dining room at about that time, and everyone had stayed behind to listen to him.

Droupadi waited for a few minutes and then began. We went through a basic routine of chanting and brief meditation. When it was over, I continued to sit for awhile. Suddenly I felt Rudi's presence. I knew he was not in the room, there was no one there but Droupadi. But I began to burn and feel that I had been absorbed into Rudi's belly. I didn't think much about it; if I had, I probably would have doubted the reality of the experience. But later in the day I casually asked him about it. "Was it real or was I having a daydream?"

"Of course it was real," Rudi said, slightly irritated with me. "How do you think a teacher is created? He has to be born. Who is the parent? The guru. I am carrying you inside me, John. The fact that you didn't realize it until now doesn't mean it wasn't going on. Now that you know, it should help you to have more faith in the reality of the process."

As part of the general preparation, Rudi decided to celebrate an Indian holiday devoted to the guru, Guru Purnima. It was like a birthday party for all gurus, regardless of when they were born. I arrived at Big Indian without knowledge of what was to occur and consequently was totally unprepared. Rudi himself was ambivalent about the ceremony, because he resisted situations that placed him in an exalted position. Nevertheless he accepted it as part of the preparation for Muktananda's visit.

My first inkling that anything unusual was going on was a sign on the kitchen doorway listing people who were fasting for the day. But even then I did not know it was in preparation for any particular event. It did not begin to dawn on me to ask about it until I noticed several people making gifts.

"What's going on?" I asked.

I received surprised looks. "It's the Guru's day. We are having a ceremony after lunch."

"What does it involve?" I was totally at sea.

"No one knows exactly, except that we each give gifts to Rudi," I was told.

Lunch passed. I volunteered to help wash dishes with a crew of seven. It had been a festive meal and had generated an endless number of dirty dishes. One by one, people began to disappear. I gathered that the ceremony was to begin at 2:00 p.m. It got to be 2:25. I began to feel slightly sick. I had no present and would be late besides. I knew I shouldn't leave until the dishes were finished, but that didn't solve my problem. I couldn't say, "I'm sorry, but I didn't know about it and have nothing to give." Such an excuse might be reasonable, but psychologically it would cut no ice. I continued washing the dishes, getting more and more upset. Finally, I took myself in hand and decided to trust that a solution would come.

I finished the dishes at about 2:35. And then I had an inspiration. For some reason, I had brought my checkbook. It was in the back of the car. I ran outside like a madman, opened the trunk, and ripped the strap off my briefcase in my excitement. Inside was the checkbook. I wrote out a check, started for the meditation hall, stopping only to pick one orange flower that was growing in a window box. I folded the check around the stem of the flower. I was ready! I arrived in the meditation hall a nervous wreck, only to discover there was no hurry. A long line of people, old and young, waited to present their gifts, one at a time. They approached the front of the stage where Rudi was sitting, bowed down, gave their gift and waited to receive his blessing. The ceremony had been going on for at least thirty minutes and more than half of the people were still in line.

I waited, enjoying the opportunity to relax and absorb the scene. It was quite beautiful. Whatever Rudi's initial misgivings, he was radiantly happy. His presence filled the room. Each person approached him differently: quickly or slowly, with a half-bow or a complete prostration. He looked on each serenely, accepting what they gave him, sometimes giving one of the gifts he had already received in return, or touching the person in a blessing.

Slowly the line shortened and I moved toward the front. As one or two were still ahead of me, I began to feel strange. Was my gift appropriate? I thought it would be all right. In any case, he could use it as needed. The thought of bowing to him didn't bother me, though I had known him for so long and never had done it before. But this was not the Rudi I had known.

The person before me in the line moved ahead. I watched, waiting with a sense of anticipation, though I did not expect anything in particular. Now it was my turn. I moved forward and came down on my knees. At that moment, a picture was taken, although I didn't know it at the time. I presented my gift, bowed to the floor, came up and waited. Rudi looked at me seriously for a moment and then gave me a garland and smiled happily. I smiled too and moved away. Shortly thereafter, the last of the people passed before him and were seated.

There was silence for a few minutes as Rudi sat within the vibrant spirit that filled the room. Then he spoke briefly:

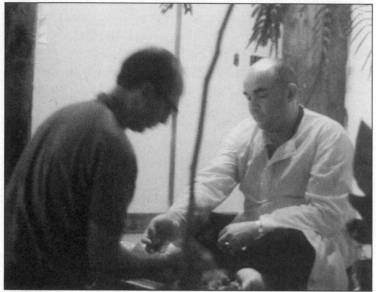

"I presented my gift, bowed to the floor, came up, and waited."

"I know that these gifts are for the force that works through me, not for me. It is in this sense that I have accepted them. It makes me deeply grateful to have experienced this day. I want to share my happiness with you.

"A few of you will find yourselves in my position in the future. When it happens, remember that it is not for you. Otherwise, you will be in danger of believing in yourself instead of knowing always that it is only through your nothingness that the force flows."

He looked around the room at each person separately, mirroring in his own face what he saw before him. The atmosphere shone. Then quietly but abruptly, he left, leaving his presence shimmering in the air.

Later when photographs of the whole day were shown, it turned out that the moment I had been with Rudi was the only picture taken during the actual ceremony. When Rudi saw the picture, he said, "John must be coming up in the world."

A few weeks later it was announced that we would have a puja. No one understood what was involved but Rudi, who had witnessed the ceremony on a recent trip to India.

"It was," he explained, "a week-long fire purification ritual during which many holy men gathered to renew their inner commitment to God."

Rudi had some doubts about the wisdom of attempting to duplicate such an ancient ritual under western conditions. But again, he was urged to do so by others as part of our general preparation. On the day before the ceremony, he described what would happen.

"In my last letter from Swami Muktananda, he gave Big Indian the title *Shree Gurudev Rudrananda Yogashram*. It is a great honor but it is also just a name. It represents a possibility, not anything that really exists. The purpose of the puja is to begin to make it real.

"Today we are going to dig a great hole in the upper field. Tomorrow it will be filled with logs and in the evening after dark, we will have a great fire. There will be a full moon. It is the right time. I cannot tell you exactly what to do beforehand; I don't even know whether anything will happen."

I had no doubt that something would happen. Rudi never did anything that didn't work. If it didn't happen easily, he just worked harder until something gave way by the sheer intensity of his effort.

As the day of preparation stretched out, expectations mounted. A vast pile of logs was thrown into a large pit that had been gouged out of the earth with a bulldozer.

At eight in the evening, we met in the meditation hall. While we worked it rained briefly — a good sign, someone said. At the end, Rudi spoke.

"As you leave here, walk quietly up to the field. A puja is a ceremony of ritual purification. It represents the nature of our work. It is also a means of attracting the attention of great beings who must be enlisted into the atmosphere of the ashram. As the light of the flame ascends, we also can rise to attract the spirits down on us. The fire itself is not important. It is only a visible symbol. It is the burning within your heart that attracts the cosmic energy with which we work. Just as a statue is dedicated through a ceremony designed to make contact between the image and that which it represents, so this experience has the potential of making contact between the whole physical structure of this ashram and great powers in the universe. I can't be sure that this will happen, but I have seen something very like it occur during the puja ceremony I witnessed in India.

"For each of you it is an opportunity to deepen your sense of dedication and surrender. As I talk, the wood is already being lit. We will shortly begin to walk around the fire. If you wish, you may hold burning branches. That is not important. But as you walk, ask to place in the fire everything within you that is obstructing your own growth. Throw in your whole personality if you wish. It's an opportunity to get rid of a tremendous amount of garbage from the past. Each step can be a different item. Each great circle around the fire can be a whole phase of your past. As for the rest, follow my lead."

Rudi got up and walked out the side door into the night. Slowly, we followed him. It was quite light outside. The ground was damp, and the full moon threw the scene into relief. The mountains surrounding Big Indian loomed like dark organic presences. The air was cool, and the great fire was already visible in the distance. The figures around it were silhouetted, and the sound of the damp wood crackling, spitting, and sparkling filled the atmosphere.

As I reached the pit, I felt the overwhelming heat of the fire. People chanted as they walked slowly around the blaze. I felt awkward, but I tried to surrender. There were certainly things in myself that I wanted to drop. As I thought of them or felt them, I threw them in the fire. I could imagine them sizzling and then disappearing in the huge swirling flames. I didn't know what anyone else was doing or whether anything was actually happening, but the mood was extremely intense.

The moon appeared and disappeared behind the gentle clouds. The fire roared and the light stretched into the heavens. People stopped moving. I stared into the flames for a time. I looked at Rudi. His eyes were reflecting the orange light. He was in some kind of abstract state. I walked over to be closer to him. He sat facing the fire for a time. Others sat down around him. He did not look at them.

The vastness of the outdoors, combined with the intensity of everyone's inner effort, seemed to be converging in some direction I could not see. I asked to be part of whatever was happening. Rudi went into the kind of spasm that often occurred when the force became particularly intense for him. Then he walked off into the darkness. The puja was over.

Later, he said, "A vast figure of Shiva appeared. It stretched up several hundred feet into the sky. We always think of higher beings on our own human scale. But that is ridiculous; they are huge.

"If we can build on what happened tonight, Big Indian can become a place that attracts such beings from the astral plane and is enriched by their energy. It is a great and important possibility that people scarcely understand. If we can bring down the energy of another level of existence, the quality here will rise beyond anything you can imagine. That is one reason I wanted Muktananda to come. Everything he has within him can be absorbed by the atmosphere and remain here after he goes."

All of this faded into the background as August ended. The necessary work at Big Indian had been accomplished. It had been a huge job. A special sign had been made in copper for the meditation room which bore our new name: Shree Gurudev Rudrananda Yogashram.

The stage was set. It remained only for the protagonist to appear.

16

Swami Muktananda Comes

I HAD LIVED IN THE SHADOW of Swami Muktananda for over a decade, but the reality of the man was unknown. I awaited his arrival with hope, curiosity, and uncertainty.

I arrived at Big Indian early in the evening on the Friday of Labor Day weekend in 1970. It seemed deserted. I looked in the meditation hall. No one was there. I entered the main house and heard the distant sound of chanting, to the accompaniment of an unfamiliar stringed instrument. I followed the sound into the small living room, which overflowed with people. In the front of the room was Swami Muktananda singing and chanting as if he had always been there. He seemed the essence of friendly power. I sat down quietly in the back of the room to absorb the scene. I was overwhelmed; it was so totally different from anything I had expected.

"You can't judge him by your standards," Rudi had said. "You will see what he appears to be and get involved in what he appears to be doing. But Baba is perfectly capable of doing a number of things at once, some of which you can't see. He has more angles than a hall of mirrors. If you get involved in trying to understand what is going on, you will go down and never come up. None of it matters. Absorb what you can use. Let him worry about the rest."

As I sat there, I forgot about everything Rudi had said as Baba's singing transformed his surroundings into an Indian temple. After fifteen minutes, he stopped and spoke through his interpreter.

Baba (Swami Muktananda).

PAINTING BY WENDELL FIELD

"I am very pleased to be here and will see you all after supper." He smiled happily as if he had made a subtle joke and quietly made his way out of the room. The weekend had begun.

Swami Muktananda's arrival in the United States received a good deal of advance publicity. This was his first trip outside India. By Saturday, 250 people, representing several different spiritual groups, had assembled in Big Indian. Swami Muktananda seemed to accept, and probably enjoy, the activity and excitement that surrounded his presence. He gave classes through his translator, and led chanting in a generally festive atmosphere. Watching him totally at ease before all these people, I was tempted to think of him as a kindly, elderly yogi, full of love and charity. But as I looked more closely, I saw a smiling tiger, or a friendly serpent, whose actions might completely change at any moment. At Big Indian on that weekend and later, he was kindly, captivating, and patient, at least in public. I didn't see him in private.

During the first day, after one of Muktananda's classes, Rudi started to work with some of his students in a totally new way. At first, all I noticed were people approaching Rudi and then collapsing onto the lawn. Then as I watched more closely, I saw that he put his fingers on the person's forehead, and shortly thereafter they seemed to become dizzy and fall to the ground in some kind of fit. It was scary. I stood around in the narrowing circle, watching with mixed emotions as he worked with one person after another. And then Rudi turned toward me. I had no idea what to expect. Two of his fingers touched my forehead; they seemed to burrow in. My hesitation had no power over them. My head went back, he touched my heart center, and then the base of my spine. Without knowing quite what was happening, I felt myself arching backward and falling to the ground. Someone caught me to break the fall. I lay still, occasionally racked by a spasm. It reminded me of the occasion so many years before, when Rudi had raised the kundalini in my spine during the great northeastern blackout. I lay on the ground for a minute or two, conscious of great energy moving through me. Then I slowly got up. The whole scene looked like a spiritual battlefield, with people strewn across the lawn in various stages of recovery. Rudi was slowing down. He had worked with about twenty people. He took on one last person.

As evening approached, I realized that the Labor Day weekend was proving to be the least likely time for me to start teaching. There were so many people moving in as many directions, that it would be ridiculous and inappropriate to begin under these circumstances. Rudi seemed to have forgotten ever having said anything to me about it. Why should he remember? It was up to me. I got sick at the thought. He was terribly busy and constantly involved with Swami Muktananda, as was natural. I could imagine the response I would get if I could find the opportunity to talk to him. But I also knew that the situation had to be clarified. So I bided my time, afraid but determined.

My opportunity came after dinner in a crowded hallway. Rudi was rushing past on some errand. I reached out to catch his attention.

"Could I speak to you for a moment?"

He obviously didn't want to speak to me or anyone else. He had something on his mind. But he halted.

"What is it?"

"A month ago, you said if all went well I could start teaching on the Labor Day weekend. Is that still true?"

He looked at me as if I were some particularly loathsome bug that he had just uncovered under a rock. I didn't care. It was no time to hesitate.

"I felt that if I didn't say anything," I persisted, "the opportunity would just go by. I know you have a lot of things on your mind."

"Remind me tomorrow if I forget about it," said Rudi. "Perhaps you can begin after class in the early afternoon."

He didn't wait for my reaction but disappeared in the direction he had been going. I stood there, shaken but happy that I had apparently achieved my objective.

That evening, Rudi heard Baba was disturbed about movies that were being taken of the weekend. Bruce, one of Rudi's older students, was the cameraman. While Baba had given his permission for the filming, Bruce, in his enthusiasm, had been taking a good deal of footage of Rudi as well as of Muktananda. This Baba did not like.

Rudi took the matter very seriously, and he spoke to Bruce about it.

"I don't care how you do it, but go to Swami Muktananda and apologize. Don't be misled by his apparent egotism. He is the honored guest. He has the right. No one told you to start taking my picture instead of his. Your future is at stake. Obtain his forgiveness."

Bruce didn't argue. He went to Baba's room. After a lengthy wait by the closed door, he was informed that the Swami was not to be disturbed. He waited for several hours more. Finally he was told the Swami had retired for the night. Bruce was grim, but not discouraged.

The next day, Sunday, was varied and exciting, but I couldn't get involved in it. The question of what would happen in the afternoon haunted me. Swami Muktananda gave a long class. Everyone was absorbed in his words. Everyone but me. I was scared of teaching and scared that the opportunity would get lost in the shuffle. Finally, after an hour and a half, the session began to break up. Rudi stayed with Baba. I waited. Some people approached Baba for his blessing. He gave it. Rudi drifted away slightly. I moved up to him. He looked everywhere but at me. It might have been intentional, but I didn't think so.

"What about it?" I asked.

He looked puzzled. Then he smiled.

"This is the time, isn't it?"

"Yes."

"See if you can find Lucas, Natalie, and the others who are preparing to teach. You can all start at once. Tell each of them to round up a few people and give a class somewhere on the grounds."

I waited to hear more, but Rudi had no more to say. Somehow I accumulated twelve to fifteen people. They sat in a semicircle near a large tree, in the middle of a field near the entrance to the main house.

I had taught many times before at Geneseo, but this was the big time, and these were all students who had studied directly with Rudi. I knew it had better be good.

I would have found a reason for delay if I could, but there was none. I started working. Once I started, I forgot everything else. I was aware only of the flow of energy.

After class, I hugged each of the students as was customary. Rudi always compared it to burping a baby. As I did it, I felt a totally new sensation in my chest. My heart center was opening for the first time. It seems incredible, in retrospect, that I could have worked twelve years with a closed heart. Some people have their hearts open the first time they work, others after a relatively short time. I had heard Rudi talk of the importance of opening the heart, not only as a means of relating to other people, but also because of the treasures hidden in the heart center itself. Now it had finally happened. Jack, who was in the group and was one of Rudi's oldest students, told me later, "You came on like a tiger." I left the group feeling deeply content.

On Monday morning, people began to disperse. Some left early to avoid the holiday traffic jam, but classes and the general festival atmosphere continued. I left after lunch for the trip back to Geneseo. The incredible mixture of Rudi, Muktananda, and the sense of climax of all the effort and heartache that had preceded the weekend rose up in me, and then began to settle. Beyond all the varied impressions, the crucial fact for me was that I had been allowed to teach. It had been squeezed in as an afterthought, but it would not be taken away from me unless I did something really terrible. And I had no intention of letting that happen.

Shortly before leaving, I had bowed down to Muktananda and he had blessed me in his slightly abrupt way. Then as I walked off, I heard someone calling my name. He wanted me to come back. I returned, and to my surprise he gave me a rose. I still had the flower in the car as I drove away from the ashram. I didn't know what it meant, but I was pervaded by an increasing sense of inner contentment.

Still at Big Indian, Bruce continued to seek an audience with Baba. He told me later that as the weekend drew to a close, he grew desperate. He decided to put all that Rudi had ever said about accomplishing a goal to the test. He sat down by Muktananda's door, determined not to leave until he was forgiven.

Soon after taking this determined stance, he was ushered in. Bruce quickly went into his prepared speech before anyone could interrupt.

"I have come to apologize for anything that I did which caused Swami any displeasure. It was the last thing I intended. It was only my own ignorance. I will destroy the film if you wish."

Swami followed the translation with interest, smiled slightly, and waved Bruce away. It was the nearest he would get to forgiveness. Bruce left with relief to tell Rudi that the mission was accomplished. Rudi was very pleased.

"You see," he said, "it wasn't very difficult. All you had to realize was that you had no other alternative. If you can keep that attitude Bruce, your success in this life is assured."

.   .   .

On my next trip to the city I was immediately struck by the intense atmosphere in the ashram and the increasing number of people. I was thoroughly lost in the crowd.

Swami Muktananda was holding four meetings a day, in the early morning, at noon, in the afternoon, and in the evening. In between these, Rudi, Michael A., Stuart, and Calvin squeezed in a few kundalini classes. It was a marathon, sometimes not ending until after midnight.

I saw relatively little of Rudi during this period. He was exceptionally busy attending to his normal business and to all the additional demands created by Swami Muktananda's presence. It soon became evident that Baba was preparing him for some kind of extraordinary ceremony that was to take place in Ganeshpuri later in the year. Rudi spent several hours a day receiving the necessary background in Hindu tradition and spiritual understanding.

Swami Muktananda never expressed any particular interest in the nature of Rudi's teaching. His own approach was very different. He told stories, chanted, wrote letters, received gifts, gave blessings. From all this, those present received his energy. The only direct contact that he made came through shaktipat. It involved his touching a person briefly, usually on the head or heart, to start a psychic or spiritual process that was on the verge of unfolding.

Although most of us were prepared to draw from Muktananda through the methods Rudi had taught us, it was hard to see how someone without that knowledge could obtain much from him. Probably they couldn't. But the aura of energy, music, chanting, and stories with which he surrounded himself was enough to keep most people interested and enchanted.

In his lectures, Baba described a form of inner work that he called Siddha Yoga. He said the mere presence of an enlightened soul was sufficient to confer blessings on others.

At one of his evening classes, Rudi made the public announcement, mostly at Muktananda's subtle insistence, that henceforth he would be a vegetarian and observe sexual continence. I was not greatly impressed by the announcement. Rudi had always maintained that one could and should be able to eat anything, but that it must be adjusted to the particular phase of growth occurring at the time. As for sexuality, he had been relatively quiet in that sphere for a number of years. He felt that sexual continence was necessary for his growth during that period, but he had never looked at it as a general principle.

All of these things went through my mind as Rudi announced his pledges, with Muktananda's obvious beaming approval.

A month before Muktananda's arrival, Rudi had talked to us about the significance of the relationship between student and teacher. He made a particular point of telling us how we should relate to him during Muktananda's visit. "A student's loyalty is to his own teacher; your loyalty is to me. Baba is my teacher. My loyalty is to him. You honor him because of the level that he represents and because he is my teacher. But do not forget that I am your teacher and that without me you would never even meet Baba."

All of this seemed fairly obvious. It was hard to see why Rudi made such a point of it. But he knew Muktananda, we didn't.

The closest person to Rudi at that time was Michael A.
During a momentary lull at the store, Michael approached
Rudi: "I have been talking with Baba and have arranged to
go to Ganeshpuri to spend a lengthy time in his ashram
and receive his training."

Rudi described the scene to me a few days later.

"I said nothing to Michael. I couldn't. I was too
shocked. He had taken it on himself to do this. He hadn't
come to me beforehand. Maybe he was afraid of my reaction. But in any case, it was an absolutely wrong thing for
him to do. That Baba went along with it was his business.
But Michael is my student. He had to have my permission
for anything of that nature.

"There are certain things that are entirely wrong. This
is one. But Michael doesn't know it. He may change his
mind when his romance with Baba wears off and he wants
to return. Then I will say to him, 'I don't know you.'"

I listened in paralyzed silence. Michael had done so
beautifully up to this point, but he had evidently just
walked off the side of a cliff.

Late in October, Rudi went with Muktananda on a trip
to Texas and California. Classes continued in New York,
but the spiritual force had moved elsewhere. No one knew
precisely what was happening. Rudi's own communications were brief. He was apparently going through an intense and painful experience.

By a strange coincidence, I found that I needed to fly to
California on business and return at virtually the same
time that Rudi was scheduled to leave Muktananda and return to New York. I left word with his mother to tell him
what plane I would be on. The opportunity to be on a
transcontinental flight with Rudi just after he had been
traveling with Muktananda seemed like a wonderful good
fortune to me. But our paths did not cross. I returned to

New York on Sunday evening. He had left Saturday afternoon. Later, he apologized for not waiting.

"To tell you the truth, John, it wouldn't have been any treat for you. I felt I was getting seriously ill. I had gone beyond my own endurance. So I just excused myself and took the first plane back."

On his return, Rudi was very subdued. He stopped giving kundalini classes. He lectured and encouraged chanting and meditation with eyes closed. I was amazed. The whole nature of the work had altered.

Rudi himself said little. He seemed to be recovering from a spiritual operation and wanted to conserve his strength. But gradually, as we sat in the store, parts of the story slowly emerged:

"When Muktananda was in New York, he generally made himself agreeable and captivated almost everyone. But I was going crazy working with him, doing my business, and keeping the ashram going. When we went West, I thought it would be easier, but that was naive on my part.

"He began by asking me to give up meat and sex. As we left New York behind us, he proceeded to systematically deprive me of other aspects of my life.

"A number of my students had followed him down to Texas. He told them that they should leave me and come with him. I didn't mind because all of them were old students who had been dragging on for years. If they left, I could accept it as long as they went of their own free will. But the situation didn't give me a very good feeling.

"Though I was the traveling host, I was treated as if I was not even a member of Muktananda's party. No place was saved for me at the table. I was often ignored in conversation. I had been through all this before. I didn't like it, but if this scourging was part of the preparation I had to undergo, I welcomed it.

"If you don't accept what the guru does unconditionally, there is no basis for the relationship. I accepted that. I had created the situation by bringing him to this country. It was not for me to question him. My present life was being dismantled so that something new could be built. It was brutal but I did not protest.

"In the end, he demanded that I surrender my connection with Nityananda. I can't really explain to you what that meant. For many, many years Nityananda would come to me when I needed him. In the depths of my loneliness, he would descend from heaven to give me strength. He was Muktananda's guru, but he lived in me. We even grew to look alike. Nobody could avoid seeing it. But Muktananda made me give up this inner connection. It was a horrible experience. The Indians in his group were really amazed that I was willing to do it. They had never seen anyone go through such an ordeal of inner destruction of every living tie. But I want to grow. It has always been my central objective. I have never bargained about the price, and I was not about to start then.

"After that connection was destroyed, I could not conceive of anything that remained to be sacrificed, but that was just because I failed to see the obvious. Muktananda's last demand was that I give up my form of teaching. He said it would be replaced by something much greater after my next trip to India. That was the hardest thing I had to do. My teaching is closer to me than any person. But I did it. There was nothing left, except my life.

"The last thing that Muktananda said to me before I got on the plane to come home was: 'The next time I come to America, I will do to everyone what I have done to you.' It was scarcely a reassuring statement."

Almost two years later, in 1972, Stuart, who had been on that trip with Rudi, filled in some additional details:

"I remember one day when I was sitting near Rudi, I looked over at him and suddenly he turned into Nityananda. Then he turned back to Rudi, then back to Nityananda. It went on like that for maybe ten minutes. I was used to seeing Rudi manifest in all kinds of ways; when I started with him, I would see him turn into weird space monsters and various ancient creatures. But somehow this was different. It must have been about the time that Muktananda asked him to surrender Nityananda.

"The climax came for me when Muktananda began to ask me to come to study with him in Ganeshpuri. Every time he asked, I would put him off with some polite response. But he was insistent. I finally did what I usually do when I need an answer. I went deep inside and found Nityananda in my heart and asked him. The answer was simple. The next time Swami Muktananda approached me, I said, 'I would certainly like to come, but I cannot do anything like that without asking my guru's permission.' He looked at me with sudden respect and never brought up the subject again. He knew what Rudi's response would be," Stuart concluded.

.　　.　　.

During the next few months, Rudi recuperated. He was inwardly preparing for the ceremony that was to occur early in the spring when he returned to Ganeshpuri.

In parallel with this effort, the number of people living with him in the ashram steadily increased. A small group from Bloomington, Indiana came about this time. I met them along with everyone else, but paid no particular attention. One Saturday morning after an early class as I was walking to the store, one of the men from Bloomington passed me, going toward the house. I glanced at him and was very struck by the intensity of his gaze. That was the moment when I first became aware of Michael S.

When I got to the store, Rudi was reading a letter from India, but he did not disclose its contents. While he was working ceaselessly to ready himself for the unknown events that were to come, most of it was behind the scenes. I was not directly involved.

Soon Rudi went on his long-awaited trip to India. On the eve of his departure, he announced that he was going to be honored as Muktananda's spiritual son before a great gathering of Hindu religious dignitaries. A statue of Nityananda was also to be dedicated in a Hindu ritual designed to bring it to life.

Rudi was scheduled to be gone for a month. After two weeks, he cabled his mother: "I have left Swami Muktananda." There was no further word. Everyone was in a state of suspended animation until he returned.

Rudi flew in a little ahead of schedule. He looked good. He sounded good. He seemed much younger. He had worked with Swami Muktananda for more than twelve years. Now it was over. I knew he would talk about it when he was ready. It didn't take long.

"I went directly to Ganeshpuri," Rudi began a few days later while sitting in his store. "Swami Muktananda had told me there was to be a great festival. Thousands and thousands of people were to attend. All of the Hindu hierarchy were to be represented. He had been building it up for months.

"But when I got there everything was quiet. I didn't know what to make of it. Then he started to treat me like dirt. I was used to that from the past. But now I was supposed to be coming as a Swami to receive a high honor. It didn't make sense. I was willing to be ignored if it served some useful end, but I had already surrendered everything.

"The final blow came with the dedication of the statue of Nityananda. That was supposed to be a crucial event. I kept asking when it was to occur and was told not to worry, I would be informed.

"One day I went into town for an hour. When I returned, I discovered that the ceremony had just occurred. Inside me something gave way. My twelve years with Swami Muktananda had made me very, very strong. I was ready for a higher and more merciful approach.

"I packed my bags and told someone who was passing to say goodbye to Swami Muktananda for me, and I left."

Rudi, 1971.

BARRY KAPLAN

17

Advanced Work

AS RUDI SETTLED BACK into his familiar routine, he was faced with a mounting pile of correspondence. In 1971, he hired a secretary and spent an hour or two a day answering letters from across the country and around the world. As he got used to dictating, he discovered that he could easily extend the process to include a description of the experiences he was undergoing at the time. Such dictation became a regular feature of his day. As his dictations accumulated, he conceived of the idea of a book. He was attracted and repelled by the prospect. He preferred to keep a low profile for as long as possible. But he started looking for a publisher.

If a customer interrupted him in the middle of a sentence, he would pause to see to them, wave a student to an inconspicuous seat, take a swallow of cooling coffee, and fifteen minutes later continue with the sentence where he had left off. To a newcomer it probably looked like total confusion. But Rudi loved to have a number of things going on simultaneously, preferably on different dimensions. He always seemed to have sufficient attention for all of them. Whenever I visited he had something new to tell me.

"I was looking at Sam's head the other day while he was mopping the floor," he said on one occasion. "I would never have believed it, but the whole shape is different than it used to be. If he can change, anyone can. It gives

me a great feeling of satisfaction to see some concrete results in other people.

"Speaking of heads, I am having Barry photograph my
own head every few weeks to document the changes that
are occurring. One of my friends who is an expert on Eastern art and mysticism suggested it. I don't know how it will
turn out, but some of the pictures are really interesting.
You can see different channels in the brain, shapes on my
forehead and a snake emerging from my neck. Remind me
to show some of them to you next time."

· · ·

With the first signs of spring, Rudi began to talk of advanced work that he would give that summer. He referred
to this work intermittently, and urged us to prepare ourselves
for the opportunity. During this same period he began for
the first time to tape-record his lectures.

In mid-June, he announced that on the July 4th
weekend he would teach astral flight. I had no idea what
that meant. If I searched through my memory, I could recall
Rudi talking about being "far away" or "in a different place"
occasionally, but he had never explained how or why, nor
did he suggest that it was important. I took it, as I did with
most of his experiences, as something unique to him. Consequently, I waited in limbo, having no idea what to expect.

When July 4th came, it began like any other long weekend, with a full day's work. In the evening, Rudi walked to
the front of the classroom amidst growing expectation.

His first words were, "Please don't record the exercise I am
about to give you. Nothing that is given here tonight must
ever leave this room. You must never share it with anyone.
If you do, I can assure you that you will live to regret it. I
have never said this before about any of the work that has

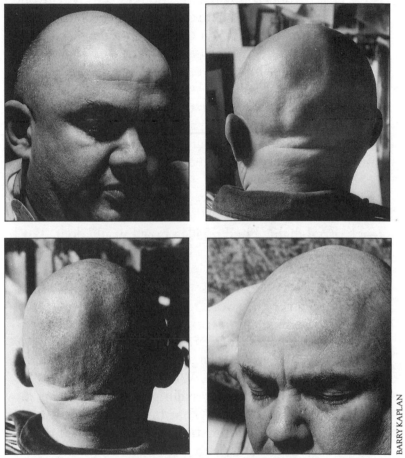

BARRY KAPLAN

"You can see different channels in the brain, and a snake emerging from my neck."

been given, though no student should ever give anyone else what he has learned here without express permission.

"But this is quite different. If you attempt to give to another what I am giving to you tonight, you will take on yourself a responsibility beyond anything you can realize and you could fatally injure your own spiritual growth.

"If this seems too strong a statement, it isn't. I can't put it too strongly. Some of you are unbelievably stupid. You won't think I really mean it unless I put it this way. I really mean it! If you can't accept these conditions, please leave."

No one stirred.

"What I am going to give you has not existed in the world for many centuries. When I announced that I would teach astral flight, I had no idea how I would do it. But I knew that if I obligated myself, a means would be found. In order for me to be able to give it to you at all, I have had to reorder the whole universe. The cosmos is a vast combination lock. For this work to be transmitted, all forces must be in perfect alignment.

"Some of you who read spiritual books are probably puzzled by my making such a large production of astral flight. You have heard of it before. Why all the secrecy? Right? But I am not talking about traveling out of the body to different places on the earth. That might have been useful before modern communications were developed, but it really has nothing to do with growing. Conditions on the earth are pretty much the same over the whole surface. The whole point of astral travel is to get off the earth to a better place where the energy is richer, purer, cleaner, and of a more refined character. Symbolically, we all live in the slums. The air is contaminated, the streets filthy and cold. People are crowded together. It is very difficult for anything of a higher nature to penetrate into such a setting. But if you can take an airplane, in a matter of two minutes

north from Delhi toward Hardwar, Rishikesh, and into the mountains.

"What can I do to prepare other than what I am already doing?" I asked.

"Nothing. Just try to open more so that there is a greater space in you to receive the contents of the trip."

"But," I said, "you seem to be going through all kinds of inner preparations. Shouldn't I do some of that?"

"Your trip and my trip are two different things. I am working to attract a great unknown experience. When it occurs, I will pass on to you whatever happens, to the extent that I can. If I didn't want you to get as much of the direct impact as you could, I wouldn't have invited you to come."

The rest of the summer is covered by a veil. Perhaps my sense of anticipation put all else in the shade. Rudi certainly did not diminish his pace. He continued to present new ideas and new experiences.

In particular, he began teaching a series of deeper psychic cleansing methods for surrendering negative psychic tensions.

"I am giving these methods," said Rudi, "as I work them out. They are coming through to me now because I need them. Before this time, it didn't matter too much about the state of my own purity. There was so much movement inside that nothing could really poison me. But now I feel a need to grow much quieter. I am cleansing myself to be able to relate to the purity in the ancient man I will meet. Otherwise, my chemistry will not adjust to his and nothing will happen."

Rudi gave three exercises. The first involved absorbing energy through the hands and feet, and then releasing it after it had dissolved some of the accumulated psychic poisons of the past. Another consisted of approaching the psychic mechanism as if it were a complex huge toilet that could be completely flushed in one lengthy but simple operation. The third involved opening a valve at the base of the spine to drain the accumulated poison in the spinal cord. Each was very different from the others, but all required work in depth.

"When you are doing this work," said Rudi, "you must understand that you are not just dealing with the negative tensions of the present. As you use these exercises, you will begin to loosen the accumulated debris and poisons of a lifetime and beyond that into past lives. It is hard to over-emphasize how important this is."

Over the long Labor Day weekend he continued to pursue this theme:

"I am giving you this work on inner purification to do while I am away in India," he said to the 150 to 200 people who were gathered in the meditation hall. "It will prepare you to receive what I will bring back. If you don't do it, you will not have sufficient purity to connect with me when I return."

"How long should these exercises be done?" someone asked.

"Don't do too much at any one time," said Rudi, "but each time you work, the force will begin to break up the poisons that are crystallized. It's like dissolving an ice jam. Sometimes only a little may be released; sometimes a great deal. For most of you, it will be a slow and gradual process.

"But one thing you will realize as a result of this work is that you don't know who you are. People who devote a lot of time and money to psychotherapy may learn something about the crap that is in them. But that is not who they are.

"We are all petrified souls lying deep in the earth. If we succeed in breaking down the layers of poison, fear, and paralysis that surround us, we will eventually come to the living being at the center, who is probably frozen. Then, and only then, do we need to decide how to revive him. All the work up to that point has been excavation. None of you can work deeply enough to let the energy get to the center, where it could begin to awaken this being who is really you. Most people spend their lives creating conditions around them that make such an awakening impossible and then wonder why it doesn't happen. It will never happen unless you want it more than anything else. It is not a question of words. The wish must be real because it will surely be tested. If you say you want it, ten situations will appear to distract you from your desire.

"The difficulty is compounded by the fact that until a person forms some communication with the unknown being buried within him, he really can't know what he wants. If and when you ever get to that point, you will cease to take two steps forward, one backward, three sideways, and then lie down and go to sleep. You will know what you need, and you will inwardly continue to pursue it in every situation in which you find yourself.

"Everything in your life is there to show you what you have so far refused to learn. When you begin to look at it in that way, then those things you have avoided or thought pointless will reveal their secret. Mostly what they will show is how stupid and weak you are. It isn't pleasant to see, but it is essential. To build on a weak foundation is the ultimate stupidity. It is bound to come tumbling down on your head sooner or later."

The talk ended with everyone doing one of the new cleansing exercises. Rudi sat quietly watching and looking beyond the scene.

20

The Ganesh Festival

RUDI DECIDED TO LEAVE during the last week in September, 1972. I gathered the necessary money together and bought an airplane ticket. There were four of us in the party besides Rudi: Stuart, now the principal teacher in Texas; Buford, who would stay in France after the trip; Peter, who lived in Paris and was going to work with Buford in setting up a Paris ashram; and myself. I was to travel with Stuart directly to Bombay. The others were stopping in several European cities on the way and would meet us there.

I thought I was calm on the day of the flight, until I quietly locked my keys in the trunk of my car. I had to call a locksmith to get them out. After that, I met Stuart at the New York ashram and we were driven to the airport by Bruce, who had spent six months in India and was full of advice. I sat in the back seat and talked my head off, which was a good indication of my excited state. I was usually quiet. At the airport, my own anticipation was absorbed by the impersonal shuffling of people and baggage, until I was seated in the plane and the engines began to roar.

The flight felt endless as the jet raced into the path of the sun. Life became a mixture of meals, movies, accumulated sweat, and the slow passage of time. Several days later, we staggered out into the relatively primitive Bombay airport at 5 a.m., exhausted. The ride to the hotel was punctuated by the sight of people living in what looked like abandoned sewer pipes, by cows sitting in the road, reluctant to budge, and the teeming hoards of Bombay.

When we were briefly held up by a religious festival in the streets, I asked the driver what the occasion was.

"It is the Ganesh festival," he said, in exotic English. "It will go on for the rest of the week. Today is the beginning."

I did not think much of it then, but a pattern emerged that dominated the time in Bombay. Nityananda had been known as the incarnation of Ganesh, the "elephant god," and we kept bumping into images and experiences related to Ganesh throughout the week.

We got to the Taj Mahal Hotel, checked in, went upstairs and collapsed. We were grateful that Rudi and the others were not due until the next day.

When Rudi arrived he immediately began to contact people he knew. Then he proceeded to set a pace for which I was totally unprepared. In New York he was always inwardly busy, but he sat quietly all day long in his store. In India, he was constantly running around, and slept only three hours a night. This, in itself, would not have been so extraordinary, but the nature of his inner work required a great deal of sleep. He always got at least eight hours in New York, as far as I knew, and didn't hesitate to take more if he needed it.

The rest of us were drawn in his wake as he visited shops, friends, and psychics. From the start, Stuart and I felt we had to make a choice. Either we had to attempt to relate to everything Rudi was doing, or to forget all that and concentrate only on him. We decided on the latter. If he objected, he would let us know. Looking at him intently wherever he went, we concentrated on drawing the energy that flowed from him into ourselves. We continued this effort under an extraordinarily diverse set of circumstances: in a store, during a dinner party, at the house of a friend, on the street. India became a stage set as we followed him around. Occasionally when he went away for a short trip, or to a place where he preferred us not to go, we either collapsed gratefully into a hot bath or visited some of the local stores where the goods were cheap.

When he was present, the atmosphere was never restful. At any moment, Rudi might stop what he was doing and start to teach. God forbid if you did not respond immediately.

"What the hell do you think you are doing?" he would say to the offending person who had taken five seconds to loosen his belt and cross his legs in preparation for the class. If the individual were smart, he said nothing. But even if he kept his mouth shut, that was not the end of it. Rudi continued relentlessly.

"You are here to work. You have to be ready at any instant. It is for me to worry about all the other people. They have nothing to do with you. Sit up straight and stop feeling sorry for yourself."

India was a kaleidoscope. We were being exposed to first-class hotels, a wide variety of business establishments, and many forms of home life, some simple and others highly luxurious.

Watching Rudi with art dealers filled in a gap in my own understanding of his operation. I had only seen the final results when the shipments arrived in the warehouse. Now I saw him buying the art. I realized the degree of personal relationship that lay behind the commercial transactions.

To one man in particular who specialized in Indian textiles, Rudi talked at great length about beginning to buy folk art. They both agreed that art antiques had become too risky to import.

As part of the visit, we were measured for orange shirts and dhotis by the dealer's wife. Rudi used these clothes as a teaching uniform for his work.

When we were ready to leave, the dealer placed his car at our disposal. Rudi gave the driver instructions. After ten minutes we stopped in the middle of nowhere and got out. We walked another five minutes to our next destination, which turned out to be an antique dealer. It seemed like a striking contradiction to everything Rudi had been saying to the first dealer about the end of importing antiques.

"Why did we have to walk the last five minutes when we had a car?" I asked as we entered the next shop.

"So that the first man wouldn't know where I had gone. When I am with him," said Rudi, "I am interested in folk art. Now that I am here, I am interested in antiques. Keep your mouth shut and wait in the store." He disappeared behind closed doors.

The next day we returned to the first man to pick up our clothes. We tried them on, had some adjustments made, and left amidst general excitement. Everyone in the garment factory seemed to have stopped work to bid us goodbye. Only Rudi appeared subdued.

When we were outside the front door he began to talk.

"People are so strange. I have known this man for several years. He and his wife are a truly beautiful couple. But this time when I saw them together I immediately sensed that something was wrong. Their marriage was disintegrating in front of me. I asked the man about it yesterday in a private moment. And he confessed something he had told nobody else, that he thought he was dying of cancer. His wife could sense that something was terribly wrong, but he had kept his fears to himself.

"I worked with him and could sense nothing inside him that corresponded to his fears. I told him that I felt whatever was wrong, it was not serious. He went to a doctor after I left and discovered I was right. He was too frightened to go before, so he put himself and everyone

Left to right: Buford, Peter, John, Stuart, Rudi, Chakrapani and his wife.

else through hell. Now he is very grateful. But the stupidity of it all is that in a few months he might have talked his body into a real cancer and then it would have been too late."

One of Rudi's oldest friends was a man named Chakrapani. He had been his personal forecaster at the ashram in Ganeshpuri. Rudi was anxious to see him. I had been hearing about him for ten years.

"When you meet him, John, you may not be very impressed," Rudi said. "He is very modest, but he really works hard for me."

We went to his house, which was probably upper-middle class by Indian standards. His wife was gracious, insisting we eat authentic Indian food and drink water of unknown origin. The food was super hot. The water I didn't touch. I ignored all social amenities, waiting anxiously to hear what Chakrapani would say to Rudi. Finally, he began to talk in a low voice that I could hardly follow.

"You have come through a great period," he started.

"I know," said Rudi. "But what should I be working for? What should I expect?"

"It will come like a lightning bolt," said Chakrapani. "You will form an organization that will involve millions of people. It is very soon that the change will occur that will make it possible."

Rudi listened to all this quietly. It was nothing less than he expected. I probably also expected it, though I had never projected his life in such terms. Perhaps I hadn't wanted to. It was enough trying to keep up with him from hour to hour.

After two hectic days following Rudi through cross-sections of Indian life, we suddenly had a free day. He was flying up to a Maharajah's palace to look at some art. Stuart and I decided to see the caves at Elephanta, which were about an hour and a half from the hotel by ferry.

During the previous days we had continued to run into signs of the Ganesh festival, but it wasn't until I was on the small boat, being tossed around with Stuart and a number of Indians who were making the trip, that I realized the connection. The Island of Elephanta was part of the same pattern! It was named for the elephant. Also, as we discovered when we got there, it was dedicated to Shiva, of whom Rudra was an early form.

The next day when Rudi returned, it was again an endless mixture of stores, friends, social occasions and work. Squeezed within this continuous treadmill of activities were visits to several fortune tellers, including Mr. Thomas. My own experience with psychics was extremely limited. I had never been attracted to astrology, palmistry, or any other form of forecasting. I felt a personal distaste for pseudo-science. And in any case, Rudi knew all that was necessary to know about me and didn't hesitate to inform me as the need arose. But I began to change my mind when I saw that he took these things seriously.

I was particularly keyed up to meet Mr. Thomas. Rudi spoke highly of him as direct, simple, and very perceptive. We arranged to have enough time together so that he could give each of us a reading. Mr. Thomas was certainly not unusual in any obvious way. His manner, surroundings, and approach were almost matter-of-fact, which in the end only made them more extraordinary.

Rudi went first. Mr. Thomas repeated, almost word for word, some of the things Chakrapani had said. He talked of what Rudi had gone through and of the tremendous expansion of his work that was to come. He described the meeting that Rudi would have on the trip and its importance to his future development.

Stuart came next. He had little interest in predictions of the future. He looked on them as likely to produce more problems than they resolved, if they were taken seriously. But his interest grew as Mr. Thomas began to describe certain of his qualities, all of which were essentially correct. Then abruptly, he shifted into the future. He said that in six years Stuart would create a great ashram or series of ashrams.

"At the end of that time, it will all be destroyed," he said. "People who you thought were your friends will do it. Nothing will remain. For the next six years, your life will be quiet. You will recover to do something greater."

Stuart was not disturbed. He was delighted to be told that he would achieve a great result, have it destroyed, and then after a period, produce something even better.

Buford had already seen Mr. Thomas on the previous trip. This time Mr. Thomas spelled out certain exceptional features of Buford's capacities and then went into detail about a number of time periods that would prove particularly difficult for him.

Finally it was my turn. I was quite nervous.

"Life has been harder for you than anyone else here," Mr. Thomas began.

That sounded very true in one sense, and absurd in another.

"But that is essentially over," he continued. "You will shortly enter a very important period of your life, starting in March through June. A major change may come. It can be a new beginning for you. There will be difficulty with someone close to you from February 15 through the month. It will be a rough period.

"During the time from March to June, you may have a possible marriage. You will meet someone whom you will know for four years, name of K. This will be in June. The opportunity to marry will exist until you are 49."

Mr. Thomas continued. "You are rarely appreciated. You are a genius whose ideas are not usually accepted. Only after you leave the scene will people begin to realize your value."

"That's all right, John," Rudi interrupted, "you don't give a shit what anyone thinks of you anyway."

That was essentially true. I smiled. Mr. Thomas paused to draw some diagrams, and then added, "You will have name and fame from the age of 47 through 71."

"We are all going to have great lives," Rudi interrupted again. "I don't want to be surrounded by nonentities."

"There will be a return of something from the year 1958 into your life," Mr. Thomas continued. "A cycle that began then will be repeated. Someone you knew at the age of 22 will also return."*

---

* Within a year and a half, all of the statements that were time-coordinated

We all left the reading in a slight state of shock, except for Rudi, who took such things in stride. He immediately began discussing with Stuart ten different ways that the destruction of his work in Texas could be avoided six years in the future. Stuart wasn't too enthusiastic. The idea of a Gotterdammerung appealed to him.

On the way back to the hotel, Rudi said, "A little psychic reading can go a long way. For most people, it only produces a great deal of confusion, even if it is true. You have to be very stable and work hard to take in what was said and not be disturbed by it. What will happen in a year depends on what you do now. If you hear about something wonderful in the future, you subtly begin to believe that it is about to happen or has already happened. Then you stop making the necessary effort. And then it never happens. But Mr. Thomas is very fine. Really remarkable.

"And tomorrow," he said, abruptly changing the subject, "we will get up at five-thirty and visit Ganeshpuri."

I absorbed his words slowly but with mounting excitement. After twelve years, I would see the town that Nityananda had created, and visit his tomb and the places where he lived. It would also be the first time that Rudi had been back to Ganeshpuri since he left Swami Muktananda almost a year before.

I went to bed early and was grateful to be able to sleep. The next day was bound to be extraordinary.

By 5:45 the next morning we were all seated in Rudi's room having tea and buns. He had arranged for us to bor-

---

proved correct. I did have a difficult time at the end of February. The period from March to June was a great new beginning. I did meet K. during this period. We were eventually married for a short time. The return of a situation and a person I knew from 1958 is embodied in this book. It was the year I met Rudi. The return of a figure I knew at the age of 22 occurred with the recent death of Dr. J. L. Moreno, who, after Rudi, was probably the major influence in my life.

row a small station wagon that belonged to one of his Indian friends.

The car arrived at 6:00, complete with driver. Soon we were winding our way out of Bombay. It was still quiet. The sun was beginning to rise. Sleepy people were moving toward their daily tasks, and those few who had been up all night were returning gratefully to their beds. The traffic conditions were relatively good at that hour, so we moved rapidly out of the city. Rudi was quiet. The rest of us took in the scenery and worked inwardly. I had never seen the Indian countryside. It was not particularly inspiring, but it was endless. As we progressed, the road slowly deteriorated.

"Another fifteen minutes," said Rudi as we turned onto the worst road yet. The sense of anticipation was growing. I felt totally unprepared.

I asked, "Is there anything we should know before we get there?"

"Just stay close to me. Do what I do. Don't get distracted by anything, and open as deeply as you can to the atmosphere."

And then abruptly we entered the town. We passed a temple but kept moving. It was Swami Muktananda's ashram. We drove on as far as the road went. Ahead was a marble building. We got out of the station wagon and entered Ganeshpuri. My initial reaction was one of disappointment. It was just another little Indian village. The only thing that set it apart were the number of holy men wandering around, and the stands that sold garlands of flowers with pictures of Nityananda, Muktananda, and others. By Western standards, it was almost primitive. But that was my prejudice. Nityananda had been indifferent to material values. He had lived in a mud hut, slept on a straw mat, and asked for nothing.

We bought some garlands of flowers and approached the building made of white marble. It was Nityananda's samadhi tomb, where his body was enshrined. We took off our shoes and entered. Immediately I was engulfed by a radiant ringing sound. We approached the tomb, placed the garlands on it, walked around it several times, finally touching our foreheads to the casket. Then we withdrew and for perhaps ten minutes absorbed the energy in the room. I could feel the presence, but couldn't really tell what or how much was happening. While I was trying to decide, Rudi, Stuart, and Buford moved on. Peter and I rose to follow. They had stopped to buy some more flowers. We stopped also. When we finished the transaction, they had disappeared. Peter and I began to search. We walked down the street, into a building that a passerby had pointed out to us. It was some kind of shrine, but Rudi wasn't there. We walked back the way we had come. Suddenly, Buford appeared and motioned us into a little building. It was where Nityananda had lived and taught. We were almost alone. I placed the flowers near Nityananda's bed, bowed down, and worked. It was a very different feeling from the shrine, much stronger and more intimate. After we left I felt dazed.

Stuart said later, "Nityananda was sitting there on his bed working with us."

Rudi decided to relax in the town. We walked down the line of stalls, looking at photographs. Then we entered a crowded cafe to have a cold drink. Immediately people whom Rudi knew approached him.

"In five minutes," he said in a low voice, "Muktananda will know I am here."

We finished our drinks leisurely, found our driver, and slowly proceeded out of town. As we approached Swami Muktananda's ashram, a figure moved out into the road and flagged down the car. It was an American whom Rudi knew. He had a message from Baba for Rudi to stop and say hello.

"No, I can't," Rudi politely declined.

"Baba has no bad feelings," he persisted.

"I am glad," said Rudi. "Thank Baba for me."

The conversation continued that way for a few minutes. The man was growing frightened. Finally, he took hold of Rudi's jacket collar. Rudi looked at him coldly and said, "Please take your hands off me before I slug you."

The man was shocked by his own actions. In one last desperate effort he said, "At least come into the anteroom and look at the new statue of Nityananda we have just had installed." Much to his and our surprise, Rudi said "Sure!" and proceeded to get out of the car. The man was delighted and went ahead of us to spread the good word.

"After we see the statue, we leave," Rudi commanded. "Don't look to the left or right; just follow me."

We entered a large, partly darkened room. In one end was the figure of Nityananda. It was very impressive. We sat for three or four minutes working with it. Then Rudi got up. We followed him. A number of people had entered the room during that time. We ignored them all and made for the front door. They were too surprised to react. Before they had regrouped, we were back in the car.

The same man came running out and started talking again. Rudi paid no attention, but nudged the driver, who did not respond. Rudi shook him. He hesitated.

"If you don't start this car and get us out of here," he said, "we'll dump you and drive ourselves."

That gentle urging seemed to convince him. He started up and we slowly moved away. No one said anything for five minutes. I was filled with an extraordinary mixture of impressions.

Then Rudi spoke. "Why didn't he just leave me alone? I had no desire to hurt him. We just came to pay our respects to Nityananda. Was it an anticlimax, John, after all these years?"

I shook my head no.

After a few minutes Rudi spoke again. "That was a beautiful statue. I have ordered a copy of it. Maybe when we get back to Bombay we can go see if it is finished."

After a few minutes the atmosphere changed and Rudi began to work with Stuart, who went very quickly into convulsions and arched backwards over the edge of the back seat into the baggage section of the station wagon. After about ten minutes Rudi turned to me and put his hands on my forehead. I found myself arching upwards over the back seat. Rudi followed me over, working on various chakras. All of the power that Rudi had drawn from the contact with Nityananda was demanding to be exerted.

I slowly settled back in my seat in a dazed condition. Rudi had meanwhile worked briefly with Buford and Peter, and was casually talking to Stuart about the experience at Ganeshpuri. I didn't pay too much attention until I heard my name mentioned. It had something to do with a book. Rudi repeated what he had said.

"I want you to write a book about me, John."

I still didn't quite take it in. "It would be impossible," I said.

"No," said Rudi, "just write about your experience with me over the years, from your own viewpoint."

"Perhaps it could be done," I thought.

"It is very important," he said. "It will teach you how to write and give you a foundation for the rest of your life."

"If you are telling me to do it, then I will."

"I am telling you," he said. Then he turned to Buford and changed the subject. I knew at that moment that I would have to write the book. The circumstances were extraordinary. Anything said at such a time had to be accepted as binding.

The rest of the trip was intense, but quiet. We got back to the hotel, had an early lunch, and collapsed for a few hours. In the late afternoon, we were off to see the statue of Nityananda that Rudi had commissioned.

The sculptor lived in a relatively small apartment. Almost as soon as we walked through the front door, the statue was upon us. It was larger than life-size and overwhelming in power. It filled the living room as we sat down before it. No one said anything for a time. Then Rudi spoke to the sculptor.

"It is a great work of art. We were in Ganeshpuri today. I feel Nityananda as much in this statue as there. It is an extraordinary accomplishment."

We continued to sit silently. It was a totally unexpected climax to the day. We left Bombay early the next day for New Delhi. On the way to the airport we asked the driver if the Ganesh festival was over. "It ended yesterday," he told us. The cycle was complete.

Rudi went on to Indonesia, Hong Kong, and Singapore to search for merchandise. The rest of us decided to go to Benares and Nepal. Rudi had never been to Nepal, even though he owned the greatest collection of Nepalese Tibetan art in America. He had never found the time. He hadn't even been to the Elephanta caves, though Bombay was his home base in India.

The period in Nepal was completely self-enclosed. It did not directly relate to Rudi, but we were constantly aware of his presence and knew that when we came together again, the climax of the trip would occur.

21

Meeting above the Ganges

RUDI WAS JUBILANT: "I bought a million dollars worth of goods for almost no money; fabrics, furnishings, rugs. It was the most remarkable trip I ever made. I just happened to go at the perfect time. A month from now is the international trade fair. The Japanese will buy everything.

"It was a whole new beginning, particularly in China. India is more or less finished. But when something ends, something else begins. It always works that way for me."

We listened, happy for him and excited at the magnitude of what he had achieved while we were resting in Nepal.

"I brought you each something." He searched through his luggage and brought out various presents. We were surprised, but that was like Rudi; he never returned empty-handed.

We immediately made arrangements to hire a driver for the third phase of the trip. We were going to travel north from Delhi up the Ganges, and probably finish in the foothills of the Himalayas.

That night Rudi asked us about Nepal. We spoke enthusiastically of its exotic mountain beauty. While we had been in Nepal, Buford had chosen to fly to a monastery on Mount Everest. As he told of his experiences he still looked a little shaken.

"They set down on a landing strip in the middle of nowhere," he began. "The plane carried supplies for the monastery I wanted to visit and for a hotel that is being built nearby. It is supposed to be the highest hotel in the world. They give the guests oxygen tanks at night. I started out in the direction they showed me, but the going was slow. By evening I was alone under the stars. I pitched my tent and spent one of the most ghastly nights I can remember.

"I had altitude sickness. Every muscle in my body was in agony. But the real climax came when I staggered into the monastery the next morning. Someone had a tape player going. You know what was playing in the highest monastery in the world? The Beatles! I was really disgusted. But the setting was incredible. I'm glad I went."

As I listened, I was glad I hadn't.

After we had talked for a while about what we had seen and things we had bought in Katmandu, a strained silence developed.

"What is wrong with all of you?" Rudi finally demanded. We didn't know what he was talking about. "Didn't it occur to any of you to buy me a present?"

"I thought about it," said Peter, "but I decided you already had everything. The last time I gave you something you gave it away."

"What I do with a gift is up to me. But that none of you should have enough humanity or sensitivity to bring me something is really terrible. Don't you think I need it? Even if I don't, it betrays your total lack of awareness of the situation.

"None of you would be here except for me. If you don't feel this inside yourself, you are completely unworthy to receive anything. I don't care about receiving gifts. I would much rather give than receive. You all know me well enough to be sure of that. But it is absolutely crucial that you should have some sense of gratitude. You owe me.

That fact gives me no particular pleasure, it just is. You can never repay me directly, but you can give love. A gift is a material manifestation of love. Your failure to be aware of that limits you terribly."

Rudi stopped talking. We all slunk out of the room and tried to forget what had happened.

The next morning we left at sunrise. None of us knew exactly where we were going or how long we would stay in any particular place, but Rudi was happy to get started. This part of the trip was the nearest thing he was going to have to a vacation. The night before was forgotten as we squeezed ourselves into the typically small Indian car he had borrowed for the occasion.

We drove all day through the endless panorama of Indian villages simmering in the heat. As the hours unwound, any sense of destination or purpose began to dull. But finally the atmosphere altered, the temperature cooled, and the road signs indicated we were nearing Rishikesh, a holy city along the Ganges where many ashrams were located. As soon as we pulled up by the river and left the car, we were absorbed by a crowd of Indians intent on buying and selling religious articles. There were stalls selling beads, pictures, and all manner of religious paraphernalia. We followed Rudi as he walked along the boardwalk. We were continuously approached by various beggars and tradesmen. We ignored them all and kept on moving. Finally, Rudi stopped to buy some malas (beads). He sent Buford to buy more: "All of you get some and I will bless them in the Ganges."

I waited until last, and had a hard time finding any. The nearby stalls were sold out. I had to wander several blocks away. When I returned, I discovered that the others had already undressed and entered the Ganges, so I quickly followed. Our nude bodies attracted considerable attention.

Whether it was friendly or not was hard to tell, so we ignored it, and after a few minutes, the curiosity-seekers dispersed.

The water of the Ganges was remarkable. I had heard of its unusual properties and knew it was considered holy by the Hindus. I quickly discovered why. In the coldness of the rapidly moving water there was a tangible vitality that went through my body like psychic champagne. I gave my ten newly purchased malas to Rudi, who touched them to his forehead to transmit his shakti to them and then dunked them in the river for a few seconds.

We emerged from the river, cold but totally invigorated. We dressed and started to walk slowly back to the car the way we had come. Rudi would occasionally wander off, but always returned in a short time. At about three in the afternoon, we got back in the car and headed toward Hardwar, an hour away.

Rudi was eager to visit the Divine Light Mission, the ashram of the late Swami Sivananda. The current director was a good friend. Rudi felt he might be an important connection in his quest for the ancient saint. When we arrived, we learned that he had left the day before and was not going to be back for three weeks. We stayed for half an hour, sat briefly in Swami Sivananda's room, and departed.

"Sivananda was one of the last generation of truly great yogis to which Nityananda also belonged. They died almost at the same time," Rudi said.

We drove on until we came to an arched bridge across the Ganges where we saw an extraordinary sight. Arranged in a curving line from one side of the bridge to the other was an incredible assemblage of beggars. They all stood there waiting. Rudi took one look and said, "It looks like the casting office for *El Topo*."

We walked across the bridge to the other side of the river, looked around, bought a few trinkets and left. There were many beautiful temples, but none that we were seeking. We got back in the car, thinking we were at a temporary dead end.

"Let's go on to Maussorie," Rudi suggested. "We can still get there by nightfall. It would be great to sleep in the mountains."

It was another two- or three-hour drive. We settled back, uncertain as to what, if anything, was happening. As we approached the first foothills, Buford and Peter remembered a Tibetan temple school they had wanted to visit. We inquired and found it was on the way, so Rudi agreed to seek it out.

When we finally arrived, we received only a lukewarm welcome. The main teacher was busy; if we wished to see him, we were told to come back the next day. Rudi shrugged and began to play with the many Tibetan children who attended the school. He was soon surrounded by thirty of them who were enchanted by his smiles, ear-wiggling, and blowing on their bellies. Their enthusiastic calls and waves followed us back to the car.

The remainder of the trip was uphill on a winding mountain road. The weather was clear and the temperature dropped as we climbed. It felt wonderful to be leaving the tropical plains.

The sun was fading by the time we arrived; a slight mist was rising from the valley, but the sky was clear. The hotel was marvelous, a great rambling structure obviously built for the English, and more or less kept up by the Indians. It was the off-season and there were only three other guests in the whole place. We settled into two large rooms with fireplaces and quaint baths, and were surrounded by well-trained servants who asked only to serve.

Rudi told Stuart and me to get settled and then join him for a walk into town. It was about 5:30 when we returned to Rudi's room. He was sitting on a couch and had started work with Buford and Peter. We quietly sat down and joined the class. I could hear the gentle mountain wind and smell the pines around us. It was with a great sense of inner surrender that I happily sat in this old hotel room high in the Himalayan foothills, absorbing the force coming from Rudi. The air was highly charged, but that seemed natural. The setting alone could account for it.

Gradually it became obvious that something unusual was happening. Rudi was in great pain, or appeared to be. He started moaning and crying as I had never seen him do before. I watched, trying not to get emotionally involved, while at the same time opening to whatever was happening. Perhaps it was only his own sense of disappointment. But this was just the first day. We had a whole week in which to search. If necessary, we could go to the origin of the Ganges by jeep.

Rudi continued to be wracked by terrible suffering, but he worked with us unless it temporarily became too much for him. I didn't doubt that he could come through anything, but what was happening? Was he being attacked by some invisible being? Was he undergoing some kind of terrible spiritual birth pangs? The process continued for perhaps ten minutes.

When it receded, Rudi motioned to us to sit in front of him one at a time. He worked with us using his eyes and hands. It was completely overpowering, as if a dam had been suddenly broken and the vast water pressure released.

When I finally got up from where I had fallen to the floor, Rudi was sitting quietly with his eyes closed as if nothing had happened. We all sat for another few minutes. The he said, "Let's walk into the town, but stay very quiet."

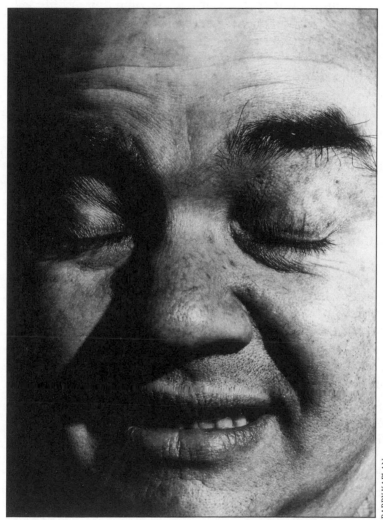

BARRY KAPLAN

"I didn't doubt that he could come through anything, but what was happening?"

We put on our coats — it had become quite chilly — and headed for the town. It was quaint, exotic, completely out of the world, but we paid little attention to it just then. Finally I asked, "What happened? Are you all right?"

"Ask me tomorrow," Rudi said. Shortly thereafter, we returned to the hotel and slept well that night.

The next day Rudi looked very strange, that is, he looked like himself and someone else. It was hard to define.

"Can I ask you now?" I was completely in the dark about what had happened.

"Yes," he began. "As I was working, a great human head of a very, very ancient holy man materialized near the ceiling. I worked intensely to bring it closer. Finally it came into me. Did any of you see it?" No one spoke.

As the day wore on, we explored the town and decided to drive back down the mountain to the Tibetan temple school. This time, we saw the principal teacher (Rimpoche), who was quite high in the Tibetan hierarchy. He complimented Rudi on the discipline of his students, as we all stared at him with concentration, attempting to draw out of him every bit of energy we could find. He had probably never been subjected to that kind of treatment before. Rudi and the Rimpoche talked for a time, then the Rimpoche excused himself. He had to go to his meditation. We filed out.

As we walked down the stairs, Rudi said, "The only thing he had to do was eat lunch. I saw them preparing it. It is really disgusting to me; he had no sense of what we are or our openness to him. He really didn't care."

An assistant asked if we would like to visit the temple. We agreed, and sat there for a few minutes. Then Rudi rose, went forward, and left some bills in the offering box. We followed. Outside, every child in the place had somehow heard of Rudi's return. They were jumping up and down and shouting around him. It was a beautiful sight. As we drove away they were all going crazy.

"Where I was sitting in the temple," Rudi said, "I noticed that we were being watched through a peephole in the ceiling. I left a hundred-rupee note in the offering box. I wanted to give them something to think about. Maybe the next time they won't take visitors so casually. I could have really helped that man expand his work if he had shown the slightest openness to me. Everyone is so intent on defending their own little pile of shit that life just goes right by them."

We returned to the hotel and had supper. Then we reassembled in Rudi's room. There was a fire crackling. The air was very cool. He began to work for a few minutes. Then he paused and announced, "We will go back to Delhi tomorrow. I have told the driver."

I did an inner doubletake. Had I missed something?

"What I came for has already happened," he continued. "There is no reason to stay."

I was flabbergasted, but it was just like Rudi. The climax could come in a flicker of an eyelash. If you were looking elsewhere at the time, you missed it.

"I expected to meet a living person who was 700 years old," he said. "I looked, I waited. It never occurred to me until the experience began that it might be the soul of someone who had died that long ago. The experience has been going on all day. He comes in and moves out, comes in and moves out. Now he has begun to settle in me. My whole chemistry is completely disturbed. I have never been in this condition. It is tearing me apart, but I am deeply grateful. It represents a quantity above and beyond anything I have known before. I don't know where it will lead, but I am certain it is the beginning of a totally new phase in my growth.

"But what really shocks me is that with all the Indian holy men devoting their lives to spiritual work, such a being should come to rest in me. I am not saying I am something great. I am what I am. But it doesn't say much of everyone else. I have just worked harder than anyone and am inwardly prepared for the fantastic jolt that such an experience produces."

Rudi was quiet for a time. Then he smiled at Buford and Stuart.

"Can you see it now?" he asked.

They both nodded: yes, they saw. I didn't expect to see it. I never saw anything, not even an aura.

"I am deeply happy to share this experience," said Rudi. "I could never go through the pain and effort that is necessary if I were doing it just for myself. It is too endless and brutal. It is my love for you that makes it possible for us to be together at the beginning of the next phase of our work."

I sat looking at Rudi with tears rolling down my cheeks. There was no weighing this man.

We left in a very subdued state. We drove back to Delhi only stopping for lunch.

That night Rudi decided to go to the movies, something we had not done since arriving in India. He chose *The House of Dracula*. He always loved a good horror movie.

"Indians are movie addicts," he said. "They would rather not eat than give up the movies."

We got to the theater and discovered the truth of this statement: there were no tickets left. We were approached by a scalper. Rudi told me to buy the tickets from him, even though they were two and a half times the regular cost. When we got inside we discovered that the tickets weren't together, but the usher assured us that he could fix us up, for a price. We waited for half an hour in the lobby. Finally, he reappeared and asked about twice as much as the tickets had cost from the scalper. We were seated in time to enjoy the last two-thirds of the movie. It was a strange story to be watching under the circumstances. The Dracula theme of draining the blood of the living in order to achieve immortality was a sinister counterpoint to the whole experience Rudi was undergoing, but he enjoyed such strong contrasts. As the climax of the movie approached, Rudi passed the word: "When I say leave, we all leave. No questions."

Buford began to object.

"If you don't want to come," said Rudi, "you can find your own way home."

Five minutes later, when all the forces of good were about to descend on Dracula, Rudi said, "Now!" in a loud whisper. We all rose. Buford was obviously reluctant. Rudi grabbed him by the arm. We dashed out of the theater and hailed the first available taxi. Once inside, Rudi said, "When I say move, move! You don't have to understand why, but I will explain it. There is a law in India that everyone must stand at attention when they play the national anthem. If you sit or leave they can throw you in jail. The split second after they finish the movie the national anthem comes on the screen. Everyone has to wait while it plays and then everyone leaves the theater at the same moment. The chances of our getting a taxi would be nonexistent. Maybe you would like to walk, but I can't right now. I am in a very delicate condition, and I can't stand the tension of four different people each with their own opinion. You have to accept the fact that when I say something, there is a very good reason."

We traveled back to the hotel in an unsettled silence.

The next day, Rudi announced that he was going back to Bombay to conduct some business and to see Mr. Thomas. He suggested that Stuart and I stay in Delhi to rest up. We agreed, since that was obviously what he wanted us to do. We were going home in two and a half days in any case. On that last day, Rudi took us aside one at a time. First he spoke to Buford, When he came back to the poolside where Stuart and I were relaxing, he said, "I just gave Buford something to think about." We were silent. "He is going to Paris at the end of the trip. I showed him how many opportunities he has thrown away and how disgusting it is to have the ability to grow spiritually and not use it. I think he got the message. He was crying when I left."

Then Rudi started on Stuart. I listened, trying to be inconspicuous. He criticized him for his egotism, for his not wanting to take from Rudi but preferring to run his own show in Texas. Stuart sat listening stonefaced and then finally broke down and cried.

"And when I come down to visit, I want to feel that I am truly welcomed and deeply loved, not some visiting power you have to tolerate." Stuart protested weakly, and Rudi subsided. There was a pause, then he turned to me.

"Don't sit there feeling superior, John. You have thrown away more opportunities than anyone else. The fact that you were too crippled at the time to benefit from them is not greatly to your credit. You leave death behind you wherever you go. That has to change. It doesn't matter whether I can accept it. You cannot afford to accept it any more. When you return, I want you to start an ashram in Livonia. It is crucial. Then when you leave Geneseo, something living can remain behind you for once."

"How about the book?" I asked. " Do you still want me to write it?"

"If you want to have a life," said Rudi, "then write it! Personally I don't care. There have been plenty of people eager to write books, articles, do interviews with me. I have always discouraged it. I have postponed fame as long as I could. It is better to delay something, so that the foundation is strengthened and one is mature enough to endure it. I want you to write the book for your sake, John, not mine."

"How have you ever put up with me all these years, Rudi?" I asked hesitantly.

He looked right through me, "It doesn't matter, John. The past doesn't matter. All that counts is that somehow you have survived. That is the test of time. I love you very much, John."

That did it. I was completely demolished.

Later in the day I ran across Stuart outside the florist shop. Startled to see him there, I asked him what he was doing.

"I was paying for some flowers I sent to Rudi. I wrote to thank him for what he said to me and to tell him that I love him. I was just up in the room. He didn't say anything, but he had them in a vase. I asked him why he said that he wasn't welcomed in Texas. I really couldn't understand that. You know what he answered? He said, 'That was a great line, wasn't it?' I didn't know whether to slug him or hug him. It was like that for a whole year when I lived in New York. He just tears me to shreds."

The next day Rudi, Buford and Peter departed. Stuart and I remained resting and growing bored by the pool. We were both eager to return to America when we finally got on the plane at four in the morning and entered the twilight land of jet travel.

22

Transitions

ON MY NEXT VISIT to the city, Rudi filled in the missing pieces of the trip.

"I went to Mr. Thomas as soon as we returned to Bombay. He asked just when the experience with the ancient saint had occurred. Then he disappeared into his books for a while. Finally he said, 'It is remarkable that you could see what happened. It was extremely subtle. It marks the beginning of a great new cycle in your inner development. It will be a three-part experience. Each part will be clearer and stronger than the next. The second phase should be around your birthday and the third in early spring.'

"Then he told me certain things about the future, which time will tell. But at the end, he gave me a remarkable mantra. You know that I have never been very interested in anything like that. But this was quite different. As soon as I began to use it, my head started to split open. It has been driving me crazy. But it is the first time that I have ever received anything spiritual without paying a great price. I hope that it is a symbol of how things will come to me in the future."

About that time, Rudi gave a talk in Big Indian about his possible future departure from the United States, for the Middle East or elsewhere.

"I may go away," he said. "It could happen by boat or train or plane. If I go, you will be on your own. You should prepare yourselves. Don't assume I will always be here to tell you what to do and straighten out every problem that arises. If I were gone, you would find out what you have really learned. You don't own anything unless you are able to hold onto it."

When I was next in the city, I went to the store on Saturday morning. It was relatively deserted. Rudi appeared to be sitting quietly, but from the first moment, I felt that something was radically different. I sat for perhaps fifteen minutes trying to relate to him in the familiar way, but I couldn't connect. He was there, but he wasn't there.

Finally, I asked, "Am I crazy or is something totally new going on?"

Rudi smiled abstractly and said, "You're not crazy. I am working in time and space."

As soon as he said the words, I resolved that this was a form of work that I must learn. Hesitantly I asked, "When are you going to begin to teach it?"

"Possibly on the July 4th weekend," he said. "Maybe I will begin with a few people next spring. If you want it, John, prepare yourself. Work harder and more seriously than you ever have before. How is the ashram coming?"

"I'm getting the house ready. The ashram should come into existence early next year."

"Fine. How about the book?"

"I'm thinking about it."

"Great! But do it."

I nodded in assent.

"I've found a publisher for my own book," said Rudi. "I thought of a great title."

"What's that?" I asked, thinking that nothing would surprise me.

"Spiritual Cannibalism!" *

"That should get plenty of attention," I said.

Rudi just smiled.

Throughout this conversation, the extraordinary quality in the atmosphere persisted. It fit in with my impression that Rudi was able to be completely normal and yet not be there at all. Finally, he stopped whatever he had been doing, and shortly thereafter I left.

November and December were quiet months. Rudi used the time to allow the crucial experience he had undergone in India to settle in him more deeply, as well as to prepare himself for an even stronger period on and around his birthday.

I continued to visit regularly. Rudi always had something new to tell me.

On one day in that period, Rudi and I took a walk in the East Village. He liked to get out of the store for ten or fifteen minutes to help break up his day. As we walked across Fourth Avenue, he said, "What are you doing inside, John?"

"Nothing in particular."

"That's what I thought," he said with a disgusted shake of his head. "You are wasting the opportunity. How many chances do we have to walk together these days without a hundred other things going on?"

That was true. The last time I had walked with him, he was so busy that I had to wait thirty minutes before I could ask him a simple question.

"What should I be doing?"

"First of all, absorb energy through the top of your head. The lotus chakra can receive energy that comes from above. Bring it down into your heart and circulate it from there. Then let your hands hang down and keep your

---

* Swami Rudrananda [Rudi]. *Spiritual Cannibalism.* New York: Links Books, 1973. Reprinted 1987, Cambridge, Massachusetts: Rudra Press.

fingers open so that you can drop negative psychic tension at the same time."

"Is that what you do when you walk?"

"Sure. Do you think I am just killing time?"

I tried out what he suggested and immediately discovered that it worked. It made me feel pretty stupid.

"Can I ask you something else?"

"Anything you want," said Rudi.

"When you are talking to people in class, you sometimes tell them their heart isn't open or they are not functioning somewhere else. How do you know?"

"It is very simple. I open my heart. Then I psychically contact their heart. If they are closed, the echo comes back to me like a dull thud. If their heart is open, there is an immediate flow between us. Try it, it works."

I took a breath into my chest and began to feel my heart center expand. Then I tried to sense Rudi's heart. The impact was immediate.

"It is so simple when you know what to do," I said.

"Like most things. It is just doing them that is difficult," he said. We were almost back at the store.

"How about psychic operations that you sometimes perform? Are those easy, too?" I asked as I warmed to the opportunity.

"You'd be surprised," said Rudi, opening the front door to his store, "but that is enough for now. Ask me again some other time." The walk was over.

At the end of December, I attended the usual Christmas party. It was quiet, warm, and peaceful. There was the deepest sense of fulfillment in the room of any such time I could remember. I felt thankful just to be present.

On the 30th of December I happened to stop at the store. Rudi said hello and motioned me to a chair. When he had a moment, he came over, "Nityananda's statue has

LINDA SAXTON

The statue of Nityananda, adorned with garlands.

arrived. I have it upstairs in my room. It is even more extraordinary than I thought. His spirit lives in the statue. I have tried working with it for a few minutes at a time. That is about all I can take. No one else has even seen it yet. In the future, I can visualize it being used as an initiation piece that will help to give hundreds and thousands of people the initial contact with the energy used in our work. It is really extraordinary."

At this moment, a striking young man came in. I later learned his name was Tom B. Rudi went over to talk to him. I was not part of the conversation, but as I was sitting nearby, I couldn't help overhearing it.

"It is part of my nature to need someone close to me," Rudi said. Tom nodded in silent understanding. "There are riches in me no one has touched. It is just a question of whether you are willing to work."

"I want to work," said Tom.

"Each day you have to demand a fresh result and go beyond anything you did the day before," Rudi said. Tom didn't flinch.

"There is so much going on inside that I have to give. There are thousands of souls in my being. There hasn't been anything like me on the earth in the last ten thousand years."

The last sentence froze me. I was perfectly willing to accept it. At the same time, I knew that most people would find such a statement insane. I had never heard Rudi say anything like that before. I knew that I was in no position to evaluate it, nor in any position to really doubt it. So I kept my peace.

I returned to Geneseo to work on the development of the ashram. I had been giving classes in Kundalini Yoga for several years. Many students had come and most had gone, but I had never attempted to establish a school where a central core of people lived and worked together. I started working toward that objective in November. The situation finally crystallized in the middle of January. I gave classes every morning and evening, and experienced for the first time the feeling of being responsible for and living with others — all of whom shared the same basic aim. Then on January 24th I went to the city for Rudi's forty-fifth birthday party.

As a birthday present I had my lawyer prepare incorporation papers for the Shree Gurudev Rudrananda Yogashram, Inc. It was Rudi's nonprofit corporation for his work in New York City and Big Indian. He hated legalities, but both situations were getting too complex to be anyone's personal property.

There were fewer people and less outward show for this birthday than for the previous one, but the sense of achievement, closeness, and love was if anything fuller as we gathered together in the aura of our teacher, whom none of us could really fathom.

"For the first time in my life," Rudi said, "I am out of danger. All along I have been following an unknown treacherous path. That is over. I may still have to go through great trials, but there is nothing that has the power to stand in the way.

"The last year has been the greatest in my life, but my position wasn't stabilized. With this birthday, my foundation is secure."

As Rudi talked, his words were mirrored in the faces of his students who shone with happiness and gratitude. Everywhere was a sense of ripening in midwinter.

"I am having the second part of the experience that began in India," Rudi continued. "It is still growing and settling in me. I didn't realize its significance at the time.

Everything I have done before is a prelude. What more wonderful realization could I have at this time."

The next day I stopped at the store. Rudi was sitting quietly, working and waiting for whoever might walk through the door. Finally he spoke.

"A new channel has been opening in my temples during the last month. For weeks I felt like there were two oil drills coming in from either side of my head. Finally they met and the pressure eased.

"Last week Danny Cook was in from Texas. Even though I felt pretty strange, I worked with him. Gradually everything began to darken. It was as if the whole room was filled with black ink. But I didn't stop working. Then suddenly, from a vast distance, a blue light cut through the darkness. It slowly approached me and eventually connected with this new channel in my head. I have read of blue cosmic energy and seen it in pictures of Krishna and Buddha. But I thought it was just symbolic. Now I understand it is very real."

At this moment Tom came into the store, and as he saw him, Rudi said, "Tom has been going crazy. He is around me so much that the channel has begun to open in him too."

I looked at Tom more closely. He seemed in pain and somewhat disoriented. While I was talking with Rudi he didn't say anything, but when he thought I was leaving, he said, "Isn't there anything I can do for the pain?"

"Yes," said Rudi. "Be grateful!"

Tom shrugged and left. It probably hurt more when he was around Rudi.

"I no longer feel that I am going to the Near East," Rudi continued after a sigh. "I have grown so fast in the last few months that it has made a great bridge to fill in the void I needed to cross. There are so many new people and such activity going on inside me that nothing else is necessary. The Near East is right here."

Rudi paused again.

"I don't know if I mentioned it, but the leading Tibetan historian from Germany has been visiting the ashram for the last week. He has studied with three or four Tibetan Lamas in the past, but he has been keeping his distance from me until he makes up his mind about my capabilities.

"Yesterday I worked with him for the first time. He has a remarkable inner quality. All I could see were a series of great doorways slowly opening, one after another...."

There was another pause as Rudi put his hand on his head and rubbed it gently.

"You often hear people talk about the thousand petaled lotus in spiritual work. In Kundalini Yoga we speak of it as the reservoir of the refined spiritual force. Once or twice I have heard people mention the ten-thousand-petaled lotus, but I never knew what they were talking about until a few days ago. Now I understand because the whole top of my head is beginning to open like one gigantic flower. I can feel it separating petal by petal. Each time I circulate the force and bring it up my spine, I draw the energy to the next petal and help it open."

He lapsed into silence again. Then he raised his arm, smiled, and said, "Have you seen these Tibetan paintings?"

He pointed to a vase that held several tankas.

I walked over and unrolled the largest one. It was a great picture of a thousand-armed figure, Avalokitesvara.

"I had that upstairs in the house for a long time. Do you like it?"

"Of course. It's great." I paused reluctantly. I owed Rudi $20,000 at that time. "I'd ask how much it is, but I can't buy anything more."

"It's $3,000. If you want it, you can have it."

"But what about what I owe you?"

"That is the past. This is for what your life is going to become."

I stood staring at the beauty of the image, feeling wonder and gratitude. Then Rudi asked if I wanted to see the Chinese tapestries he had just received. We went to the back of the store. There were six huge, gorgeous dragon tapestries, hand sewn and embroidered.

"They're incredible. I've never seen anything like them," I said.

"I picked them up in an estate a few weeks ago."

"They must cost a fortune."

"No."

"How much?"

"I'll sell all six to you for $2,000."

I was staggered. I assumed they were each worth that much.

"I got a bargain. I want you to have them. They will be in the Institute that I want you to form one day. All the art you have bought will be there. It will be wonderful. I can't wait to help you decorate it."

In a daze of gratitude and puzzlement about the Institute, I left to get my car and carry away my treasures for the future.

The next day I stopped at the store at about three in the afternoon. We talked casually. Then Rudi asked me to get something from the house. On the way, I met another student who asked if I were going to the concert. It was the first I had heard about it. I returned to the store. At about 4:00 Rudi started to leave, even though he usually stayed open until 6:00.

"Where are you going now," he asked, "to your parents?"

"I guess so. Isn't there a class tonight?"

"No. I'm going to a concert." As an apparent afterthought, he asked, "Are you free to come?"

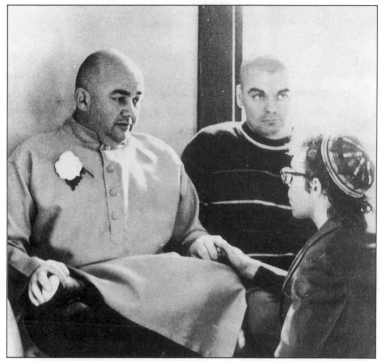

Rudi with Michael S. (Swami Chetanananda) and Jordan Shifriss from the Bloomington ashram.

"Sure," I said, glad to be included.

There were about twelve people waiting for transportation outside the store. Rudi motioned me into the car he was taking. Michael was visiting from Indiana. He and I were in the back. Rudi and Tom were in the front, along with Norman, who was driving. We were headed toward Westchester to pick up Norman's wife.

Rudi talked for a time with Norman and Tom. He asked Michael some questions about Bloomington. Then he began to work with us as he had in the station wagon in India coming back from Ganeshpuri. He came to me last.

He simply took my hand in his. It contained an incredibly strong force. I didn't want to let go, but it was like holding lightning.

When it was over, I closed my eyes and settled back to absorb the effects. Rudi was talking to Tom and Michael: "When should we go? I was thinking of late June." At first I didn't pay much attention, but it slowly dawned on me that he was talking about his next trip to India. Evidently Tom and Michael were going. It was the first I'd heard of it. Rudi talked on. Abruptly, he turned to me, "Would you be free, John?"

"I'll make myself free," I said.

"You don't have to do that," he said. "Just tell me when is good for you and we'll go then."

A moment before, I was overhearing plans in which I had no part. Now I was not only included, but the departure time was to be arranged at my convenience. The combined effects of the work and the invitation welled up in me and I started to cry. Rudi took my hand again and smiled, "You are included in my future, John." I cried some more. So many years of watching and waiting! So much time spent in half-hearted attempts to start moving, and for so long, so little result. All that seemed behind me. As I cried for what I had been, I felt it return and then fall away.

"No matter how many times the work has changed," Rudi said, "you have managed to change with it. That alone entitles you to a place. You have always felt insecure. I understand that. It has kept you moving. You are going to have to work harder and harder. But the place is yours. You have survived everything."

I settled back again, feeling a sense of great spreading happiness as the car moved on into the country.

The following day, January 27th, Rudi was leaving to visit the various Texas ashrams and asked me to drive him to the airport. It was a special treat for me, because I had never driven Rudi to the airport alone. I decided to relax and enjoy it, but that wasn't so easy. The traffic on 4th Avenue was heavy and the drivers unpredictable. I said to Rudi, "I guess I don't have to worry, with you along nothing could happen."

He smiled. "Nothing can happen to me," he said, "but that doesn't mean that someone might not hit your side of the car. Don't take anything for granted."

I was slightly dismayed, but I still felt protected. As the traffic finally began to thin, Rudi spoke again: "I've been thinking some more about the Institute you are going to establish. I assumed that it would have nothing to do with the ashrams. But last week I began to see how the two are connected."

"What do you mean?" I was intrigued.

"They can help each other. Certainly the Institute can help the ashrams. I'll talk to you some more about it another time. It is still forming in my mind.

On his return three days later, he said:

"I have never been happier in my entire life. It is with enormous gratitude and joy that I prepare for the much more intense period ahead." It was then January 30th.

During the next few days, Rudi's arms felt stiff and swollen, as if hundreds of rubber covered wires were being put into them. He had students massage his forearms to ease the pain. Enormous amounts of energy shot out of his fingers in the process. A psychic rewiring process was occurring.

By the second week in February, Rudi began to sense an enormous increase in the life force that was flowing in him. He realized that a new inner mechanism was being evolved to handle it. This mechanism required much greater quantities of energy. The two were unfolding in parallel. He fought to open to the reality of the experience, and to break the resistance of feeling that he had already done enough.

During the same week in February, Rudi began to plan for a European trip that would be the basis for establishing several ashrams on the continent. Buford had been doing some spade work in Paris, and Rudi had various other contacts in Sweden, Vienna, and elsewhere that were waiting for his appearance.

One of his major concerns was that such an expansion should not occur at the expense of the work that already existed in the United States. For this reason, he invited Stuart from Texas, Michael from Indiana, and Buford from Paris to come to New York for a week to reinforce his connection with them and thus strengthen the foundation for his European venture, scheduled for late February or early March.

He spent the weekend of the 17th in Georgia with close friends. Upon his return he settled many business matters including signing the papers that turned over the property at Big Indian to Shree Gurudev Rudrananda Yogashram, Incorporated.

23

The Meeting Ends

ON WEDNESDAY, FEBRUARY 21, 1973 I had a question about my inner work. There was nothing pressing about it, but I decided to phone Rudi, which was unusual. I had only called previously when I needed immediate advice.

I dialed the number. Rudi answered, sounding slightly distracted. "Hello, John. How have you been? When are you coming in next?"

"I'm fine," I said. "I'm going to Bloomington this weekend. It's the first time I've been back there in over a year. I'll probably come in the weekend after that. Are you very busy right now?"

"I'm always busy. What is it?"

"I wanted to ask you something."

"Go ahead." I could hear Rudi yelling at someone off the phone to do something or not to do something. But I went ahead.

"When I was fifteen years old," I said, "I had an experience that is returning now in a different form. I want to know whether it has reality and how to relate to it." He didn't say anything, so I continued: "The original experience happened while I was walking along a country road. A voice began talking inside me. I knew it was inside, but it was extremely real. The thing that struck me most was the totally alien quality of the person behind the voice. He could have been from another galaxy.

Rudi in his store, February 1973.

BARRY KAPLAN

"The basic thing he told me was that I would be alone in a haunted house for a long time, and that there was nothing that I or anyone else could do about it. He said some other things, but it wasn't the content that held me. It was the realization that this alien being was myself, and that everything else I had ever identified with had no existence. I am beginning to sense that being again more strongly. I have had a taste of it intermittently, but now it has a more permanent feeling." I paused and then asked, "What do you think?"

"I'm sorry, John," said Rudi. "There is a lot going on. Could you repeat what you just said?"

In all the time that I had known Rudi, I had never heard him ask anyone to repeat themselves. Usually he interrupted them after the first few sentences, having heard enough. But I did as he asked. Then he said: "John, I have been telling you for fourteen years. You have to work deeper. If you don't, you will spend the rest of your life in a backwash of shit."

I said nothing, and he continued: "The experience was real. It was your higher self. That is what you have to try to bring into your work, your relationships, your writing of the book. How many times have I told you this over the years? You never listen. You never try hard enough. If you don't do it now, everything you have done could be for nothing."

I was happy that he had confirmed the importance of the experience, but disturbed by what he said. I couldn't reply immediately.

"John. I wouldn't bother saying this if I didn't want you to have a wonderful future. The easiest thing for me to do is to sit back and watch you go over a cliff. But I won't do that. I care. But that isn't enough. You have to care, too. You can no longer live your life on the surface. You must dig and dig until you get into contact with this being and begin to let him function. Then everything will be different for you.

"I have to go now. I love you very much. Goodbye." He hung up as I said: "Goodbye and thank you."

I sat by the phone for a minute after I had hung up, silently digesting what he had said.

Late that afternoon, Rudi boarded a small plane piloted by one of his students. He was scheduled to give a talk in upstate New York. As the plane took off in the waning winter twilight, Rudi relaxed for the first time in an otherwise hectic day, but after the flight was securely underway, he began to dictate to Mimi, one of the students who was accompanying him:

"2/21/73: Today has been a particularly exhausting day. I knew I was going through a transition but could not quite determine where it would carry me. I am now en route to Glens Falls in a small plane, to teach a class in Fort Miller, New York. It is a good way to travel.

"I have been sitting for at least seven or eight hours today, letting negative psychic tensions flow through my fingers, which it continues to do unceasingly.

"I seemed to doze for just a moment or two and could see the faces of several of the people I love most deeply. A great warmth opened in my heart, and I felt positive energy move down from my brain to my heart and my sex organs. It immediately clarified the reason for the amount of the outflow of these negative psychic tensions. It was my system making room for the transfer of this finer energy by removing the heavier energy which previously occupied those areas.

"Although it is just a few minutes since this experience took place, I feel refreshed and renewed and once again strong. It is exciting to look forward to the way the energy expresses itself, as all of these changes have the capacity to reflect a higher creativity. It is not within my mind to try to guess, but I am deeply looking forward to teaching the class tonight.

"It has always been a great strength for me to do a simple exercise for a long period of time, allowing it to go deeper and deeper. Improvisation is not a substitute for discipline. It is continually the inability of students or teachers to do what is given to them that brings about problems. They wander through the basic exercises, not having the ability to sustain them. Involved and dramatic methods allow us to lose in their elaborate nature the basic responsibilities and disciplines from which we receive our strength. It is the ability to check ourselves by our deviation from our constant that not only guides us but also perpetuates the line of energy which makes for elasticity as well as an extraordinary deep strength.

"I am leaving for Europe this weekend to begin a deeper commitment toward my European ashrams. Most of the teachers in the United States were brought to New York for additional work and strengthening of existing connections. I feel this exemplifies the above principles. I do not wish to exchange the loyalties in this country for loyalties in another. It is easy to look to the glamour of a foreign culture as a means to expand. The success that our spiritual work has will be based on the depth and growth and love and reality between myself and those with whom I have connected my life. From that, the integrity of our European ashrams and brothers and sisters will grow. It is the investment of those people who have been with me that allows me to consciously deepen and expand that which exists. It is not the neurotic need to go off to the glamour of other ashrams and countries. I feel I need to strengthen and simplify relationships with all of those close teachers that I have before I leave. It is always a principle of growth that simplification conserves energy and allows it to rise to a higher level. I do not wish to see what will happen in Europe as anything except the rising of a total spirituality that reflects the maturity of my surrender to God.

"I am deeply grateful for this opportunity, and feel the last year of my life preparing me for the understanding that expanded consciousness can only come through expanded nothingness. This has to do with the ability to surrender tensions that bind and restrict our physical mechanism from expressing the power of creation. This is God flowing through us and showing us how we are connected to him. It is the expression of higher creative will and a deeper sense of surrender. . . ."

. . .

The next day I was in an encounter group. During the meeting, a woman described her dream of the night before. She had walked up to the attic of her house. The door was closed. She could sense spirits behind the door calling to her; she wanted to go in, but was afraid that if she opened the door she might not be able to return. Suddenly, as she described the dream, she realized who was on the other side. It was a man she had loved and their child, both of whom had died. I listened to her and started to cry. The sadness of it held me. Other people were also affected, but not to that extent.

During the group, I led a guided fantasy. Each person was told to imagine a door, which they would open and walk through. When I did, I found myself on a kind of airfield. I started to rise like a rocket, flying and flying and flying out into the universe. I felt concerned about whether I could return and retrace my steps through the door. Then I realized it didn't matter. I was launched and could go on forever. It was a wonderful feeling.

I spent Friday quietly in the country. I returned to Geneseo about 5:30 and for some reason decided to stop at my office. I had spent a few minutes at my desk when the phone rang and I picked it up.

"Hello, John, this is Jack Stewart." (I had known Jack for almost ten years. He was one of Rudi's oldest students.)

"Hello, Jack, you're the last person I expected to call."

"We've been trying to reach you for two days."

"Me? Why?"

"I don't know how to say this. Rudi was killed in a plane crash Wednesday night." I went blank and said nothing.

"His plane hit the top of a mountain in the fog. Beau was the pilot; Mimi and Stuart were there. Rudi died instantly — his heart exploded in his chest. He was dictating to Mimi at the time. The others are all right."

Finally I said, "I'm sure you mean what you say, Jack, but it isn't possible."

"That was my reaction at first," said Jack. "I'm afraid it's true. I've seen his body."

He said more, but it was of no matter. Inwardly, I still did not believe him for a moment. It might appear this way, but it would be shown to be entirely different in time.

"Thank you for calling, Jack," I said when he paused. "It must have been difficult."

"Will you be at the funeral?"

"Of course."

"Rudi's mother particularly asked that you come quickly."

"I'll be there tomorrow."

"She wants you to say something at the funeral as one of Rudi's oldest friends."

"Of course. I'll see you soon, Jack."

I stood there by the phone feeling rather disconnected, but realizing even then that the rest of my life had been altered in an instant. That evening I talked to the students at the ashram:

"Rudi has been dead for two days and nothing in me felt anything. That is really extraordinary. The nature of the work is such that whatever is happening to the teacher inevitably affects the students, even at a distance. I have seen that happen thousands of times. When Rudi has a headache, others do. When things go well for him, they go well for them. I don't know how I could be untouched when he died. But my strongest sense is that it makes no difference. His work was done."

In New York City, everyone was attempting to remain calm, but the situation was charged with disbelief. Our immediate task was to make the funeral arrangements. On Saturday night a small group of us went to the Riverside Chapel to make the final arrangements.

"Would you like to view the body?" the director asked.

We nodded. He took us into another room. The coffin was open. In it was a large body. I remember it very clearly. There could no longer be any doubt in my mind that Rudi had actually been killed in the crash. But this was not him. It was a shell. I felt nothing toward it — no pang, no sadness.

The funeral was held in a large chapel that overflowed with people, most of whom I had known. They were a living cross-section of Rudi's life: students, customers, dealers, friends. Through it all my inner calm persisted. Perhaps it had begun with the experience of flying into the universe the day after Rudi's death.

Michael, Buford, Stuart, and I sat together in the first row to represent the teachers of Rudi's work, along with Hilda and Taisan Maezumi Roshi, both of whom Rudi had known and loved for many years. Each spoke briefly. Michael said a few words for the rest of us.

In front of the room was Rudi's coffin. Even in death he seemed oversized. The ceremony passed quickly. Finally each person came forward to say farewell to Rudi before they left the room. I watched the endless procession, noticing how each individual approached the coffin in a different way, standing up, bowing down, with tears, in a meditative state, touching their forehead to the closed lid, placing a flower on it.

The farewells began to take longer than the ceremony. Toward the end, people were asked to hurry, so that preparations might begin for the next funeral.

When it came to my turn, I bowed to the ground for a moment, remembering a similar occasion on Guru's day in Big Indian. But that was long ago, and the doors were closing.

Afterward, Buford accompanied the body to the crematorium. The rest of us returned to the ashram where we talked in muted voices, and two teachers gave class simultaneously. It was intense and slightly crazed, but it was better to work than stand around and pretend that nothing had happened.

I returned to Geneseo that evening to face an uncertain future.

24

Return to India

MY DAILY ROUTINE carried me through the spring of 1973. I occasionally thought of the book, but felt partially paralyzed. On my less frequent trips to New York City I saw that a struggle for ascendancy was brewing. The city had been Rudi's home. Big Indian had been his country retreat. But the respective teachers in each ashram began to view each other with suspicion. Their students could do little but await the outcome.

Shortly after Rudi's death I went to Bloomington. The situation there was radically different. There was strength and love in abundance and no struggle for power. In a quiet moment, Michael and I made plans to return to India in the late spring. He wanted to retrace some of Rudi's steps and take the trip that Rudi had promised him a month before.

During this period, Rudi's mother, Rae, gradually recovered from her loss. He had been the mainstay of her existence. On several occasions, he had literally saved her life.

At the reading of his last testament the remarkable truth was revealed: he had left her everything. The will that I had witnessed a decade before was still in effect.

Rudi knew his mother would take care of his brothers. He seemed to assume the ashrams would take care of themselves. Whatever he had in mind, Rae found herself in the center of a confusing empire that Rudi had been building.

She inherited his art, his debts, his tax problems, his buildings, his customers (most of whom owed Rudi money), and all the complications that follow when a will is probated.

Two major issues of concern to her were the disposition of Rudi's ashes and the statue of Nityananda. Both were finally sent to Big Indian for safekeeping. Rae was afraid that someone might steal the ashes. This did not seem terribly rational, but it was possible. The room that held them was securely locked and only Dean, who was in charge of Big Indian at the time, had the key.

In March of 1973, I visited Big Indian. Michael was also there. I happened to be present when he was having a conversation with Dean. As I listened, it slowly dawned on me that Michael was planning to spend the night in the room with Rudi's ashes and the statue of Nityananda. Without pausing to think about it, I asked if I might join him. He agreed, but urged me to say nothing about it to anyone else, since a slight air of paranoia surrounded the ashes and the statue. It was understandable. Their future was uncertain. It was in Rae's hands and she was still partially overwhelmed by her responsibilities and her grief.

As night approached, I borrowed a sleeping bag and, in a quiet moment, gathered with Michael and Dean before the closed door of the room in which we were to stay. Dean opened the double lock and let us in. His last words were, "Please speak softly."

I had seen the statue in India in the living room of its creator. It had seemed large then, but now it occupied three-fourths of the available space. There was barely room for the two of us to stretch out in front of it, nothing more.

As soon as the door closed behind us, I glanced at the statue. A torrent of energy struck me. I felt as though I had been grabbed by the shoulders and was being shaken. The thought of spending the night in the company of such intensity frightened me.

Michael proceeded to light a candle and burn some incense. He bowed before the statue and consecrated some tantric instruments he had brought with him. I followed his lead silently. On one side of the room was a shelf with a small box of Persian design. I realized, with a chill, that it must contain Rudi's ashes.

As we settled down, I said to Michael, "I don't know if I can take a whole night in here."

"I'm not so sure myself," said Michael, "but if it gets too much for you, leave."

I lay there in the dark, aware of the energy that continued to pour from the statue, wondering whether my system could absorb it without being injured, vaguely aware of the small box by the window. I knew that Rudi was dead, but it was hard to believe in the presence of such energy.

I did not sleep that night, but gradually the force receded, or I became used to it, so that it was like resting under a waterfall.

We left as the sky began to lighten. The next time I saw Michael, he looked radiant.

"Nityananda descended into the statue while we were there," he said. "It was a great honor, John. It wasn't just his energy. He was really present in the room to meet us."

I wasn't entirely sure what Michael meant, but I could certainly feel the energy burning in me for the rest of the day.

·   ·   ·

For several years before his death, I had invited Rudi to come to the Rochester area to talk and teach. He had always put me off. He did not feel the situation was ready to receive him. But finally, in the beginning of January, he had agreed to come. I had made preliminary arrangements for him to talk at an ashram in Rochester. When the time came, I had to appear in his place.

It was a fiery day. I could feel his energy on me as I introduced his work. There were many in the audience who were to become my students in the following months. Mr. Thomas had predicted this period as the beginning of a whole new phase of my life. I could not have visualized the circumstances, but there was no doubt that it was true.

One of the indirect effects of Rudi's death was that people began to consult psychics to get some sense of contact with the future. Rudi had used psychics to help chart his own possibilities, but he had done so carefully and with a conscious sense of skepticism. This was abandoned in the search for emotional reassurance.

Chief among psychics who were discovered was a woman named Beula. Many stories began to circulate about what she had said. Different people were named as the inheritors of Rudi's work. Contact with Rudi himself was established. It was very difficult for me to sort these stories out. If anything, they only made the situation more precarious, as they put fuel on the hopes and ambitions of different people, and intensified their conflict with each other.

I purposely held back. I didn't want to be involved in the uncertainty and struggle that was occurring. But in late spring, after the initial excitement had subsided, I made an appointment with Beula, calling from upstate New York so that she would not connect me with Rudi in any way.

I duly appeared for my appointment on my next visit to New York City. She lived in a large suite in a West Side hotel. The living room was overflowing with objects and upholstery. It looked like she stayed there for days at a time without leaving, which might well have been true. But I didn't have much time to think about it as she quickly ushered me into her office. In an abrupt and businesslike way, she sat down behind her desk and motioned me into an armchair.

I said nothing. She shrugged her shoulders and closed her eyes.

"I feel a strong presence. Someone you know. Very high energy. It is someone I have come to know in the last months: Rudi!"

I was shocked. I hadn't said two words to her since I entered the apartment.

"He greets you as an old friend," she continued. "He sends you his love. Do not be sad."

I waited. I wasn't sad.

"Is there anything you would like to ask?"

"Why did you die?"

"My work was done," was the immediate reply.

I had never believed that Rudi could die accidentally.

Beula continued on.

"He is gone, but I hear singing. It is in a large place like a cathedral; many people. It is a ceremony for you, in your honor. You have completed your transformation."

Shortly thereafter, she concluded.

I didn't really want to think about what she had said.

Toward the end of May, Michael and I left on our trip to India. On the airplane I asked him what he thought of Beula. I had gained tremendous respect for Michael since Rudi's death.

"She said that I would inherit the mantle of Rudi's work."

"What do you think of that?" I asked.

"Time will tell," said Michael.

"Then you take her seriously?" I persisted.

"I just want to do my own work. When we get to India, I will talk with Mr. Thomas. I am not going to drive myself crazy about what to believe or not to believe. It will all take care of itself."

Two endless days later, we were in Bombay. Michael went off to meet Mr. Thomas while I caught up on my sleep. When he returned he didn't want to talk about it, except to say, "Mr. Thomas is coming over later in the afternoon."

We took a walk around the neighborhood. It was all the same; the overcrowding, the decayed exotic odors, the shops, the beggars, and the heat. But Rudi's name, like an unanswered question, hung in the air. To come halfway around the earth and see things that only reminded me of him was extremely strange. The ashes had not yet settled.

I stopped in Michael's room later in the day. Mr. Thomas had indeed come. He didn't seem to remember who I was, but in a lull in the conversation, he started to make a few comments about me: "You are the kind of person," he said, "on whom most of what you have gone through is wasted. But you will gain great benefit in sharing it with others. As you do that, you will come to understand and appreciate what you have known. And others will benefit greatly also."

I immediately thought of the book, but Mr. Thomas had shifted his conversation to other things.

Later in the evening, as we sat eating some papaya fruit, Michael said, "Mr. Thomas gave me the mantra he gave to Rudi on his last trip. It is very intense."

"I don't suppose. . ."

"Don't even ask, John. Let me work on it. When the time comes, we will see."

The next day we hired a car and driver to retrace the route that Rudi had taken toward Hardwar, Rishikesh, and into the mountains. It rained continually. The roads turned to mud and the heat intensified. Finally we came to the Ganges; cold, vitalizing, bubbling with pure energy.

But we did not delay. There was no 700 year old man waiting for us in the foothills of the Himalayas, but our destination was still Maussorie.

When we arrived, the hotel was almost full. It didn't look like the same place. I rested while Michael disappeared into the mountains. He wanted to be alone. I didn't really know why until later, but when he returned, he was enthusiastic.

"I ran across a Tibetan who invited me to his village. There is a whole Tibetan colony nearby. The man's uncle is a famous tanka painter. I commissioned him to make some huge paintings for the ashram in Bloomington. He is going to send one of his best students to stay with us and teach painting. They are wonderful, wonderful people."

Michael went to bed early, complaining that his head was splitting open and he couldn't see straight. I decided to take a walk in the surrounding forest. As the sun was setting I caught a glimpse of the Himalayas, but the mountain mists quickly blotted them out and I turned for home before I got lost in the dark.

The next day I went with Michael to the Tibetan village, but most of the people he had met were gone. We sipped buttered tea, ate small cakes, and decided to move on.

Our next stop was Benares. As we made our way through the maze of temples, shops, and people. I listened as Michael talked to Indians about our work, describing himself as its leader. It was strange for me to hear him say it, but I discovered that I had already accepted the fact. Evidently Mr. Thomas must have reinforced the idea for him, though he hadn't specifically said so. But who else was there? Stuart had retired to Texas and took no part in any struggles. Buford was in Paris and didn't seem concerned. And no one else really had the strength. I had purchased a ticket to Bloomington before Rudi's death and accepted the transition easily. Therefore I said nothing. Michael's biggest problem was that he was only 25 years old, though his youth could become a great source of strength if he could survive the maturing process.

Finally I asked him directly: "Just what did Mr. Thomas say?"

"He said that because I was starting so young I would grow beyond Rudi."

"How do you feel about that?" I persisted as we walked through twisting alleyways, trying to keep our guide in sight.

"It sounds very impressive, John, but it is also endless work and a lot of pain. I don't think anyone else could stand it. Rudi and I have a similar chemistry. I loved him completely. A few weeks before he died, he said to me: 'I know where everyone fits into my past lives, but I can't place you, Michael. You must be more ancient than anything I can remember.' Maybe it's true."

"Was he talking about space and time work when he said that?" I asked.

"Yes."

"It's a tragedy that it died with him."

"It didn't," said Michael. "He gave it to me a few days before his death. He said I was the only one who had worked hard enough to receive it."

I was stunned. I had assumed it was lost.

"Don't misunderstand me," said Michael. "Like anything else it takes time to mature. But he gave me the basic method. The rest, I hope, comes with time."

"Is this something you are free to share?"

"Sure," he said. "I thought you would never ask. But don't stop dead in your tracks or we'll lose the guide. Ask me about it when we get to Darjeeling."

We flew to Calcutta and shifted connections to fly to northern India. The trip was nearly aborted when we found that permission for Darjeeling was difficult to obtain without long advance notice, but the customs officials finally decided we were too naive to be dangerous and waved us on.

The drive from the airfield to Darjeeling took three hours on a narrow mountain road that wound upward, continually criss-crossing a small railway that followed a similar route. It was rainy, with intermittent fog. We could see very little, just enough to realize that our safety depended on the memory of the driver.

Darjeeling was a little like Nepal, a world of its own, peopled by a unique mixture of exotic racial types. The tourist season was over. Fog almost totally obscured the view of the Himalayas for which the area was famous. But the manager of our empty hotel was happy to see us as we settled in to explore the surroundings.

Nearby was a large Tibetan settlement. Many monks had been forced to sell their most precious religious possessions to survive. When it became known that we were interested in such things, merchants began to appear at the hotel, uninvited. We followed them in fascination through the fog to small huts and houses where they stored their wares. It was hard to tell what we were looking at in the dim light. But they were happy to mail or ship anything we might wish. In the end we bought some paintings and small statues that we could carry out by hand. It wasn't clear whether they would be seized by Indian customs, but so far as we knew, Tibetan objects were not of concern to Indians.

Michael was scheduled to return to Bombay shortly to meet Danny Cook, the teacher from Dallas, who was coming over on business. And I had to return home. Sitting in my room in Darjeeling, with a warm fire burning and fog obscuring the view, we talked of the trip.

"The night that Rudi crashed, I knew instantly what happened," said Michael. "Ever since then I have been paralyzed inside. During this trip I have begun to thaw. The immediate effect has been a terrible pain in my head. If I seem a little strange at times, that is the reason. I feel like a great wounded water buffalo charging around India.

"When I was in the mountains, I began to let my grief emerge. It wasn't very pretty. I just wanted to pull some trees out by the roots. I had to come to India or I would have gone crazy.

"The first time I met Rudi, I didn't know what to expect. One of my friends had told me about him so I decided to go to New York to see for myself. I just walked into the store; Rudi was sitting behind his desk. All he said was, "Hello. I've been waiting for you." But inside, I began to have incredible experiences. Voices started talking in different languages, images of other lives flashed; it was like something straight out of science fiction. I used to think that Rudi was Maitreya, the Buddha who is to come, but that no longer matters."

We sat in silence and listened to the crackling of the fire. Outside, it had begun to rain. Finally I asked, "Are you still leaving tomorrow?"

"Yes. I want to meet Danny at the airport when he gets in."

"I think I'll stay," I said, " and try to get into Gangtok, even though the border is closed. The head of the Red Hat sect has settled there."

"The Red Hats originated the Lamaist tradition in the eighth century," Michael said. "You should have an interesting day. I'll see you for breakfast before I go."

He paused and looked at the pattern of raindrops on the window.

"In Benares, you said that. . ."

"I know," Michael finished for me, "space and time. I haven't forgotten. I'll give you the exercise now."

When he finished, I sat there feeling the characteristic sense of hovering in emptiness that the experience brings and thinking of what Rudi had written in *Spiritual Cannibalism*. In many ways he had explained the process. But he hadn't given everything. You needed all the pieces or it didn't work. Now it was complete.

"I don't know what to say," I began.

"Just be thankful that it wasn't lost and use it well," said Michael, dropping the subject.

The next morning he returned to Bombay and I left for the border of Sikkim. Much to my surprise, I was allowed to cross. I spent the day in territory closed to westerners, visiting several Tibetan monasteries and finally meeting the Chief Lama of the Red Hat Sect. He dictated letters and asked me questions through an interpreter.

Before I left, he signed and presented me with a picture of Padmasambhava, the originator of Tibetan Buddhism. As I looked at it I suddenly remembered the first tanka I had bought from Rudi fifteen years before. It was a painting of the same man.

When I returned from India, the pattern of my life began to alter. I visited New York only infrequently. The next time I saw Rudi's mother, a year had elapsed. She scolded me for having stayed away so long, but then forgave me. She was going up to Rudi's old apartment where some of his Tibetan statues were still kept. On Friday night the apartment was open to old students who wished to go there to meditate. She wanted to arrive early to avoid the crowd.

We both ascended the familiar stairs. I had not been inside the building since the day of Rudi's funeral. But the room that we entered was still alive. I sat quietly and opened to the energy in the atmosphere and all the memories that the room evoked. Rae closed her eyes and seemed to fall asleep. She was very tired. After a few minutes, she stirred and said: "I haven't felt Rudi's presence since his death. But he just came to me and said he would return later to deliver an important message."

We left the room as others started to assemble. I gave Rae a big hug and returned to Geneseo.

Over the weekend, she had a heart attack and died.

AFTERWORD

Rudi's shrine at Big Indian, New York.

JULIANA WRIGHT

Afterword

Hello, John.

Where am I?

Where we can talk.

But you don't seem the same.

I'm not. Your personality is coloring my words. Try to surrender more deeply.

I'm not sure that any of this is happening.

You never were. That was part of your difficulty.

You seem impersonal.

No, John. But you must understand. This conversation is like a dream to me. I will wake up when we stop talking.

Don't you care what has happened to your work since your death?

It's not my work. It's the work that the creative spirit of the universe did through me. Use what was given. That is the only way to absorb it. Take my life. I left it to you in the only way I could. Isn't that enough?

But there is so much I want to ask.

There is nothing to say.

Then why have I written this book?

To offer what you have been privileged to witness to an audience beyond yourself. You may not have appreciated it in one sense, but you knew from the beginning that it was basically extraordinary.

I'm still having difficulty accepting your reality.

That is your limitation. When you look at one of my photographs, do you feel a flow of force?

Yes. And it always surprises me.

Why should it? You have been working with statues and paintings for years.

I just don't know you anymore.

No one knew me. A hundred different books could have been written about my life, each by people convinced of their version of the truth. If I had lived longer it would have happened.

How could I be with you for so long and not know you?

You knew enough. My force is impressed on you indelibly. That's what counts, alive or dead. You must either feel yourself begin to burn or know that you are a dead hunk of shit. Which is it to be? Do you want to spend the rest of your life apologizing for your inadequacy in comparison to my example? That would be terrible!

I looked forward to talking with you. I was a little scared, but I needed to do it.

And now?

You keep backing me up against a wall. I have done what you asked. I have written the book.

Good!

Is that all?

Sure.

What do I do next?

Open to your own depth. It will attract the future.

I thought that seeing you would answer all my questions. But you are doing what you always did, pushing me in a direction I can't see. And I am fighting inside to hold back.

And it is stupid! Stupid! Stupid! I am not trying to prove anything. Every time you feel resistance and fear, John, take a stick and hit it. No one can inflict anything on you. Don't you understand that yet? You have to be a chorus of voices pleading for growth and energy. You have to get out from behind the clouds and live in the sun.

I want to.

Then do it. You can cooperate with creation by raising the level of energy in every situation you attract. If you do that, the rest will take care of itself.

I'm beginning to feel better.

You are starting to relax. You can't do anything unless you are very open and full of force. Work for that. It will keep you busy.

Isn't there more?

You haven't even scratched the surface and you ask is there more. What more do you want?

I don't know — fragments of the past are scattered around me, but I begin to feel resolved.

Fine! I never wanted to burden you with my memories. Absorb their nourishment. Eat me.

I don't know if I want to do that.

You've been doing it for as long as you have been writing this book, dummy! Now aren't you going to ask me about the future of the work I left behind?

Do you want to tell me?

Sure. If I were vulnerable, it would bother me a lot to see what has happened since my death. Every personal weakness in the people around me has manifested. Some of it was terrible. But I knew it would happen. It was part of the price for my own freedom. And at this point, I am no longer concerned. A new generation is emerging. The work will go on.

Then what should I do?

Breathe me in. Put me in your heart. Feel my radiance as you have known it in my lifetime. We are all bubbles. The Rudi bubble may shine brighter than the John bubble, but it is the light that counts, and what do either of us have to do with that? Behind all patterns are atoms of vitality that bind us together and make us brothers. Accept the past and move on.

The only thing that anyone can leave behind is a pathway through the wilderness. Follow it. That will help to justify my existence. But don't expect me to be waiting at a turn in the road. I have never waited for anyone.

Is there anything else? I can't stay here forever.

Are you on a schedule?

I have things to do. Don't you?

Nothing important. And I may not get this chance again.

You could have had the contact any time you really needed it. I wanted to help. All you had to do was find me — think of it this way: You have a friend in high places.

I would like to believe it.

I'm telling you!

Oh, Rudi! It is really wonderful to be with you. I was never able to remember what you were really like from week to week. You are more real than I am.

Then open to my energy. I have never tried to hide. It is not my nature. The problem is just the other way around. Who could take my radiance? It is still there. Can you feel it?

Yes. It is growing strong. I am very grateful to be talking with you.

It wasn't easy. You had to write this whole book to create the need.

Wasn't the book necessary?

I don't mean that. Its function will become clear in time. I mean, you could have talked to me before. But I got my message through one way or another.

That's what I figured.

And if you open more completely, I can manifest within you in the future.

That would be wonderful!

Then attract it. But don't get caught in that possibility either. Open and grow. Transcend everything you have ever known, including me.

And then?

And then, nothing — you will be free.

Index

OTHER BOOKS BY THE AUTHOR

Mann, J. *Changing Human Behavior.* New York: Scribners, 1965.

——. *Encounter: a weekend with intimate strangers.* New York: Grossman, 1970.

——. *Frontiers of Psychology.* New York: Macmillan, 1963.

——. "Human Potentialities." In *Human Potentialities: the challenge and the promise.* H. Otto, ed. Mississippi: Warren Green, 1967.

——. *Learning to Be.* New York: The Free Press, 1972 (paper, 1974).

——. *Louis Pasteur: father of bacteriology.* New York: Scribners, 1964.

——. *Sigmund Freud.* New York: Macmillan, 1964.

——. *Students of the Light.* New York: Grossman, 1973.

——, and M. Richard. *Exploring Social Space.* New York: The Free Press, 1973.

——, and H. Otto, eds. *Ways of Growth.* New York: Grossman, 1968.

Also From Rudra Press

Video Tape
LILIAS! ALIVE WITH YOGA

"An instructional videocassette by America's best-known yoga teacher . . . informative, and non-intimidating to the beginner. A great gift for a loved one who is out of shape or non-physical and is looking for new ways to relax." – *Yoga Journal*

With a warm and vital teaching style, Lilias Folan, star of the popular PBS-TV series "Lilias, Yoga and You" teaches us to stretch, strengthen and relax. Two 30-minute lessons include warm-ups, exercises for strength and flexibility, and a full range of yoga postures. Instructions in breath and relaxation to reduce stress and increase vitality!

Safe and easy to follow for practitioners of all ages. Music by Steven Halpern.

60 minutes, VHS or Beta $39.95

Audio Tapes
HATHA YOGA IN MOTION

Developed by the teaching staff of the Nityananda Institute, these hatha yoga audio tapes give balanced workouts for home practice. Two 30-minute practice sessions on each tape include warm-ups, asanas for strength and flexibility, and instruction in breath and relaxation.

Both tapes feature *vinyasa*, a graduated series of movement and breath which leads the student to a sense of ease and strength in the poses. By combining breath and movement, *vinyasa* practice also enables the student to develop a meditative understanding of hatha yoga. Each 60-minute tape includes a fold-out guide to the postures.

Beginner, Level 1 $9.95
Intermediate, Level 2 $9.95

Books
SPIRITUAL CANNIBALISM
by Rudi (Swami Rudrananda)

Originally published in 1973, *Spiritual Cannibalism* is an American spiritual classic. Rudi approached spiritual work with total intensity and dedication. In his direct, no-nonsense style, Rudi cuts through the fantasies of spirituality and directs us to the reality of spiritual work. Includes meditation instruction. This book is a must for every spiritual student.

New paperback edition $10.95

BEHIND THE COSMIC CURTAIN
edited by John Mann

A fascinating close-up view of Rudi's extraordinary spiritual journey. This book combines personal experience with practical spiritual guidance, covering such topics as *Creativity and Detachment, Growth and Transcendence,* and *Death and Rebirth.* Also includes dictations from the last days of Rudi's life.

Original paper $9.95

SONGS FROM THE CENTER OF THE WELL
by Swami Chetanananda

A wonderful collection of short, inspirational verse that speaks to the heart of living a conscious, spiritual life. Written from the unique perspective of an American kundalini yoga master, *Songs* offers fresh insights on the discovery of the transcendental as we face the challenges and struggles of daily life.

Second edition, paper $6.95

NITYA SUTRAS: The Revelations of Nityananda from the Chidakash Gita
by M.U. Hatengdi and Swami Chetanananda

Nityananda's own words in an inspired translation of aphorisms recorded during the 1920s. In his terse, powerful style, Nityananda speaks of that inner awareness that is the goal of every spiritual student.

Informative introduction, commentaries, comprehensive glossary, and 20 rare photographs complete this remarkable volume.

Original paper $11.95

NITYANANDA: The Divine Presence
by M.U. Hatengdi

This book powerfully documents the life of one of India's greatest spiritual masters. Fascinating eye-witness stories and rare photographs trace Nityananda's life from the turn of the century to his mahasamadhi in 1961. These vivid stories compel us to suspend our rational assumptions as we meet one who is totally absorbed in the Absolute.

Original paper $10.95

To Order

Call or write Rudra Press, P.O. Box 1973, Cambridge, MA 02238 (617) 576-3394

When ordering by mail please include the following shipping charges with your payment: video/$3.00; books and tapes/$1.50 first item, $.50 each additional item. Thank you.